G. D. H. COLE:
SELECTED WORKS

EARLY PAMPHLETS AND ASSESSMENT

EARLY PAMPHLETS AND ASSESSMENT

With a new introduction by
NOEL THOMPSON

Volume 1

LONDON AND NEW YORK

Pamphlets first published between 1921 and 1956

First published 2011 by Routledge

2 Park Square, Milton Park, Abingdon, Oxfordshire OX14 4RN
711 Third Avenue, New York, NY 10017

Routledge is an imprint of the Taylor & Francis Group, an informa business

First issued in paperback 2017

Copyright © Pamphlets 1921, 1932, 1943, 1944, 1948, 1951, 1952, 1954, 1956 H A Cole
Copyright © New introduction 2011 Noel Thompson

All rights reserved. No part of this book may be reprinted or reproduced or utilised in any form or by any electronic, mechanical, or other means, now known or hereafter invented, including photocopying and recording, or in any information storage or retrieval system, without permission in writing from the publishers.
Notice:
Product or corporate names may be trademarks or registered trademarks, and are used only for identification and explanation without intent to infringe.

British Library Cataloguing in Publication Data
A catalogue record for this book is available from the British Library

ISBN 13: 978-0-415-56651-3 (Set)
ISBN 13: 978-0-415-59726-5 (Volume 1) (hbk)
ISBN 13: 978-1-138-56449-7 (Volume 1) (pbk)

Publisher's Note
The publisher has gone to great lengths to ensure the quality of this reprint but points out that some imperfections in the original copies may be apparent.

Disclaimer
The publisher has made every effort to trace copyright holders and would welcome correspondence from those they have been unable to trace.

An Introduction to the Selected Works of G.D.H. Cole

Guild socialism

George Douglas Howard Cole was born in Cambridge on 25 September 1889, the son of a jeweller, who subsequently moved to Ealing and became a surveyor. In his own words he 'became a socialist as a schoolboy a year before the general election of 1906...converted quite simply by reading William Morris's *News from Nowhere* which made me feel suddenly and irrevocably, that there was nothing except a socialist that it was possible for me to be...I became a socialist as many others did in those days on grounds of morals, decency and aesthetic sensibility.'[1]

In 1908 he went to Balliol College Oxford to read classical history and philosophy, before being elected to a fellowship at Magdalen College in 1912 and focusing on the study of economic and political thought. During his time as an undergraduate he became involved in political activities through his membership of the Fabian Society and the I.L.P., 'agitating for the Workers' Educational Association, to which he was to make a lifelong contribution, and editing the *Oxford Reformer*.[2]

The period between Cole's embrace of socialism and the publication of his first major work, *The World of Labour,* 1913,[3] was one of declining real wages, an aggregation of capitalist power by way of a concentration of industrial ownership, growing threats to the status of skilled sections of workforces, in consequence of skill-destroying technical change, a growth of industrial unrest and a rise in trade union membership which tripled between 1888 and 1910. Moreover this period saw both the emergence of new national unions and the growth of inter-union co-operation culminating in the Triple Alliance of the railway workers, miners and transport workers in 1914.

In such circumstances it is unsurprising that there emerged, both in Britain and elsewhere, socialist political economies that looked to a decentralised socialism brought into being by the efforts of the workers themselves rather than by the prior conquest of state power. All the more so, as the political route was one that seemed to have signally failed to advance the cause of the working class, despite the emergence of the Labour Party and its electoral success in securing 29 M.P.s in the 1906 election.

Syndicalism was one manifestation of this antipathy to the political road to socialism, with its emphasis on industrial struggle as the essential means of vesting ownership and economic decision-making power in the hands of the producers. Its influence was most potent in continental Europe, particularly France and the United States,[4] but it was also felt in Britain. James Connolly, for example, was influenced by the work of Daniel de Leon during a period he spent in the United States and was effective in spreading syndicalist ideas through organizations such as the Socialist Labour Party. Tom Mann, who established a paper, the *Industrial Syndicalist*, in 1910, and a year later, the Industrial Syndicalist Education League, also played an important role in disseminating syndicalist ideas within the British labour movement in the period prior to the outbreak of the Great War; a period which saw both an unparalleled wave of industrial unrest and the growth of rank and file movements challenging trade union hierarchies. It was indeed one such group, the Unofficial Reform Committee of the South Wales Miners' Federation, which produced a classic text of British syndicalism – *The Miners' Next Step*, published in Tonypandy in 1912.[5]

More importantly, in terms of its impact, the decade prior to the outbreak of the Great War also saw the emergence of guild socialism. A.J. Penty's *Restoration of the Gild System*, 1906, had articulated many of the elements of this. There was the setting of the producer centre stage, with the concomitant rejection of the notion 'that government should be conducted solely in the interests of man in his capacity as consumer.'[6] There was a focus on creative and fulfilling labour as the essential objective of any transformation of society. There was the rejection of the use of state power as a means of achieving this, and an emphasis rather on producer guilds as the motive force of social transformation; these guilds, like their medieval counterparts, were to regulate their trade, assume responsibility for the quality of what was produced, the price at which it was sold and the remuneration and social status of its members. Penty's work was, though, tinged with an atavistic medievalism and imbued with an antipathy to commercialism, international trade and mechanised mass production, that often spilled over into a more general antipathy to industrialism and all its works.

It was, therefore, S.G. Hobson's *National Guilds, an Inquiry into the Wage System and the Way Out*, 1914, based on a series of articles in A.R. Orage's, *The New Age*, 1912, that precipitated the emergence of a guild socialism applicable to an industrial civilization: a guild socialism that in condemning the commoditisation of labour inherent in the wage system, also rejected that collectivism which threatened to replicate it in an economy characterised by extensive public ownership. Thus what Fabian socialists proposed would merely replace private capitalism with state capitalism, with the decision-making and controlling authority retained by the manager or bureaucrat. Fabian collectivism failed to extend the application of democratic principles to industry, while the Fabian attitude to democracy was 'arrogant and supercilious' and inimical to the concept of an active and informed citizenry which Hobson saw as integral to socialism.[7]

Guild socialism alone could effect the destruction of the wage system and 'trade unions' would be both the means of its destruction and 'the natural nuclei of future industrial organisation'.[8] To achieve this Hobson looked to the widest possible extension of the trade union movement and the unification of its fragmented structure into a number of powerful industrial unions. Such unions would 'make tireless and unrelenting inroads upon rent and interest', press for the co-management of industries to erode the power of existing managers and owners and so lay the basis for the transfer of that power to the guilds.[9] Guilds would, in Hobson's view, assume responsibility for all aspects of the organisation of production and 'instead of the State...for the material welfare of its members'.[10] That said ownership of the means of production should be vested in the state which would, in effect, co-manage the economy with the guilds. So while guild socialism 'rejects State bureaucracy...it [also] rejects Syndicalism because it accepts co-management with the state...subject to the principle of industrial democracy'.[11]

As noted Cole's socialism was inspired by Morris's *News from Nowhere* and at the core of guild socialism, whether that of Penty, Hobson or others, was an embrace of the Morrisian notion that work should be about the expression of humanity's creative capacities and, therefore, about 'the intelligent production of beautiful things'.[12] Capitalism was a system essentially inimical to this, and was therefore not just materially, but also morally and aesthetically, impoverishing. Fabian socialism did not address these, the most fundamental failings and inequities of capitalism, because it did not seek the kind of worker autonomy that made creative labour possible. Of Sidney Webb Cole wrote, 'he still conceives the mass of men as persons who ought to be decently treated, not as persons who ought freely to organize their own conditions of life; in short, his conception of a new social order is still that of an order which is ordained from without and not realized from within.'[13] Only a democratisation of the industrial process of the kind proposed by guild socialism would make possible such creative self-realization.

For the young Cole, the focus was on the need to effect a transformation of industry and society that replaced 'useless toil' with 'joyful labour'. 'The crowning indictment of capitalism was that it destroy[ed] the freedom and individuality in the worker, that it reduce[d] man to a machine, and that it treate[d] human beings as a means to production instead of subordinating production to the well-being of the producer.'[14] 'The greatest task of the present [wa]s the awakening of individuality and spontaneity in the worker' and it was the desire to accomplish this that led Cole to embrace guild socialism and, in works such as *The World of Labour*, 1913,[15] *Self-Government in Industry*, 1917, and *Guild Socialism Restated*, 1920, establish himself as its most important theoretician and effective populariser.[16]

To reawaken creativity, spontaneity and individuality in the worker it was imperative that 'the individual worker [should] be regarded not simply as a "hand"...but as a man amongst men, with rights and responsibilities, with a human soul and a desire for self-expression, self-government and personal freedom.' And, for this to occur, it was imperative that 'the control of industry should be democratized; that the workers themselves should have an ever-increasing measure of power and responsibility in control, and that capitalist supremacy...be overthrown only by a system of industrial democracy in which workers will control industry in conjunction with a democratized State.'[17]

It was freedom, autonomy, individuality and the opportunity for creative self-expression, not the generalisation of material affluence which should be the primary desiderata for socialists. This was the error of the Fabians and other collectivists. They had prioritised the latter rather than the former. 'Inspired by the idea that poverty is the root evil, socialists have tried to heal the ills of society by an attempt to redistribute income.' But 'higher wages will not make less dreary or automatic the life of the worker who is subjected to bureaucratic expert control and divorced from all freedom and responsibility.'[18] The extension of public ownership and the enhanced efficiency and output which it would allow might have its place in the socialist commonwealth of the future but socialists must never lose sight of the fact that ownership was a means to an end and not an end in itself.

Like Hobson and other guild socialists Cole was sensitive to the danger of the centralisation of decision-making authority which state ownership could precipitate; particularly so with the onset of the Great War. This saw the state assume control over significant areas of war-related economic activity. However, for Cole, 'the fact was that capitalism had broken down under the strain of war, and the efforts of the State to make up for [its] deficiencies had raised more problems than it had solved.'[19] For, as he saw it, in 'round[ing] in the end the Cape of State Capitalism, we shall only find ourselves on the other side in a Sargasso Sea of State Socialism, which will continue *to repress all initiative, clog all endeavour, and deny all freedom to the workers.*'[20] The experience of the wartime role of the state had therefore confirmed all Cole's reservations about collectivism but, in particular, the view expressed in *The World of Labour* that 'the extension of the powers of the state may be merely a transference of authority from the capitalist to the bureaucrat.'[21]

What, then, was to be done? As with Hobson, Penty and other guild socialists, the trade unions were to be a critical agent of progress. But to realise that role they needed to change and the issue of trade union structure therefore became fundamental. As he wrote in *The World of Labour* 'today the question of trade union structure is the central problem before the labour movement'[22] because, on the basis of the existing structure and trade union policy, the possibility of trade unions playing such a role seemed remote. In the 1917 edition of the work, Cole referred to 'the lamentable flabbiness, the fatal indecision and the childlike gullibility' of British trade unionism describing it as a movement bereft of ideas and policy.[23] Yet there was evidence of change and in particular a realisation on the part of some that to be effective in a period which witnessed the marked concentration of industrial ownership, trade unions too had to become organised on an industrial basis. And, for Cole, this was the way forward: 'out of trade unionism today must arise a Greater Unionism, in which craft shall no longer be divided from craft, nor industry from industry. Industrial unionism lies next on the road to freedom'.[24] And the logical outcome of this Greater Unionism was guild socialism.[25] In that regard, as Cole put it in *Chaos and Order in Industry*, 1920, 'trade unionism itself' would become 'the nucleus of a new industrial order'.[26]

Pari passu with this should go a process of what was termed encroaching control. 'Only through their own organizations', wrote Cole, 'can the workers hope to counteract this tyranny of industrialism'.[27] And the method these organizations would deploy was that of the progressive invasion of capitalist control; a progressive wresting of the right to make decisions from Capitalism and a vesting of it in the workers themselves. A process that would effect 'a progressive atrophy of Capitalism corresponding to a development of function and opportunity and power for the proletariat.'[28] As trade unions grew in size, ambition and the range of activity they encompassed, so a growing self confidence and power would allow then to subvert and assume the prerogatives of management. Thus, for Cole, 'the two movements towards control and amalgamation must go on together, for each will lend to the other a momentum which neither could by itself acquire.'[29]

And there was already evidence that the trade union movement was evolving to accommodate ambitions that involved not simply wages and conditions but also those relating to the organisation and control of industry. As Cole put it in *The World of Labour*, 'there are the first beginnings, in Trade Unionism today, of an attempt not merely to raise the standard of life or "better "conditions, but to change the industrial system and substitute democracy for autocracy in the workshop.'[30] The very 'experience of collective bargaining has given the unions confidence in their powers and the tendency continually to extend the sphere of such bargaining...it can be used as a means of getting a share in the actual control of the management.'[31] In this way capitalists would be rendered socially functionless and the basis for the system's transcendence established. 'The workers, having learnt how to interfere in control, will then assume actual government, just as modern democracies have begun by enforcing concessions by insurrection and have then gradually forced their way to recognition and habitual control.'[32]

This, however, raised the issue of the role of politics and the state in this socialist transformation of society. For Cole, 'in the Commonwealth today, power in the economic field is the key which alone can unlock the gates of real political power' and parliamentary democracy, to have substance, needed to be underpinned by economic and social democracy.[33] Cole's concerns about the power of the state have already been noted and, in terms of the location of power and authority, Cole embraced a pluralism that saw the state as one, but only one, association within which these could reside. No one authority should be supreme. And just as humanity was multifaceted in terms of its goals and activity, so that should be reflected in the associated representative organisations in which people participated and the power which they wielded. In this regard power should follow function.

In this context, one of decentralised control and decision-making, the state had a constructive if circumscribed role to play. To begin with Cole's guild socialism was predicated upon the ownership of the means of production by the state.[34] So, 'expropriation is the state's business; and the development of the new forms of industrial control must be coupled with the growth of state ownership. Nationalisation retains the importance assigned to it in Socialist theory; but it becomes a means and not an end in itself.'[35] Indeed Cole opined that it was 'inconceivable that, even in a single industry, the workers would reach such a stage as to be ready and fitted to take over the control of industry before the state has actually stepped in and nationalised the service.'[36]

In his earlier works Cole also saw the state as having a critical role to play in representing the interests of the consumers. Thus, as regards major investment decisions, 'the State as a representative of the consumers must have...a voice equal to that of all the producers'.[37] Also, while a National Guilds' Congress might assume responsibility for 'the organisation of demand and supply...[and] the control of prices', this function should be performed 'in consultation with the consumer', represented either by the state or, in terms of the position he was to take up in *Guild Socialism Restated*, 1920, by institutions such as co-operative societies, representative of consumer interests.[38] In this regard the determination of prices was a 'social function'.[39]

In contrast to the syndicalists, therefore, Cole believed that ownership of productive capacity should reside with the state, and the interests of the consumer should be represented and institutionally embedded. He recognised, as the syndicalists did not, the potential conflicts of interest between producer guilds and society as a whole. So what was required was not just workers' control but a partnership between state and guilds or between the state, guilds and consumer organisations. 'Syndicalism', in contrast to Collectivism, 'lays all the stress on the producer and none on the consumer. It...refuses to recognise the function of the great league of consumers we call the State. But this refusal, where it is not an unjustifiable theoretical development, is an unreflective antipathy to the bourgeois state of the present.'[40] Yet for all its deficiencies, and in particular its failure to engage constructively with the political dimension, 'syndicalism' was, for Cole, 'the infirmity of noble minds', while 'collectivism is at best only the sordid dream of a businessman with a conscience.'[41]

This then raises the question of where Cole stood, as a guild socialist on the issue of revolutionary as opposed to gradualist change. That Cole in his guild socialist period articulated clearly the notion of irremediable class conflict, there can be no doubt. In *The World of Labour* he wrote, that it should be 'understood once for all, that the interests of Capital and Labour are diametrically opposed and although it may be necessary for Labour sometimes to acquiesce in "social peace", such peace is only the lull before the storm.' And again, 'industrial peace then must not be permanent. There is a real class-antagonism, a quarrel that can only be adjusted by the overthrow of capitalist society.'[42] Yet the combination of encroaching control, if aggressively pursued, together with the use of political power to secure the transference of the means of production to the ownership of the state, held out the possibility that a socialist transformation of society could be effected without violence or bloodshed. And he believed that, 'provided the Labour Movement keeps its ultimate revolutionary aim clearly in sight, it will get on better with discipline than without it.'[43] Cole did not rule out the possibility of violent struggle but his vision of revolutionary change was predicated on the possibility that it could occur without it.

Cole's attitude to the notion of a revolutionary transference of power also raises the question of his attitude to Marxism. For, like many on the Left in this period, he had to engage both politically and ideologically with those who articulated a Marxism which had at its core a commitment both to revolutionary struggle and the violent overthrow of the capitalist system. This engagement is a complex question spanning the whole of his intellectual life and it can only be touched upon briefly here. Cole certainly viewed favourably Marx's method of analysis seeking to understand the trajectory of social development in relation to the material drivers of historical change. And, as Wright has indicated, there were points during the 1930s when he was willing to apply a Marxist label to himself.[44] Moreover he recognised that class antagonism might indeed reach a pitch that would precipitate a revolutionary struggle for power; though this was an attitude that was more apparent at some historical junctures than others.

Yet in the final analysis he was antipathetic to much in Marxism[45] and, in particular, to its conception of an intensified class struggle based on increasing social polarisation in a capitalist context. For Cole, Britain's social structure was more variegated and complex than that which informed Marx's view of capitalism. Here in particular he pointed to the new salariat that owed no ideological allegiance to capitalism and might be recruited to socialist purposes within a planned economy. He was also critical of what he saw as Marx's determinism and the elevation of class above the individual. He also saw fascism as a complex phenomenon that could not easily be reduced to a last desperate attempt to maintain an imploding capitalism.

His *The Meaning of Marxism*, 1948, based on *What Marx Really Meant*, 1934, represented a relatively sympathetic engagement with Marxism. However, part of that sympathy can be explained by Cole's own rendition of Marx. The Marx who emerged from the former work 'was a Marx humanized by Cole's basic beliefs in creativity, fellowship, equality and liberty.' Or, as another commentator has put it, what Cole produces is, 'an activist, idealist, voluntarist, libertarian, minimally determinist version of Marxism; in fact a characteristic product of Cole's own approach to social theory.'[46]

As to guild socialism, this was to be a short-lived ideological phenomenon. In the aftermath of a brief post-war boom unemployment rose rapidly and trade unionism, the key agency of guild socialist change, was profoundly weakened. With the economic downturn also came the collapse of the National Guilds League and practical manifestations of guild socialism such as the National Guild of Builders, in 1923. Guild socialism also experienced ideological rifts, particularly in relation to different conceptions of the role of the state in its vision of the socialist future. Moreover there were different views as to the character and outcome of the class struggle which would inform and drive the transformative process. For some, it would be waged through encroaching control, for others it would assume a more violent and revolutionary form. As to the latter, many guild socialists moved into the British Communist Party when it was formed in 1921.[47]

The demise of guild socialism left Cole without an ideological cause to champion or a political economy to which to adhere. As Beatrice Webb put it in an entry in her diary in May 1924, 'G.D.H. Cole continues to write articles in the New Statesman and to carry out his duties as a staff officer to the W.E. A. with exemplary regularity but he has lost all touch with other people and has no spiritual home in, or outside, the Labour Movement. Politically, he is a lost soul – the older men have ceased to fear him; the younger men no longer look up to him...He still trots out his "Workers' Control" – but in a disheartened fashion without conviction that anyone cares about it.'[48] The General Strike of 1926 further highlighted the contemporary limitations of the trade union movement and, therefore, the extent to which extra-parliamentary action could advance the socialist cause.[49] Perhaps in consequence of this, and in a period when he lacked a political home and defensible political ideology, Cole pursued intellectual interests that were less of a theoretical and propagandist nature and more those of an historian and educationalist.[50] And certainly it has been argued that in the 1920s his aim became that of inculcating into the working class a sense of their own history, identity and historical mission; or, as one commentator has put it, 'arm[ing] the worker with that sense of his own past which would create a confidence to make his own future.'[51]

Whatever the drivers, for much of the 1920s Cole elided a direct engagement with politics and political economy. However by the late 1920s he had ended this sojourn in the political wilderness, joining the Fabian Society in 1928 and embracing the centrality of parliamentary action in laying the basis for any future progress in the direction of workers' control and socialism. In this regard he came to give a greater role to the state and conventional politics and, in 1928, played a major role in drafting a pamphlet, *Labour and the Nation*, 1928, which represented an expression, articulated in Fabian terms, of Labour's policy stance on the key social and economic questions of the day.[52] One year later, in 1929, Cole published his first major work of political economy in almost a decade, *The Next Ten Years in British Economic and Social Policy*, 1929, which effectively position him as a mainstream Fabian who sought to stabilize capitalism before progressing socialism by essentially statist means.[53]

The state and socialist planning, 1929-45

In the late 1920s and early 1930s, faced with a capitalism in crisis and in imminent danger of collapse, the imperative for Cole became the formulation of a strategy which would mitigate the suffering of the masses, prevent a politically violent implosion of the system and lay the basis for socialist advance. In this task he was influenced by the work of J.A. Hobson and Maynard Keynes. His sense of the nature and causes of the crisis was initially derived from the former though, later in the 1930s, it was also informed by the latter. And it was upon such theoretical foundations that his proposed policies rested.

Before 1931 the objective was to articulate a package of measures which would deliver social control over critical areas of economic activity, while laying the basis for a smooth transition from an economy still essentially capitalist, to one characterized by planning on the basis of an extensive social ownership of economic activity.[54] After 1931, it became necessary to advance a more radical programme, to which end Cole played a critical role in establishing the Socialist Society for Information and Propaganda[55] and the New Fabian Research Bureau. The first, as its name would suggest, focused on the dissemination of socialist ideas; the latter on furnishing the basic economic research needed to transform the theoretical rigour, sophistication and coherence of Labour thinking on economic policy issues.[56]

As to Cole's own analysis there were clearly Hobsonian inflections. Writing in *The Next Ten Years*, he made the point that 'it is not the inducement offered but the size of great men's incomes that determines the size of the savings under present-day conditions' and that 'there [was] no guarantee that the right amount will be saved.'[57] Indeed given the skewed distribution of income and wealth, it was highly likely that savings would outstrip the willingness to invest and, in consequence, a crisis of underconsumption would result. It therefore became 'vital...that the purchasing power distributed in society should be measured in accordance with the productive capacity of the community, and not left to depend upon the active production secured by the free play of the forces of supply and demand.'[58]

Post *General Theory* the analysis became more obviously Keynesian. Writing in a pamphlet entitled *Monetary Systems and Theories*, 1942, for example, Cole opined, in a quintessentially Keynesian manner, that 'from the standpoint of the community, "savings" that do not lead to "investment" – that is, to the spending of the saved money on capital goods – are not real savings at all. They are cancelled by the losses of those who cannot sell their goods at remunerative prices. This is the gist of Lord Keynes' theory of "savings" and "investment"; and most economists are agreed that this part of his theory is true.'[59]

As to remedies for depression and macroeconomic disequilibria these varied over the period after 1929. Cole was the author of *We can Conquer Unemployment*, 1929, the Labour Party's rebuttal of *Can Lloyd George do it?*; a pamphlet in which the Liberals had articulated a radical expansionary public works strategy endorsed and informed by the thinking of Maynard Keynes. Cole's pamphlet accomplished the impressive feat of castigating the Liberals for appropriating Labours' ideas, whilst at the same time rejecting them as ineffectual, financially unsound and politically irresponsible. The crux of his polemic lay in the extent to which demand could be stimulated while adhering to the prevailing fiscal orthodoxy of a balanced budget. And Cole's solution was one which utilized what might now be termed a balanced budget multiplier. Thus taxation would be used to redistribute income and wealth, with increased tax revenues being disbursed by way, for example, of family allowances. In effect, those with a high propensity to consume would be favoured over those with a high propensity to save, with aggregate demand stimulated and jobs created in consequence.[60] '*We must get the resources required for employing the unemployed mainly, and for providing family allowances wholly, from taxation* of the social income, and we must get the capital required for social development from the investible surplus remaining after taxation has been levied.'[61] Of course what was not factored into the balanced budget equation was the rapidly shrinking revenue base that came with the diminution in the level of economic activity when general economic depression finally struck. Cole therefore trod an interesting tightrope. On the one hand he did not want to fall off into the arms of the Liberals. On the other he did not want too obviously to succumb to the siren call of the I.L.P. whose proposals to increase working-class purchasing power had been soundly rejected by the 1927 Labour Party Annual Conference. On the one hand his reconciliation with the conventional politics of the Labour Party suggested the need for state action, on the other he was not yet prepared to give the state the pre-eminent role in the conduct of economic policy which he was to do in the 1930s.

In the end the circle was squared by a proposal for redistribution which, while driven by the state, would realize its beneficial consequences through the additional purchasing power deployed by the working-class consumer. As he wrote in *The Next Ten Years*, 'the bulk of the new taxation proposed is to be raised, not for spending by the Government but for direct redistribution as purchasing power among the members of the community. The sum provided for family allowances as a whole, and the bulk of the money allocated to the prevention of unemployment will become purchasing power in the hands of the recipients. It will thus serve directly to bring about an expansion of demand for commodities.'[62]

In line with the underconsumptionist analysis which informed this prescriptive position, Cole continued throughout the 1930s to emphasise enhanced working-class consumption as a driver of economic activity. Thus in relation to the expansionary potentialities of monetary policy he was clear in *The Principles of Economic Planning*, 1935, that 'whenever the need arises to increase the supply of money, I am suggesting that the increase ought to be made not in the form of increased loan credits to either producers or consumers, but in non-repayable presents of purchasing power to all the citizens, save to the extent to which the state decides to use the money itself for public purposes.'[63] That said, by the 1930s, Cole had also come to believe that the state itself had a more direct, potent and immediate role to play. For, as he saw it, state-financed public works created economic activity and thence employment without the intermediation of the private consumer.[64] In *Practical Economics*, he was particularly emphatic, 'there is only one condition on which a capitalist economy can maintain "full employment" for any length of time. This condition is that the state will so act to maintain the demand for the factors of production at the requisite level. The state can do this by a policy of public works, accompanied by monetary expansion.'[65]

In this period Cole also came to accept the need for an appropriately supportive monetary policy if the economy was to be moved back towards full employment.[66] In *The Next Ten Years* he had recognized the negative role which a monetary system in private hands could play, both in terms of the manner in which it could obstruct a socialist policy of industrial transformation, and the deleterious macroeconomic impact it could have. Thus 'the joint stock banks by discrimination in the granting of credits, could largely neutralize the effects of [a] policy of national industrial development...and the Bank of England, by manipulating the bank rate, or even by transactions in securities, could go a long way towards causing an industrial depression'. Yet Cole remained sceptical as to the efficacy of monetary policy *toute seule* in turning an economy around. Even with a socialization of the banking system and the use of monetary policy for socialist purposes, the management of money and credit could 'help but it cannot create'.[67] Similarly, in 1935, Cole wrote of the banking system that 'its power by manipulating money or controlling bank policy, even to the extent of bringing the banks under full public ownership to increase the employment of resources in production, is exceedingly limited...unless it controls the industries whose production is to be increased.'[68] He was also concerned that to the extent that an expansionary monetary policy could help bring about a fuller utilization of resources, it ran the risk of producing 'recurrently rising prices' which would 'confer advantages on every sort of capitalist monopoly'; though Cole also made clear that if such a policy could contribute to increased economic prosperity it should be supported, even at the risk of benefitting vested interests or an inflationary spiral.[69] And certainly, by the 1930s, he was convinced that a planned, full employment economy required an appropriate monetary policy. 'We cannot have planned production (or in my view, full employment) without planned finance, or without public control of the commercial banks'. 'Bank nationalization' was therefore 'needed, not for its own stake, but as the instrument of a policy of "full employment".'[70] As he wrote in *What Everybody wants to Know about Money*, 1933, 'any Socialist government which is not prepared to tackle thoroughly the question of the banks cannot be a government that means to seriously advance socialism'.[71]

But Cole was also clear that even an expansionary monetary and fiscal policy conducted on Keynesian or Hobsonian lines would simply steady the capitalist ship. It could prevent the capitalist system's catastrophic demise and it could, in consequence, materially improve the position of the working class. But, such a macroeconomic strategy would not address capitalism's inherent volatility, inefficiencies and inequities. To do that a more radical interventionist strategy was necessary; one that involved social ownership and planning. And through the efforts of the NFRB and SSIP 'the idea of economic planning emerged as a central theme of Labour's refurbished socialist ideology in the 1930s.'[72]

As we have seen the extension of social ownership was integral to Cole's conception of the transition to guild socialism. In *The Next Ten Years*, the term socialization was preferred to signal the possibility of alternatives to outright national ownership and, in that respect, his concern over the centralisation of economic power in bureaucratic hands persisted and was also to surface with renewed force in the post-war period when various forms of social ownership of a non-Morrisonian kind were mooted.[73] In the 1930s the extension of social ownership was central to his understanding of how the British economy could be stabilized, rationalized, established on a firm basis and planned for socialist purposes.[74] But that understanding was now essentially Fabian, with nationalization being seen primarily in terms of the elimination of waste and the utilization and direction of productive capacity for social purposes.

It is true that the issue of workers' control was one which surfaced periodically in his writing and the link made with that creative self-fulfilment which should lie at the heart of socialism: 'we must make men and women citizens of industry as well as the state'. And a measure of workers' control was necessary, for otherwise while 'the robots may be richer and more leisured...they will be unhappy with an unhappiness that many of them will be unable to define or to track to its source.'[75] In this regard Cole continued to articulate his vision of guild socialism as the ultimate goal. 'That a socialist economy should develop towards a system of guild control seems to be indispensible if the dangers of top heaviness and concentrated bureaucracy are to be avoided'; 'in the long run the aspiration of a planned economy must be to make each industry to the fullest possible extent a democratic, self-governing guild.'[76] And Cole proclaimed himself 'an unrepentant Guild Socialist.'[77] Nevertheless, in most of his writing in the 1930s workers' control is articulated in terms of models of representation within the structures that nationalized corporations would present. It was not seen in guild socialist terms of decentralized producer control of a multiplicity of relatively autonomous enterprises. Moreover, in line with the increasingly Fabian complexion of his political economy, there was greater prominence given to the role of the expert.[78] As he put it in *The Next Ten Years*, 'within the limits of the broad control of policy by the State it is indispensable to give the expert a wide discretionary power and a liberal freedom to experiment in new methods.'[79]

The Fabian conception of progressing nationalization, and the benefits to be expected from this, is particularly apparent in *The Next Ten Years*. First, there was an acceptance that the emergence of monopolistic arrangements was something to be embraced as it prepared areas of capitalist industry for regulation, control and, ultimately, social ownership. Thus, for Cole, 'it [wa]s of vital concern for Socialists to make capitalist industry as suitable as possible for collective regulation...in the transition from a capitalist to a socialist economy, it will be necessary to extend a progressive control over industries whilst they still remain in capitalist hands and this involves the existence of collective organizations with which the State itself can deal.'[80] This done, nationalization should proceed, though not on such a scale as to encompass the totality of economic activity. Socialising the control and direction of economic life would 'certainly involve the transference of a large number of enterprises now in private hands to various forms of public ownership and administration but it does not involve...universal public ownership'.[81] In the 1929 work there was also considerable emphasis on the possibilities opened up by a socialization of control which stopped short of outright ownership. So, once 'let the state control the nation's industries, and it need not care who owns them as long as the unfettered power of taxation is in its hands.'[82] The assumption too was of an incremental or gradualist approach. 'The socialization of industry, restated in these terms, comes to be envisaged...as a progressive transformation of capitalist industrialism into a Socialist system' and *The Next Ten Years* was conceived very much in terms of articulating 'the more important steps that can be taken *within the next few years* in order to begin straightening out the tangle of our economic affairs', rather than as a blueprint for the construction of a socialist commonwealth.[83]

However, with demise of the second minority Labour government in 1931 the tone becomes more aggressive and urgent and Cole's proposals, like those of other Labour thinkers, came to involve an extension of the scale, and an acceleration in the pace, of nationalization.[84] In the *Principles of Socialism*, 1932, an SSIP pamphlet, Cole wrote of the need for 'an immediate frontal attack on the key positions of capitalism' for 'the policy of gradual transition to socialism is in danger of meaning no transition at all, but the turning out of Labour governments, which seems only to make the situation worse.'[85] He looked therefore to the immediate nationalization of a swathe of key industries, but in particular the banking system, together with the creation of a National Investment Board which would play a critical allocative and planning role. What was needed was the power to plan and to give effect to planning decisions once made. Such an extension of social ownership was also critical for the delivery of a macroeconomic strategy, of the kind noted above, that would move the economy out of depression. Thus the destabilizing and restrictive tendencies of capitalism could not be eliminated as long as 'at any rate major industries, including the key industry of finance, remain in private hands'.[86] So, for example, 'the wider the sphere of public ownership of industry is, the greater is the State's power to carry out a balanced programme of public works.'[87] While, therefore, a strategy such as Roosevelt's New Deal was to be welcomed, 'there is no reason to suppose at all that the New Deal, in helping the United States to weather the crisis of 1929 and the following years will prevent a recurrence of such crises.'[88] A New Deal strategy could 'succeed in the long run [only] by passing beyond capitalism and superseding capitalist incentives to production and the capitalist system of distribution of incomes by effectively Socialist alternatives.'[89]

What was needed was a transformation altogether more profound than that encompassed by macroeconomic management. In this regard it should be noted that Cole, *au fond*, was part of that tradition, with roots in the very origins of socialist political economy, that evinced a deep suspicion of the market and the allocative and distributional outcomes which it generated. Prices, in the context of a capitalist system, were seen as rarely a reliable indicator of social need, and even in a socialist context social imperatives might necessitate the market's circumvention or the qualification of its outcomes. What socialists needed to work to was some concept of 'real value'; one which 'consist[ed] in the power of a thing to satisfy human needs and desires, irrespective of those who have the needs or desires to pay for it.'[90] Thus an allocation of resources which optimized social utility must be one which implied reference to a 'social standard [of value] which cannot be identified with the price standard accepted by most economists.'[91]

Under capitalism, 'the price system fails to measure anticipated satisfactions because of the unequal value of money to rich and poor.'[92] In this context the concept of consumer sovereignty, while in some ways an attractive one, and consistent with Cole's emphasis on freedom and individual self-expression, was nonetheless problematic. For while it 'would doubtless be reasonable to demand that the workman should recognize and subject himself to the demands [of consumers]... if these were determined by the community as a whole, on a basis of its needs...there is no reason why it should willingly submit to the control of productive effort if this is based on the employer's expectation of profit, *this expectation being based, in turn, on a wrong distribution of purchasing power.*'[93]

Given an equitable distribution of income and wealth, Cole accepted that the price mechanism would roughly reflect social need. But even then the price mechanism as a determinant of optimum resource allocation had its limitations, for there were certain 'basic needs' that should be met independently of consumer demand. Moreover the state must necessarily make strategic decisions, with implications for resource allocation, independently of the imperatives emanating from consumer demand. In consequence, for Cole, consumer demand became something of a residual element in the imperatives driving the allocation of resources. As he envisioned it in *Practical Economics*, 1937, it would be 'the resources of production, *beyond those employed in meeting basic needs*...and of course those required for the maintenance and increase of capital', that would 'be directed to giving consumers what they want.'[94]

As to the pricing of labour, Cole envisaged a circumscribed and diminishing role for the market. 'Remuneration for work done [would] be retained at all only to the extent to which it is necessary in order to assist in regulating the supply of labour and in eliciting the satisfactory response of effort from workers'.[95] However, Cole considered that under socialism even this circumscribed role would diminish over time. As he put it in the *Principles of Economic Planning*, 'I believe the tendency will be for a planned economy steadily to reduce the proportion of total income distributed in the first of these ways and steadily to enlarge the amount of the social dividend.'[96] In effect, with a substantial and probably growing proportion of the needs of workers furnished directly by the state, the purchasing power represented by wages would simply become less significant. And while Cole accepted 'there [was]...no objection to allowing the laws of supply and demand to operate to a considerable extent upon the relative levels of remuneration', he believed that it would be 'wiser to equalize the eligibilities of different occupations more by varying hours and conditions of labour than by establishing widely different wage standards.'[97]

As to planning it was logical therefore to argue that, 'decisions involved in the national plan ought to be made as far as possible in terms of real things, and only translated subsequently for convenience into terms of...money.'[98] Real things, real value, use value: it was by reference to those concepts that a socialist economy would be managed; no longer by reference to the shadow world of market prices flickering on the walls of the capitalist cave.

And planning was the key to the socialist economic future. It made possible the circumscription of the price mechanism and the gradual replacement of 'the monetary incentives on which capitalism relies for getting the world's work done, by other incentives more consistent with the social interest.' 'Planning under public auspices, and with a view to the satisfaction of consumer needs' also 'offer[ed] the prospect of eliminating the wastes inherent in unregulated competition, whether of the older or the newer monopolistic variety.'[99] It allowed supply to be matched with demand and therefore could ensure the full utilization of resources. And not just the aggregate matching of supply and demand, for industry would be 'rebuil[t]... with the right proportions in view of modern needs, in accordance with a definite plan, instead of trusting to the blind forces of individual profit seeking somehow to create an harmonious structure'.[100] Together with the extension of social ownership, it would also sweep away the constraints on the expansion of output that were characteristic of a capitalism whose industrial structure was inherently monopolistic.[101] Cole was also clear that planning should encompass the business of distribution and that a socialist planning authority would 'be inexorably driven to plan the distribution of incomes as a condition precedent to the just or expedient planning of production'.[102]

So on what basis and within what structures would planning take place? Cole wrote at length on the bureaucratic paraphernalia of economic planning, mooting various entities such as a National Planning Commission, a National Planning Authority, a National Investment Board, Departments of Inspection, Import Boards etc and those who would wish to pursue further this aspect of his thought can consult, amongst others, works such as *The Machinery of Socialist Planning*, 1938, and the *Principles of Economic Planning*. As to the basis for effecting the socially optimum allocation of resources and distribution of incomes, Cole's general desire to plan in terms of real things and social utility, and his aspiration for an increasingly circumscribed role for the price mechanism, has already been noted. However, he did not really engage with the socialist calculation debate which raged with a particular intensity in the 1930s[103] and his discussion of the basis on which planners might make decisions was distinctly unilluminating. He did suggest that the sale of goods and services should be at prices corresponding to their costs of production but he also opined that 'if the planning authorities have overestimated or underestimated the demand for a particular commodity, it will be possible to adjust supply and demand by raising or lowering the price.'[104] And in the same work he argued that 'over by far the greater part of the field of production...the task of a planned economy will not be to dictate what is to be consumed, but to respond to the movements of consumer demand','mov[ing] prices accordingly'.[105] And again 'both the planned and the planless economy have the same necessity to adjust their output to what the consumers are prepared to buy at prices at which the producers are prepared to sell.'[106] In this regard he seemed, at least in the short to medium term, to be prepared to envisage planners and a planning system responsive to consumer demand and market price. In truth it must be said that while the rhetoric of planning was at the core of his political economy in the 1930s, and remained so in the post-war period, he added little to an understanding of what would be distinctive about socialist economic planning in terms of the basis upon which it would be conducted, the means it would use and the ends it would serve.

This faith in socialist planning also had a particular bearing on Cole's attitude to the Soviet Union. A New Fabian Research Bureau trip to Russia in July/August 1932 strengthened Cole's and others interest in Soviet planning[107] and he certainly believed 'that planning Russian style could yet prove a practical model for a British socialist system.'[108] Like the Fabians he believed that planning meant the calculated and rational utilization of the nation's resources for maximum social benefit and, in this context, socialist planning was contrasted with capitalist disorganization; particularly in the aftermath of the Wall St. Crash. And this attitude persisted throughout the 1930s alongside disquiet about a political system where purges had become an instrument of state policy. Yet that disquiet was muted. Throughout the 1930s and into the post-war period Cole, as one writer has put it, 'sought to explain to the social democratic left that Russia remained an essentially socialist society; and a society which, if it abrogated some liberal democratic values, decisively enlarged and realized others.'[109] Writing in *Left News* in 1942 he stated "I regard the Soviet system as much more democratic than parliamentarism and I advocate it for a large part of Europe as the most appropriate way of bringing democracy about".[110] Again, in a *Plan for Britain*, 1943, he wrote that 'in a clearly realistic sense the Russian peoples are a great deal more free than we are or can be till we have abandoned our atomism and set out to make a determined pursuit after collective and not merely individualistic values.'[111] And, as he saw it, what he was proposing in the 1930s 'involve[d] some sort of National Economic Plan such as exists today in Soviet Russia and nowhere else in the world.'[112] Like many on the Left, therefore, Cole qualified criticism with equivocation: equivocation borne partly of a perception of the particular circumstances and challenges which the Soviet Union was confronting, partly of a determination not to concede terrain useful to the critics of planning and partly of a desire to believe that what seemed to be rational must ultimately be defensible. Soviet Russia was therefore 'a guarantee that, if other communities do take the task of constructing a Socialist system seriously in hand, they will not find themselves isolated in a capitalist world.'[113]

Cole and the affluent society

The post-war world was to bring different and, in some ways, more formidable theoretical and prescriptive challenges. If not immediately then certainly by the 1950s social democratic political economists such as Cole confronted those posed by full, or near-full, employment, sustained economic growth, rapidly rising living standards and a relatively stable capitalism that was seen to be delivering the goods and in ever increasing quantities. Moreover, by that decade, and courtesy of the Attlee governments, Labour had completed a substantial part of the programme which it had mapped out in the 1930s and presented to the electorate in 1945. As Richard Crossman put it, 'those who manned the defences of Jericho could not have been more surprised than those socialists who saw the walls of capitalism tumble down after a short blast on the Fabian trumpet.'[114]

So for some writers there was a need for a fundamental revision of social democracy in the light of a profound alteration in the nature of capitalism. Crosland, for example, did not believe that the social and economic character of post-war Britain merit the label of capitalism at all and other writers concurred.[115] Thus in addition to the manifest dynamism of capitalism, many saw a radically altered distribution of economic power, with the state having assumed authority in relation to macroeconomic management and having put in place the essential structures of a welfare state. Nationalisation had taken a significant section of the economy's commanding heights into social ownership, circumscribing the area of the economy over which private enterprise held sway. Further, the managerial revolution was spelling the demise of the pivotal role of the capitalist entrepreneur, while full employment significantly redressed the balance of power in the labour market in favour of the trade union movement. As Roy Jenkins saw it, the capitalist class had surrendered its power 'partly to the state, partly to their own managers and partly to the trade unions'.[116]

Cole viewed these developments differently. Socialism must be about more than the 'managerial welfare state' that had emerged in the aftermath of the post-war Labour governments and the Keynesian revolution.[117] It had to be about more than a mixed economy still heavily skewed in favour of the private sector. It must offer more than the spiritually impoverished material affluence of a consumer society. And he bridled at the extent to which so many social democrats had accepted that these things represented anything other than a reinvention of capitalism that left intact its loci of power and its demoralising *raison d'être*.

As Cole saw it, 'most of the non-Marxist socialist economists swallowed Keynes whole and became his most fervent disciples'.[118] For many, indeed, demand management had become both the essence of socialist planning and something that vitiated any need for the further extension of social ownership. As he put it in *Socialist Economics*, 1950, 'this new Keynesian economics deeply affected the thought of Socialists. Hitherto most socialists had considered that the disease of unemployment in both its long-term and cyclical form was incurable except by socialization...that is, by the State taking over industry and employing every available person and, at the same time, so distributing purchasing power as to ensure that there would be a demand for all that socialized industry could produce...But now it appeared if Keynes were right that full employment would be maintained without socialisation, merely by manipulating the correct leavers at the centre in the money and investment markets. There might be a case for socializing this or that industry on other grounds...but not in order to cure unemployment.'[119]

For Cole this view was manifestly flawed. First, he was unconvinced that demand management could keep in check the inflationary pressures which full employment threatened to unleash, 'unless it is in a position to control, broadly, what is to be produced and when, and what is charged for it, and also the broad distribution of purchasing power.'[120] Moreover, 'full employment' was a problematic concept which might accurately characterise the state of the labour market in some regions but not in others. To achieve genuinely full employment 'the State must be in a position to control the position of industry in order to bring balanced employment to the workers rather than expect them to migrate in large masses in search of work.'[121] In addition, and again with an eye to inflationary pressures, 'in a Socialist society, it will clearly not be possible to allow wage rates to be settled by a large number of uncoordinated bargains...There will have to be both some general way of determining how large an aggregate of wage payments the economy is able to afford and...how what is deemed to be available shall be divided amongst the various claimants.'[122] In short then a concerted regional policy, price and wage regulation would be necessary just to deliver on social democracy's macroeconomic objectives.

Yet that still left relatively untouched the heartlands of capitalist power. Nationalisation had certainly proceeded under the Attlee governments. But the programme of extending social ownership had proved, with the exception of steel and sugar, relatively uncontroversial. As Cole put it in a *New Statesman* pamphlet, enterprises 'singled out for socialization, with one exception, were services which can be seen as falling broadly within the "public utilities" range...and from the outset have been subject to public regulation and control...Thus there was nothing essentially "socialistic" in proposals to nationalize any one of these services.'[123] The 'proposal to socialize "public utilities" raised no real question of principle between Socialists and Anti-Socialists'.[124] Again, writing of the Labour Party's position in the 1930s, Cole stated that, 'their plans of nationalization were substantial and challenging to some great capitalist interests, particularly in the case of iron and steel: but they were plans which could be carried out without interfering seriously with the main structure of capitalist ownership and control.'[125]

That, of course, was the significance of the post-war fight over steel. Steel was something of critical importance for capitalism; an industry pivotal in terms of the power it could exert indirectly over a swathe of industrial activity.[126] 'It is a key industry: its pricing policies affect the fortunes of many other industries, including those on which the long-run success of Britain as an exporter chiefly depends... It has a naturally strong tendency towards monopoly. It is an industry in which, because of the technical conditions, it pays the profit-seeking firms best to keep total productive capacity down as near as possible to the minimum expected level of demand, and to maintain high prices rather than to pass on the benefit of technical economies to the consumers.'[127] It was an industry where 'monopoly paid handsome dividends: arms-pushing was a highly remunerative business: risks could be reduced by bribing or cajoling Ministers or politicians or kings or tribal chiefs to favour the interests of the great firms and their investing associates.'[128]

But even further extension of social ownership into areas such as steel, would not deliver that to which socialists should aspire. And here, in the 1950s, Cole once again touched base with his guild socialist roots. 'As a Guild Socialist I believe that industry will not work really well until the responsibility for its efficient control is fairly shared with the workers by hand and by brain, under conditions based on the recognition of every worker as a responsible partner in a democratically organized public service.'[129] Post-war nationalisation had not been the precursor of this. The creation of public corporations had made 'little difference' to the 'actual status and conditions of work' of their employees.[130] Cole therefore looked once again to the 'trade union movement' to 'develop as far as possible a structure through which an advance to workers' control can be effectively made.'[131] Apart from anything else this was a prerequisite for corporate efficiency, for Cole was 'convinced that there can be no way of making industry work well under socialization without enlisting the workers as democratic partners in control, above all at the workshop and factory level.'[132] It was necessary too if industrial relations were to be harmonious. It was critical if workers were to act responsibly in a full employment context and avoid exploiting their strengthened bargaining position to secure inflationary wage gains. But above all the extension of workers' control was essential for the creation of a truly democratic society: for, 'it is impossible to have a really democratic society if most of the members have to spend most of their lives at work under essentially undemocratic conditions.'[133]

And Cole's thinking on the forms which post-war social ownership should assume must be set in this context. Here Cole, like many others on the Left, was critical of the Morrisonian model. Crucial to democratisation were therefore 'new forms of social ownership and control to replace capitalist enterprise';[134] new forms which would avoid the inherent authoritarianism of the monolithic Morrisonian corporation and create opportunities for decentralised decision-making and the extension of workers' control.

The legacy

In the famous doggerel categorisation of Cole by Maurice Reckitt, he was 'a bit of a puzzle...with a Bolshevik soul in a Fabian muzzle.'[135] This contains at least half the truth. For while the Fabian muzzle was certainly apparent from the late 1920s onwards, Cole's soul was Morrisian not Bolshevik. His vision was informed by a libertarian socialism which, like Tawney's, saw humanity in terms of ends not means. What he looked to was to transform work into something that involved creative self-fulfilment, and while he came to recognise the profound restraints upon the realisation of that ideal, it was one to which he continued to adhere. In that respect Asa Briggs was correct when he saw Cole as 'the Enlightenment on the surface: the Romantic Movement underneath'.[136] And, as Wright has perceptively remarked, 'if we seek to locate Cole within an intellectual tradition, it is a tradition staffed overwhelmingly by radical individualists. It contains Morris and Whitman, Cobbett and Paine, Belloc and Chesterton'.[137] At least this is the company kept by his socialist soul, even if, in the 1930s, his mind occupied a different ideological terrain.

Assessing his legacy is more problematic. At the time of his death in 1959 industrial democracy and workers' control had a place only in the sub-literature of socialism. However, by the late 1960s and early 1970s, which saw an efflorescence of interest in these things,[138] guild socialist principles, if not guild socialism, 'found a new strength and following in Britain and the world, and the British trade-union movement and the Labour Party...incorporated the principles of workers' control into their statements and manifestoes for the first time.'[139] As Houseman has pointed out, Cole's work on workers' control was published in over a dozen languages and this literature had some influence on Yugoslav development and planning in the 1960s and 1970s.[140] In these decades too his reservations as to what might be achieved solely by macroeconomic management were echoed by a generation of post-Keynesians such as Joan Robinson, Nicholas Kaldor and Thomas Balogh whose thought, amongst others, played a part in effecting the turn towards planning which informed the Labour Party's political economy in the Wilson years.[141]

Yet with the passing of that period, and the waning of enthusiasm for both industrial democracy and planning, interest in Cole correspondingly diminished and it would be difficult now to substantiate Houseman's view that 'the years since his death have seen G.D.H. Cole loom larger than ever, as a literate and formidable social political philosopher and to some extent as a prophet.'[142]

If his works continue to be read it is more by historians: historians of socialist political economy and historians of the labour movement. In this regard, while scholarship has moved on, his multi-volume *History of Socialist Thought* will continue to be a reference point for those who work in the field and his biographies of Owen, and in particular Cobbett, and his edition of the latter's *Rural Rides*, will continue to be regarded and read as major contributions to labour history. Yet in relation to his work as a socialist theorist one final point should be made. Unlike the Fabians and the socialist revisionists of the 1950s and 1960s, let alone those of the New Labour period, Cole, like Morris, and for that matter Tawney, posed the kind of questions to which capitalism has manifestly failed to provide an answer: questions related to the nature and purpose of work, the significance and character of material affluence and consumption, the conditions necessary for creative self-fulfilment and the prerequisites of an informed and democratic citizenry.

Selecting the works

Selecting eleven volumes from his enormous literary output to convey a sense of the work of G.D.H. Cole is a formidable task and whatever approach is adopted is open to criticism. If the selection is to be thoroughly representative then it must necessarily include works of social theory, economics, political economy, economic history, social and labour history, political theory, intellectual history, detective fiction and sociology, to say nothing of the full range of literary genres from polemical pamphlets to scholarly monographs. Selecting on this basis, as this list suggests, the edition would necessarily have been more voluminous, and considerably so, than the present one, and this approach would also have carried the risk of a selection which failed to give a coherent sense of the evolution and trajectory of Cole's socialist thinking over the five decades of his active intellectual life.

There is also the issue as to whether one goes for the classic texts or those which are lesser known, or less easily available, and which have not, as some would see it, had the attention they deserve. In this regard there was a temptation to include some of the post-Great-War works that were produced under the auspices of the Carnegie Foundation and published in 1923: *Trade Unionism in Munitions*, *Labour in the Coal Mining Industry* and *Workshop Organization*: works which not only contribute to an understanding of the post-war economy and the contemporary trade union movement but also illustrate Cole's strength as an empirically-rooted theoretician.

However, in the end, I have chosen works, books and pamphlets, which I hope are representative of the three critical periods of Cole's socialist thinking: the guild socialist decade from 1913-23; the post-1929 period when his political economy was dominated by the notion of socialist economic intervention and planning and the post-war period when, like other socialist theorists, he sought to come to terms with the particular challenges posed by the legacy, positive as well as problematic, of the Attlee governments, and the emergence of an affluent society. Also, because it is representative of the historical works of a particular period (1923-29) when there was a hiatus in the output of Cole the theoretician, I have included his biography of William Cobbett. In any case, as regards the latter, no selection would be complete without an example of his extraordinary contribution to labour history and *The Life of William Cobbett*, 1927, is certainly amongst the finest of his historical works: not least one feels because of his obvious empathy with the subject.

In her *Life of G.D.H. Cole*, Margaret Cole wrote of students who having 'selected "Cole and his ideas" as a subject for their doctoral theses... got themselves so bogged down in his own published writings as to render their own work, painstaking as it was, almost unreadable by anyone other than a specialist'.[143] This is one, but only one, of the dangers of seeking to master the formidable corpus of Cole's writing. The other main one being that justice is not done to important aspects of his life and work. I hope this Introduction has avoided the first of these pitfalls and provides an understanding of the evolution of Cole's socialist political economy, but I am only too aware that to avoid the second is beyond the scope of anything other than a substantial monograph. Others have essayed these tasks and efforts, for a full appreciation of the achievements of one of the most important figures in the intellectual history of the twentieth-century British Left, the reader should consult their works which are noted below. I hope this selection of monographs and pamphlets will inspire them to do so.

Notes

1. G.D.H. Cole, *The British Labour Movement – Retrospect and Prospect*, Ralph Fox Memorial Lecture, London, Fabian Society, 1951, pp. 3-4.
2. M. Stears 'Cole, George Douglas Howard (1889–1959), university teacher and political theorist', *Oxford Dictionary of National Biography*, Oxford University Press, 2004, Vol. 12, pp. 505-6.
3. The work 'arose directly out of the discussions of Syndicalism held by the Balliol College Group and the Political Science Group of the O.U.F.S', L. Carpenter, *G.D.H. Cole: An Intellectual Biography*, Cambridge, Cambridge University Press, 1973, p. 16. The work went through four editions by 1917.
4. Syndicalism in both France and the United States is discussed at some length in Cole's first major work *The World of Labour*, 1913. In France *syndicats* of workers were federated in *bourses du travail* co-operating with each other and acting collectively through *Confédération Générale du Travail*. In the United States syndicalism was promoted through the Socialist Labour Party under the leadership of Daniel de Leon, with the syndicalist International Workers of the World being established in 1905.
5. On pre-war British syndicalism see B. Holton, *British Syndicalism, 1900-14, Myths and Realities*, London, Pluto, 1976.
6. A.J. Penty, *Restoration of the Gild System*, London, Swan and Sonnenschien, 1906, p. 7.

7 S.G. Hobson *National Guilds, an Inquiry into the Wage System and the Way Out*, London, Bell, 1914, p. 219.
8 Ibid, p. 278.
9 Ibid, p. 5.
10 Ibid, p. 135.
11 Ibid, p. 132.
12 Wm. Morris, 'Art and the people' [1883] in M. Morris (ed.), *William Morris, Writer, Artist and Socialist*, 2 Vols., New York, Russell and Russell, 1966, Vol. 2, p. 383.
13 G.D.H. Cole, 'Recent Developments in the British Labour Movement', *American Economic Review*, 8, 1918, pp. 485-504.
14 G.D.H. Cole, *Self-Government in Industry*, London, Bell, 1917, p. 24; Cole, *The World of Labour, a Discussion of the Present and Future of Trade Unionism*, London, Bell, 1917, p. 319.
15 This work also represented 'a comparative account of the development of trade unionism across the western world', Stears, 'George Douglas Howard Cole' p. 506.
16 See, Carpenter, *G.D.H. Cole: An Intellectual Biography*, p 44.
17 Cole, *Self-Government in Industry*, p. 4.
18 Ibid, pp. 112, 53.
19 Ibid, p. 7.
20 Ibid, pp. 7, 197-8; see also *The World of Labour*, p. ix, my emphasis.
21 Ibid, p. 347.
22 Ibid, p. 210.
23 Ibid, p. xiii.
24 Cole, *Self-Government in Industry*, p. 117; see also ibid, p. 69.
25 Cole, *The World of Labour*, p. 386.
26 G.D.H. Cole, *Chaos and Order in Industry*, London, Methuen, 1920, p. 45.
27 Cole, *Self-Government in Industry*, p. 151.
28 Ibid.
29 Ibid, p. 22.
30 Cole, *The World of Labour*, p. 371.
31 Ibid, p. 8.
32 Ibid, p. 383. Encroaching control would provide the workers with an apprenticeship which would prepare them to govern themselves.'
33 G.D.H. Cole, *Labour in the Commonwealth*, London, Headley, 1920, pp. 164-5.
34 'Only the state as the representative of the community had the right to bring capitalist ownership to an end', G. Foote, *The Political Thought of the Labour Party*, 3rd edition, Palgrave, 1997, p. 116.
35 Ibid, p. 389.
36 Ibid, p. 407.
37 Cole, *Self-Government in Industry*, pp. 192-3.
38 'In *The World of Labour* he nominated the state as representative of the community, while by the time he came to write *Guild Socialism Restated*, he proposed consumer associations', Foote, *The Political Thought of the Labour Party*, p. 112.
39 Carpenter sees this later stage of Cole's guild socialism as representing his 'more original contribution' to its political economy. 'In his later guild socialist writings, Cole turned to the consumer and differentiated his needs from politics', *G.D.H. Cole: An Intellectual Biography* p. 58.
40 Cole, *The World of Labour*, p. 214.
41 Cole, *Self-Government in Industry*, p. 122. As to *The World of Labour*, Margaret Cole saw 'the moral of the book' as 'syndicalist rather than guild socialist... strongly against the pure doctrine of parliamentary and municipal collectivism as expounded by the Webbs and Shaw', M. Cole, *The Life of G.D.H. Cole*, London,

Macmillan, 1971, p. 74; while, as Wright saw it, 'in syndicalism, Cole found an industrial doctrine rooted in the conception of active self-emancipation', A.W. Wright, *G.D.H. Cole and Socialist Democracy*, Oxford Clarendon, 1979 , p. 24.
42 Cole, *The World of Labour*, pp. 285, 288.
43 Ibid.
44 Wright, *G.D.H. Cole and Socialist Democracy*, p. 209.
45 'Marx also suffered rough treatment in the *History of Socialist Thought*', ibid, p. 232.
46 Carpenter, *G.D.H. Cole: An Intellectual Biography*, p, 226; Wright, *G.D.H. Cole and Socialist Democracy*, p. 211.
47 N. Riddell, '"The Age of Cole?" G.D.H. Cole and the British Labour Movement, 1929-33', *Historical Journal*, 38, 1995, p. 937.
48 N. And J. MacKenzie (eds.), *The Diary of Beatrice Webb*, 4 Vols., London, Virago, 1985, Vol. 4, 17 May 1924, p. 27.
49 On this see, for example, Cole, *The Life of G.D.H. Cole*, p. 161.
50 Wright, *G.D.H. Cole and Socialist Democracy*, p. 144.
51 Ibid, p. 147. Though his formidable literary output did not diminish. Thus 'the Carnegie Foundation for International Peace invited him to contribute three books to their enormous projected series of studies on war time organisaton...In 1923 these duly appeared, three impressive looking volumes entitled respectively *Trade Unionism in Munitions, Labour in the Coal Mining Industry* and *Workshop Organization*...The last-named of which contained a great deal about the shop stewards' movement', Cole, *The Life of G.D.H. Cole*, p. 132. It was in this period too that Cole wrote a series of 'long monographs on Morris, Keir Hardie, Richard Oastler and Richard Carlile which came out as Fabian biographical tracts', Wright, *G.D.H. Cole and Socialist Democracy*, p. 134, and also his *Life of William Cobbett*, London, Collins, 1927, perhaps his finest work of biography and on a subject with whom he clearly empathised.
52 On this see, for example, Riddell, '"The Age of Cole?"', p. 937.
53 Wright, *G.D.H. Cole and Socialist Democracy*, p. 106.
54 On this see, for example, ibid, p. 167.
55 It had Ernest Bevin as Chair and Cole as Vice Chair.
56 'By the summer of 1931 the N.F.R.B. had already set up three wide-ranging inquiries. In order to study all aspects of economics, international affairs and the political system', Riddell, '"The Age of Cole?"'., p. 948. These had an influence on subsequent Labour Party policy documents such as *For Socialism and Peace*, 1934 and *Labour's Immediate Programme*, 1937.
57 G.D.H. Cole, *The Next Ten Years in British Social and Economic Policy*, London, Macmillan, 1929, pp, 71, 72.
58 Ibid, p. 108.
59 G.D.H. Cole, *Monetary Systems and Theories*, London, 1942, p. 26; though Cole could seem to blow hot and cold on Keynes throughout the 1930s there can be no doubting the underlying respect for his theoretical contribution. His review of the *General Theory* in the *New Statesman* described it as 'the most important theoretical writing since Marx's *Capital*' and as effecting 'a revolution in economic orthodoxy which would 'sooner or later cause every orthodox text-book to be fundamentally rewritten', G.D.H. Cole, 'Mr Keynes beats the band', *New Statesman*, 15 February, 1936. He also responded positively to Keynes's *Times* articles on *How to Pay for the War*, 1939-40, see R. Toye, *The Labour Party and the Planned Economy, 1931-51*, Woodbridge, Boydell, 2003, p. 99. He also eventually came to accept that deficit financing might be a necessary prerequisite for the stimulation of economic activity. As he wrote in *How to Obtain Full Employment*, 1944, 'it is better in bad times to lower taxation, so as to give private citizens more money to spend, and to meet some part of public expenditure by incurring

budget deficits', G.D.H. Cole, *How to Obtain Full Employment*, London, Odhams, 1944, p. 18.
60 *The Next Ten Years*, p. 183.
61 Ibid, p. 202, my emphasis.
62 Ibid, p. 411.
63 G.D.H. Cole, *Principles of Economic Planning*, London, Macmillan, 1935, p. 213.
64 Cole had of course already advance the idea of a National Labour Corps in 1929, see Carpenter, *G.D.H. Cole: An Intellectual Biography*, p. 137.
65 G.D.H. Cole, *Practical Economics*, London, Penguin, 1937, p. 254. There was reference here also to the success of the employment-generating consequences of the Swedish public works programme.
66 For a fuller discussion of this and other aspects of Cole's macroeconomic thinking in the 1930s see N. Thompson, *Political Economy and the Labour Party, the Economics of Democratic Socialism*, 2nd edition, London, Routledge, 2006, pp. 103-107.
67 Cole, *The Next Ten Years*, pp. 226, 246.
68 Cole, *Principles of Economic Planning*, p. 208. As one commentator has put it, 'Cole saw banking, monetary policy and especially the trade cycle as capitalist economics. For socialist economics he viewed planning and capital supply as the central questions which arose from the need to organise production in the socialist state', E. Durbin, *New Jerusalems, the Labour Party and the Economics of Democratic Socialism*, London, Routledge & Kegan Paul, 1985, p. 117.
69 Ibid, pp. 217-8.
70 Cole, *Monetary Systems*, pp. 20, 21.
71 G.D.H. Cole, *What Everybody wants to know about Money*, London, Gollancz, 1933, p. 512.
72 D. Ritschel, *The Politics of Planning, the Debate on Economic Planning in Britain in the 1930s*, Oxford, Clarendon, 1996, p. 99. As Ritschel has pointed out 'much of the group's [SSIP's] first year was spent in attempts to define and distinguish a specifically socialist form of planning In Cole's words SSIP "set out to capture the cry of planning for the Labour Party", ibid, p. 98.
73 See below, pp. 19-20.
74 Considerable research effort was put by the New Fabian Research Bureau into the different forms which social ownership and control could take, see Durbin, *New Jerusalems*, p. 122.
75 Cole, *Principles of Economic Planning*, pp. 331.
76 Ibid, pp. 336, 338.
77 Ibid, p. 339.
78 In this period as one commentator has pointed out, Cole 'pointed to [the need for] more professional expertise in the civil service, greater Cabinet co-ordination and less reliance on Parliament, as among the ways to forward a socialist Britain', M. Taylor, 'Labour and the constitution' in D. Tanner, P. Thane and N. Tiratsoo (eds.), *Labour's First Century*, Cambridge, Cambridge University Press, 2000, p. 159.
79 Cole, *The Next Ten Years*, p. 136. This was certainly the case with the conduct of the financial sector. Thus 'the administration of a bank is the affair of experts who give their whole time to mastering the intricacies of banking policy', ibid, p. 242.
80 Cole, *The Next Ten Years*, p. 129.
81 Ibid, p. 131.
82 Ibid, p. 143.
83 Ibid, pp. 414, 152, my emphasis.
84 In any case, as one commentator has put it, for Cole, 'a socialism which was only prepared to tinker with capitalism would succeed in eroding capitalist efficiency without replacing it with anything else', Wright, *G.D.H. Cole and Socialist Democracy*, p. 165.

INTRODUCTION

85 G.D.H. Cole, *The Principles of Socialism*, London, Socialist Society for Inquiry and Propaganda, 1932, pp. 9, 8.
86 Cole, *Principles of Economic Planning*, p. 405
87 G.D.H. Cole, *How to Obtain Full Employment*, London, Odhams, 1944, p. 15.
88 Cole, *Practical Economics*, p. 216.
89 G.D.H. Cole, *The Intelligent Man's Guide through World Chaos*, London, Gollancz, 1933, pp. 614-15.
90 G.D.H. Cole, 'A short tract for the times', *Economic Tracts for the Times*, London, Macmillan, 1932, p. 5.
91 Cole, *Principles of Economic Planning*, p. 220. Cole also 'doubted whether existing market forces could be trusted to decide which countries should produce what goods', A. Booth, 'How long are light years in British politics? The Labour Party's Economic Ideas in the 1930s', *Twentieth Century British History*, 7, 1996, p. 17.
92 Ibid, p. 164.
93 Cole, 'The abolition of the wage system; in *Economic Tracts*, p. 261, my emphasis.
94 Cole, *Practical Economics*, p. 34, my emphasis.
95 Cole, *Principles of Economic Planning*, p. 317.
96 Ibid, p. 235.
97 Ibid, p. 318.
98 Ibid, p. 313.
99 Ibid, p. 326; Cole, *Practical Economics*, p. 20.
100 G.D.H. Cole, 'World economic outlook', in *Economic Tracts*, p. 145.
101 'Where monopoly tends to replace competition, it is apt to prefer restriction to plenty, because the highest profit can be secured by limiting supplies in order to maintain prices', *Practical Economics*, p. 20. 'Sectionally planned capitalism is thus, in the great majority of cases restrictive in its use of the available sources of production', Cole, *Principles of Economic Planning*, p. 199.
102 Ibid, p. 226; a view he continued to adhere to in the post-war period.
103 On this see, for example, Thompson, *Political Economy and the Labour Party*, pp. 126-29.
104 Cole, *Principles of Economic Planning*, p. 190.
105 Ibid, p. 228.
106 Ibid, p. 229.
107 Cole, *The Life of G.D.H. Cole*, p. 57.
108 Toye, *The Labour Party and the Planned Economy*, p. 41.
109 Wright, *G.D.H. Cole and Socialist Democracy*, p. 252.
110 Quoted in ibid, p. 252.
111 Quoted in J. Harris, 'Labour's social and political thought' in Tanner, Thane and Tiratsoo (eds.), *Labour's First Century*, p. 48.
112 Cole, *Practical Economics*, p. 25.
113 G.D.H. Cole, 'The debacle of capitalism' in S.D. Schinahausen (ed.), *Recovery through Revolution*, New York, 1933, p. 41.
114 R. Crossman, 'Socialist values in a changing civilisation', *Fabian Tract*, 286, London, 1950, p. 11.
115 See, most obviously, Crosland's *The Future of Socialism*, 1956 and for other writers see, for example, Thompson, *Political Economy and the Labour Party*, pp. 147-49.
116 R. Jenkins, 'Equality' in M. Cole and R. Crossman (eds.), *New Fabian Essays*, London, Turnstile, 1952, p. 72.
117 G.D.H. Cole, *Is this Socialism?* London, New Statesman, 1954, foreword
118 G.D.H. Cole, *Socialist Economics*, London, Gollancz, 1950, p. 49.
119 Ibid, p. 47.
120 Ibid, p. 50.

121 Ibid.
122 Cole, *Is this Socialism?* p. 21.
123 G.D.H. Cole *Why Nationalise Steel?* London, New Statesman, 1948, p. 3.
124 Ibid, p. 4.
125 Cole, *The British Labour Movement*, p. 13.
126 Cole, *Why Nationalize Steel?* p. 5.
127 Ibid, p. 29.
128 Ibid, p. 44.
129 Ibid, pp. 38-9.
130 Cole, *The British Labour Movement*, p. 15.
131 G.D.H. Cole, *What is Wrong with the Trade Unions? Fabian Tract* 301, London, Fabian Society, 1956, pp. 15-16.
132 Ibid, pp. 6, 21.
133 Ibid, p. 26.
134 Cole, *The British Labour Movement*, pp. 19-20.
135 M.B. Reckitt, *The Guildsman*, June 1919.
136 A. Briggs, *Listener*, 20th October 1960.
137 Wright, *G.D.H. Cole and Socialist Democracy*, p. 274.
138 Of significance here was the work of the Institute for Workers' Control and the increasing influence of the New Left, see Thompson, *Political Economy and the Labour Party*, pp. 200-203.
139 G. L. Houseman, *G.D.H. Cole*, Boston, Twayne Publishers, 1979, p. 113.
140 Ibid, p. 114.
141 Ritschel, *The Politics of Planning*, p. 339.
142 Houseman, *G.D.H. Cole*, p. 124.
143 Cole, *Life of G.D.H. Cole*, p. 10.

Price 6d.

UNEMPLOYMENT
AND
INDUSTRIAL MAINTENANCE

BY

G. D. H. COLE.

1921
PUBLISHED FOR
THE NATIONAL GUILDS LEAGUE
BY
THE LABOUR PUBLISHING COMPANY,
Limited,
6, TAVISTOCK SQUARE, LONDON, W.C.1.

Unemployment and Industrial Maintenance.

A SUMMARY OF POINTS.

Under capitalism, goods are produced, not because they are needed, but because the capitalist hopes to make a profit out of their production.

When there is no prospect of profit, the capitalist does not order goods to be produced, however great the need for them may be.

The worker's prospects of employment therefore depend upon the capitalist's prospects of profit.

In other words, although the capitalist poses as the "risk-taker" of industry, he really throws the greatest risk of all——unemployment—upon the worker.

The worker only receives wages when he is actually employed. If there is not enough work for him, he gets either no wages (unemployment) or less wages (short time).

Capitalism does not recognise that the worker has any rights in the industry he works in, except the right to wages when he is actually at work.

But the product of industry is the product of the workers' labour, and he has a right to continuous maintenance out of the product of his industry.

That is, the worker should get his pay week in and week out, whether or not the capitalist makes continuous use of his labour.

Industrial maintenance would at once improve the worker's status, and give him a sense of greater security and freedom.

It would at the same time stimulate higher production and, by raising the purchasing power of the workers, enable them to buy the additional goods produced. It would also lower prices.

In certain industries, the workers have already taken the first steps towards establishing the principle of industrial maintenance.

The Building Guilds are based upon this principle. That is one of the reasons why they are being fought so hard by the Government and the employers.

The workers in other industries can, if they will, follow the example set by the Building Guilds.

But, as Guilds cannot yet be established everywhere, they must demand industrial maintenance from their capitalist employers.

Any acceptable scheme of industrial maintenance must be based on the following principles:—

   (a) It must give the workers *continuous pay at the full standard rate*.

   (b) It must be administered entirely by the workers *through their own Trade Unions*.

   (c) It must be free of all conditions which might hamper the workers in gaining full *control of industry*

It is YOUR business to work out a scheme your own industry and your own Union.

On June 17th, 1921, there were 2,028,400 adults registered as "out of work" on the books of the Employment Exchanges. If to these are added the unemployed who were not so registered, the total number out of work at that time certainly cannot be put at less than 2,500,000. This means that at least 7,500,000 people found themselves deprived of their ordinary means of livelihood, and left, either without resources at all, or dependent on the "charity" of the State unemployment pittance, eked out in some cases by Trade Union benefits, and by the spending of the scanty savings of a life-time. The amount of misery, of semi-starvation, and of degradation of status and loss of self-respect which those facts involve is past computation.

In other countries, much the same conditions existed at the same date. In every capitalist nation, many thousands were vainly seeking work, and those who were in employment were wondering when their turn for dismissal would come.

Why were all these persons out of work? Not because they were shirkers; for they were vainly seeking for work, and could not find it. Not because no one had need of their skill and of the useful products which they might have been producing; for the whole world was crying out in vain for goods, and all the economists were busy proving that the workers of the world did not produce enough wealth to go round.

There are, of course, special causes, mainly international in character, which account for much of the abnormal unemployment of to-day. Our rulers, after the world has been wasted with years of war, have spent years more, not in healing the sores which war has left, but in preventing, by the "peace" which they have made and by their attempts to strangle the economic life of both Germany and Russia, any effective recovery of international trade. In seeking to punish Germany and to destroy the power of the Soviets in Russia, they have really punished the British workers, who depend for their livelihood under capitalism on the maintenance of foreign trade. "Reasons of State" have thus made the internal situation of this country far worse than it need have been if a real attempt had been made to restore the peace of Europe.

But "real peace" is a state unknown to capitalism, which ceaselessly breeds economic rivalries and seeks to prevent international co-operation. At bottom, the reasons for the abnormal unemployment of 1921, and the reasons for the normal unemployment which is recognised as a regular feature of the present industrial sytem, lie in the nature of that system itself. For it is a plain fact that the existence of a mass of persons wanting work on the one hand, and of a mass of persons clamouring for goods and services on the other, is not regarded, in the world of capitalist economy, as at all a sufficient reason why those who want work should be given an opportunity of supplying the needs, however pressing, of those who want goods and services.

Production for Profit.

From the standpoint of capitalist economics, the question of human wants is irrelevant. It is true that the capitalist does not order the production of goods which he does not expect that he will be able to persuade somebody to buy; but it is also true that he would be both pained and surprised if it were suggested to him that his job was to produce those things which men most need, without regard to their ability to pay. Indeed, under the capitalist system, he could not do so even if he would; for he has to reckon, not only with competitors at home and abroad, but also with shareholders and financiers whose sole interest in his business is to extract from it the maximum return for themselves. The individual employer is a helpless instrument of the system in which he is involved; and it is to the system, and not to the sinfulness of particular employers, that the evil is to be traced. But, wherever the blame may rest, the fact is plain enough. The sole reason for production which is recognised in the capitalist system is that a profit can be realised. And it is the system of production for profit only that interposes a barrier between those who want work and those who want the goods and services these workers could provide.

There was a time when the system of production for profit was confidently defended on the ground that the best test of the usefulness of a product or service was the price men were ready to pay for it, and that therefore he who made most profit for himself was best serving the common interest. It was said that the contrast between "production for profit" and "production for use" was a false contrast, and that the two really coincided in this best of all possible economic systems. This argument can still be heard in the mouths of business men and economists; but it has lost the old confident ring. In face of the fact that the system of production for profit often means no production at all, and results in the normal existence of a huge mass of unemployment in every industrialised community, it is impossible to contend that this method really succeeds in satisfying human needs.

The worker is at once a producer and a consumer. He depends for his income, that is, for his ability to consume, on finding someone who will employ him and pay him wages. If he can find no one to employ him, his ability to consume ceases, except in so far as he is saved from starvation by his Union or by a State dole. But the fact that his wages stop does not lessen by one iota his needs or those of his dependents. He still needs just as much food, warmth and clothing: he still needs a house over his head and the ability to keep his household goods together. If these needs go unsatisfied in the case of a single worker, there is a manifest sign of the failure of production for profit to correspond to production for use.

Only Semi-Starvation.

Gradually, there has been extorted from the State a small measure of recognition of the responsibility of Society towards the worker. Nowadays, the unemployed are not normally left quite to starve. They are chastised with the whips of semi-starvation, but the scorpions of utter starvation are not usually applied. It is not necessary to attribute this "moderation" wholly to the growth of a disinterested benevolence on the part of the ruling classes; for it is clearly due very largely to the growth in the power of the working-class movement, and to the fear of the rulers that starvation may mean revolt. Whatever its cause, it remains still a miserably inadequate provision, and does not save the worker from a sudden and disastrous degradation in his standard of life as soon as he loses his job.

This degradation of the life-standard of the workers always accompanies the growth of unemployment. But note the fact, that, unless the worker and his dependents are to starve utterly and die, someone must support them, however miserably, when no wages are available for them. The employer does not do this. He employs the worker when he can make a profit out of the use of his labour; but, as soon as there is no profit to be made, he flings the worker into the street. The State and the Trade Union then step in, and provide bare subsistence until some fresh employer, seeing a prospect of profit, consents to take the worker on.

What is a "Reserve of Labour,"

Think what this means. The employer only pays the worker for the time during which he actually employs him. He can work his staff "short time," and so cut down their earnings below any reasonable subsistence level. He can " stand them off," and so deprive them of their incomes altogether, until he wants them again. But, all the time, he expects the worker to be ready and waiting for employment. He cuts down his staff to-day and expands it to-morrow, according as he expects the greater profit from higher or lower production. And it is the worker's business, where there is no work for him, to wait patiently at the factory gates and register at the Employment Exchange, until the employer wants him again. That the worker should do this is essential to the maintenance of the capitalist system. These unemployed workers are the "reserve of labour," upon which capitalism relies.

Who is to Pay for It?

In other words, the unemployed worker is just as much a part of the necessary personnel of capitalist industry as the worker who is actually employed. The employer cannot do without him; but he repudiates all responsbility towards him. Is this right? The wages paid to the workers wno are employed rank, according to capitalist econmics, as an element in the "cost of production." But what about the wages which are *not* paid to the workers who are unemployed? If these unemployed workers are a "reserve of labour" that is necessary to capitalism, ought not the payment of wages to them to be recognised as an element in the cost of production just as real as the wages which the employer pays to-day! Guild Socialists have always contended that it ought. They have demanded that every worker who is prepared to do service in an industry necessary to the public shall be assured of continuous pay at the expense of that industry.

This is the system of "industrial maintenance" which has always occupied a prominent place in the propaganda of Guild Socialism. We maintain that the present system enables the capitalist to evade one of his most vital obligations, and to make profits out of the labour of the workers before he has met the real cost of producing the goods which he sells. This real cost includes the continuous maintenance by the industry of the whole body of workers in it. But, by paying the workers nothing when they are unemployed or "standing-off," as well as by docking their pay when they are on short time, the employer makes them pay, with such assistance as they can get from the State, a considerable part of the cost of production which it is his business to meet before there is any profit for him to appropriate.

Maintenance an Industrial Right.

There is a big difference between this demand of the Guild Socialists and the claim which is often put forward that the unemployed workers should be maintained at the expense of the State. It is upon industry directly, and as an essential part of the cost of production taking precedence over all claims to profit, that we hold the charge of maintaining the unemployed must fall. It is not a *State charity* that we are demanding, but an *industrial right*, a plain recognition that the workers in an industry have a claim to continuous maintenance out of the product of their common labour.

The recognition of this principle would at once enhance enormously the status and self-respect of the workers. Not only would it give them that measure of economic security without which no real social or industrial freedom can possibly be enjoyed: it would give them this security *as a right* derived directly from their position as workers, that is, from their will and ability to do useful work. It would thus give them an assurance of possessing a recognised social status, a sense of their share in the common inheritance of Society, and in the functioning of the industry through which they serve the community. State maintenance would inevitably give to the worker a sense of dependence: industrial maintenance would give him a sense of freedom. If I belong to my industry, he would be able to say, so does my industry belong to me. And the belonging in both cases would have a close and definite relation to the idea of service.

Short Time and Shorter Hours.

Consider, for example, the effect which the adoption of industrial maintenance would have on the question of "short time." At present, when the worker is put on "short time," he loses an equivalent proportion of his earnings: under a system of maintenance his pay would continue even if full time work could not be found. This would, in the first place, give the employer a very excellent reason for so organising the factory as to make more continuous production possible: and, in the second place, it would enable the problem of a productive power in excess of demand to be met by the rational expedient of shortening the hours of labour, without the burden being flung upon the worker of maintaining himself as best he can during the time of depression. Industrial maintenance must accompny any reasonable scheme for "sharing out the work," or reducing the hours of labour so as to absorb any surplus of unemployed.

Who "Takes the Risks?"

It is commonly urged, as a reason for the maintenance of capitalism and as a justification for the making of private profit, that under the present system the capitalist takes the *risks* of production. No more ghastly lie was ever told. The capitalist risks only his capital, and he usually seeks to cover his risks by a careful distribution of it among a number of different enterprises. The worker, on the other hand, daily risks his whole livelihood. If South America buys fewer locomotives, the value of engineering shares may fall; but the workmen who relied on the building of these locomotives for their livelihood lose at a blow their whole income. Every trade fluctuation reacts upon the workers far more heavily and immediately than upon the capitalists. The worker often goes supperless: the employer at the worst need usually do no more than sack his gardener, or dismiss his chauffeur. It is upon the workers that the principal risks of industry fall; but the workers, though they bear the risks, have no share in the great gains which frequently fall to the employer.

We are not demanding that the workers should share the employer's profits, as they now bear the major part of his losses. We desire to destroy the whole profit-making system and not to include the workers in it. But we do demand that the worker, who has no desire to become a profiteer, should not be made to bear the risks which result directly from the profit-making system. We demand the recognition of the principle of "continuous pay" for every worker in industry.

The Result of Maintenance.

What would happen if this principle were recognised? In the first place, the employers in a particular industry, treated as a national unit, would have to reckon into their cost of production the payment of continuous maintenance to all the workers in the industry, and would be compelled to make provision for this charge before they could distribute a single penny in profits to their shareholders. This might mean an addition, taking both good and bad years into consideration, of ten per cent. to their wages bill, on the assumption, with which we will deal in a moment, that the change of system did not cause any change in the organisation of the industry. In order to meet this charge, the employers would have to put aside, in good years, sums which they now distribute in high dividends to their shareholders, or allot to open or concealed reserve funds which later make their appearance as extra dividends or as bonus shares. A business which now seems to have made ten per cent. profit one year and five the next, would then be seen, after meeting the legitimate charges upon it, including the charge for maintenance, to be entitled only to five per cent. in each year. The other five per cent., which the employers now pocket at the workers' expense, would go to the maintenance fund of the industry.

Stabilising Production.

But would not the adoption of this system bring about big changes in the organisation of the industry itself? At present, especially since the growth of industrial combinations among capitalists, employers are constantly making calculations which involve either an expansion or a restriction of the output of their works. Will it pay us better, they say, to keep prices low and so sell a large quantity of our products, or to raise our prices at the cost of reducing our output? In making such a calculation, the employer acts in strict accordance with current business morality if he adopts the course which is the more profitable for himself and for his shareholders. And, with the growth of combines, there is an ever-increasing tendency, amply illustrated in the Report of the Government Committee on Trusts, for the associated employers to prefer the method of restricting output and working for an assured, if narrowed, market in which they can sell at a high price, to the method of extending their production and relying for their profits on a larger turnover at a smaller margin of profit for each commodity sold. Instances are not wanting in which a particular firm is actually paid a handsome compensation by a trust for refraining from production.

The growth of the practice of "restriction of output" on the part of the employers is very relevant to the question we are discussing, that of industrial maintenance. For to-day, when an employer or a combine makes the calculation mentioned above, an essential element in it is the "saving" of wages which will result from a lowering of production. It pays the employer best to produce little at a high selling price, because, if he does so, he can drastically cut down his wages Bill. He can sack so many of his workers, and put so many more on short time, and thus escape all liability for their maintenance, and for the havoc in many working-class households which is caused by his action in "restricting output." But, if the right of these workers to maintenance at the industry's expense is recognised, at once the boot is on the other foot. For the employers in the industry, if they then decide to restrict output in order to raise or to maintain prices, are compelled, out of the sums which they receive for the reduced quantity of products, to pay the whole wage bill which would have been incurred if the industry had been working up to its full capacity. In these circumstances, it would usually pay them to increase output even at lower prices rather than to maintain in idleness a large proportion of the workers in the industry.

Industrial maintenance thus offers a direct stimulus to increased output on the part of the employer. And, as it is the organised employers, far more than the organised workers, who restrict the output of commodities to-day, there is hope in this stimulus of a real increase in the amount of goods available for distribution. Moreover, if the workers are receiving continuous pay, they will have more money with which to buy the goods which are produced, and the employer will thus more readily find a market for the increased output of his factory. "Over-production," that is the production of goods which those who need them have not the money to buy, and "under-consumption," which is the reverse side of the same situation, will thus alike be checked, and a more even balance between production and consumption will be established.

Will Prices be Higher?

But, it may be said, will not the effect of "industrial maintenance" be to raise the prices of all commodities, because the employer will simply add the fresh charge imposed upon him to the selling price? During the war, when purchasers were clamouring for far more of almost every commodity than could be made available, this might have been so; but, under normal conditions, industrial maintenance would have rather the opposite effect. It would practically compel the employers to produce as nearly as possible up to the full capacity of their plant, and they would only dispose of the commodities so produced by keeping prices low; for it is well-known that the quantity of a commodity for which there is an effective demand grows in proportion as the price falls. If, therefore, the employers sought to recoup themselves by raising prices, they would be worse off than before; for they would be left with unsaleable commodities on their hands.

Or Employers Go Out of Business?

But, if this is so, will not the effect of "industrial maintenance" be even more dire? Will it not drive the employer out of business altogether? Alas, we cannot believe that the employers will be so obliging as to abdicate if the principle of "industrial maintenance" is adopted. We are not putting our proposal forward as an infallible and instantaneous method of ending capitalism, but as a means both of greatly improving the status and economic position of the workers under capitalism, and of strengthening them for more decisive assaults upon it. The capitalist system, we fear, would be able so to readjust itself as to incorporate the principle of maintenance without thereby involving its own instant dissolution. Profits would, we believe, be reduced, and the self-confidence of the workers increased; and, when the battle for emancipation was again joined, it would be joined on terms far more favourable to the workers; but there is no scheme—either ours or anyone else's—which, by a simple reform, will bring the workers straight to the millennium. The road to freedom is uphill to the very end.

We are not saying that, if the principle of maintenance were suddenly applied to all industries to-day, the readjustments that would be necessary would be in all cases easy to bring about. The artificial depression in which industry is plunged at the present time, mainly as a result of the suicidal international policy which our rulers are pursuing, has created problems with which some of our industries are helpless by themselves to deal. It would probably be necessary, out of general taxation, to apply a subvention to the various industries towards the meeting of the maintenance charge during the period of readjustment. But this does not mean that such a subvention would cost the State as much as the inadequate provision which it now makes for the unemployed by the method of compulsory insurance. Nor does it in any way invalidate the general principle. Even if subventions are needed in the early stages, every worker can, and should, be assured at once, *from his industry*, of that continuous pay which is both his human and his economic right.

If Capital Fights.

But, sound as this principle may be, is there any real chance that it will be conceded? Will not the capitalists, realising that this involves a serious inroad on their profits and also a very great strengthening of the economic position and sense of security of the working class, use every ounce of strength that they possess in opposing any such concession? It may well be that they will do so; but cannot the same be said of every proposal for change which really offers any prospect of bettering the position of the workers? Reforms which leave the relative postions of the opposing classes in Society unchanged the ruling classes may, with comparative readiness, be induced to accept, but any proposal that really menaces the class-structure of present-day Society is, we agree, likely to meet with very strenuous resistence. We are, however, quite unable to understand why this should be regarded as a reason for not pressing the demand. If we press for nothing that we do not expect easily to obtain, we shall claim nothing that is worth having; and, if we say that it is not worth while to press for anything short of complete revolution, because nothing worth having will be conceded without revolution, then, even if the reason is sound, we shall find ourselves without an army to lead forward to revolution. We must press for the measure which we see to be necessary in order to rescue the workers from their present degraded condition, whether we believe that it will be hard or easy to get what we want, And, if, in doing so, we find the capitalists obstinately resisting a clearly necessary and justifiable change, because they feel that it menaces their economic supremacy, we shall, at the worst, have found the best possible means of bringing home to the minds of the workers the naked truth about the present economic and social system.

Achievements to Date.

We put forward, then, industrial maintenance as one of the demands which should be most insistently and immediately pressed by the whole working class movement. Already, in certain instances, that movement has taken a few very hesitating steps towards the recognition of the principle. For instance, when the railway workers succeeded in securing the concession of the "guaranteed week," they were winning, not maintenance, but an essential, though small, step towards it which has since stood them in good stead in their opposition to the companies' efforts to introduce short-time. The dockers, who have suffered as heavily as any section of workers from the evil of casual employment, have at least won the "guaranteed day." The miners secured during the war the concession that the "war wages" paid to them under State control should be continuous, and should be paid even when the miner was thrown out of work through no fault of his own. And, most important of all, in the cotton industry during the war a special levy was imposed on all employers whose mills were working at more than a minimum pressure for the partial maintenance of those workers who were thrown out of employment by the restriction of output imposed by war conditions. Moreover, the partial maintenance thus conceded was paid over to the Trade Unions, and administered by them to all workers who were entitled to it, Unionists and Non-Unionists alike.

These are actual steps which have been taken in the direction of industrial maintenance. They fall very far short of the full recognition of it which the workers are beginning to demand,

and in some cases they are only temporary concessions, while in others they are now being destroyed by the employers, who see in the growth of unemployment the prospect of taking away from the workers even that scanty measure of protection which they now possess. But certain Unions have already realised the need to go further, and to establish a complete system of maintenance for all workers in their industries. The most notable plan of this kind is the scheme for the industrial maintenance, at full standard rates of wages, for all workers in the waterside transport industry. This scheme, drafted by the Transport Workers' Federation, has been placed before the port employers, who have been asked to give effect to it in fulfilment of the recommendation of the Dockers' Court of Inquiry in 1920 that a complete scheme of industrial maintenance for waterside workers should be devised. There may well be a stern struggle before the dockers before they can succeed in getting this right recognised; but it is a struggle that is far more worth while than most of the industrial conflicts in which the Trade Unions find themselves engaged.

Why the Building Guilds are Attacked.

The vital importance of the demand for industrial maintenance appears also very clearly in the struggle which has centred round the development of the Building Guilds. When the organised workers in the building industry determined to demand the right to serve the public directly, under conditions of full industrial self-government and on a basis which would eliminate all forms of profit, they based their offer to build at cost price all the houses the public required on the full recognition of the principle of industrial maintenance. Their own past experience had taught them that no decency of life or sense of assured status in the community was possible for the building operative under the old bad conditions of casual employment. They therefore insisted, as the first condition of their offer, that every worker for the Building Guilds should be assured of continuous pay, in rain or shine, in employment or in unemployment. With considerable difficulty, the recognition of this principle was secured in the Guild contracts which were at length accepted by local authorities and sanctioned by the Ministry of Health. But the employers, who at first regarded the idea of the workers organising a self-governing service of their own as a wild-cat scheme which would certainly break down, soon changed their tune when they found that the Guilds, after meeting the cost of industrial maintenance, were building houses for the people at far less than the prices which the employers were seeking to exact. They then brought all their force to bear for the purpose of smashing the Guilds, and they induced the Ministry of Health to refuse to sanction any further Guild contracts.

The point round which this contest between the building workers on the one hand and the employers and the capitalist

Government on the other centres is, simply and solely, industrial maintenance. The employers protest that the Guilds must not be allowed to give continuous pay to their workers, because they realise that the concession of continuous pay changes the status of the worker, and that, if the principle is accepted in one part of the industry, they will not be able to resist its application to the industry as a whole. They know that the power of capitalism depends on keeping the worker in a permanent condition of insecurity and subjection, and they rightly see in the rise of the Building Guilds, based on the principle of industrial maintenance, a challenge to the whole-class-system of capitalist production. That is all the more reason why the organised workers should both rally to the Building Guilds in their endeavour to establish the principle of industrial maintenance, and seek, by the methods most convenient in each industry, to apply that principle throughout the whole world of Labour.

Why not Guilds for Public Work?

It is for the workers in each industry to work out their own detailed plan of action, while it is for the whole working class to stand solidly united in support of the plan which the workers in each industry devise to meet their own case. In some instances, it will be possible for the workers to give a strong impetus to the demand for industrial maintenance by following the good example which the Building Guilds have set. There is a great mass of public work, in addition to house-building, which could be carried out, with huge saving to the public and with greatly inproved conditions for the workers, if the Trade Unions in the industries concerned would form Guilds there also and offer their service to the public on the same terms as those under which the Building Guilds are now at work. These terms are production for the public at cost price, carried out under conditions of full democratic self-government and with recognition of the principle of industrial maintenance. Why should not all road-making, bridge-building, afforestation, and indeed every form of public work be carried out under these conditions? The sole reason why this is not the vital issue of the hour is that the workers concerned in these services have not yet, like the building operatives, come forward with a definite offer and compelled the public to accept it by a convincing demonstration of the superiority of industrial democracy to capitalist profit-mongering. If the workers would realise the opportunity which lies open to them here, they could at once threaten the dominance of capitalism by showing their ability to organise industry on a better basis.

Of course, these offers of service would not be readily accepted, any more than the Building Guilds are now finding the road to industrial emancipation made smooth for their feet. Capitalism is interested, not in serving the public well, but in making profits; and any plan that menaces profits will be vigorously opposed, whatever manifest benefits it may offer to the public. But here again is only a reason the more for the working-class to press its demand with all its force. For what it will be demanding will be simply the right to use its skill and organising ability in the public service, and not for the profit of the ruling class. The fact that there will be determined opposition from the capitalists and the Government which serves capitalism means, not that it is useless to make the demand, but that it must be backed by the whole power of the Trade Union Movement, and that, in exerting its strength to break the capitalist resistance, Labour must make the whole community understand that the right which it is seeking to enforce is the right of service.

Demand Full Maintenance.

Besides taking action on the lines indicated by the example which the Building Guilds have set, the workers must make the demand for industrial maintenance from the capitalist employers. The scheme proposed by the Transport Workers' Federation is an instance of the way in which this demand can be formulated, and every Union, no matter what its industry, ought to formulate a similar scheme, varying the precise details according to the character and circumstances of the industry. But in no case ought the workers to stand for less than the principle of full industrial maintenance—that is, continuous pay at the standard rate in periods of unemployment as well as of employment, and when short time is being worked as well as when they are busy for a full week. What the worker wants, and what he has a right to demand, is the banishing for ever of the economic insecurity which at present makes a mockery of the claim that he is "fere." He demands, for the sake of his wife and children as well as for himself, an assured and recognised status in the community, and that status he can only have when his right, as a worker, to continuous maintenance out of the product of industry is fully conceded. When the workers fight for the recognition of this principle, they are fighting for a fundamental human and economic right. The wage-system, which depends on keeping the worker in a condition of permanent and degrading insecurity, is no less a form of slavery than the chattel-slavery which it has replaced. And there is no way of ending the wage-system, or of securing for the workers real freedom, that is not based upon the recognition of the right to maintenance and economic security for every worker.

Trade "fluctuates" now, and workers are periodically condemned to unemployment and at best semi-starvation, not because these fluctuations are necessary or because human needs vary greatly from time to time, but because of an economic system throughout the world of capitalism which is based on the principle of production for private profit. There is no royal road to freedom which does not involve the utter destruction of that system; but is not the first step on the right road a firm insistence by the workers on their right to continuous maintenance out of the fruits of industry? Will not the demand, strongly enough made, do more than any other to compel a fundamental re-making of the economic system? Guild Socialists believe that it will; and that is why they place it in the forefront of their immediate programme.

Administered by Trade Unions Alone.

There are certain points which it will be essential to safeguard in any scheme for the adoption of industrial maintenance which the Trade Unions in the various industries may put forward. The most vital point is that of Trade Union administration. Any scheme of industrial maintenance that is to be of use to the workers must be administered completely through the Trade Union organisations. If the employers or the State were allowed to administer, or to have a hand in administering, a scheme of this sort, there would be manifest dangers that the independence of the workers might be undermined, and that industrial maintenance, instead of proving an important step on the road to industrial freedom, might result in a security which would subject the workers, even more than to-day, to capitalist domination.

The workers must therefore insist that all forms of industrial maintenance shall be administered by the Unions, and that the sums levied upon the various industries in order to provide maintenance shall be handed over to the Unions for distribution among the workers. There is nothing impracticable in this proposal; for this was the course actually adopted in the cotton industry during the war. The cotton Trade Unions during the war dispensed the benefits provided under the Cotton Control Board, not only to their own members, but also to the non-Unionists employed in the industry. The workers must insist that this shall be the case with any scheme of industrial maintenance that is accepted.

Control the Exchanges.

Not only must the Unions administer unemployment benefit, they must also, if they are to make this administration effective, secure complete control over the working of the Employment Exchanges. The Exchanges should be, as they have been in some other countries, notably in France, not State organisations, run by bureaucrats, subservient to the employers' interests, but institutions completely administered by the Trade Unions themselves, which would thus secure an effective control over the supply of labour. Such a change in the organisation of the Exchanges would be the natural accompaniment of the adoption of a scheme of maintenance on the lines proposed.

No Concessions to the Employers.

In the third place, the workers must resist any attempt which may be made by the employers or the State to grant industrial maintenance only under restrictive conditions which would hamper the freedom of Trade Union action, or stand in the way of the assumption by the workers of an increasing control over industry. The employers have sometimes put forward schemes for the provision of unemployment pay on an industrial basis, coupling with this proposal the demand for concessions from the workers, such as the acceptance of payment by results, the abolition of all so-called "restrictions on output," or the abandonment of the demand for control. Needless to say, no such conditions can be tolerated by the working-class movement. Maintenance is demanded as a right, and as a legitimate charge upon the industry, and not as a benefit to be conferred in return for concessions which the workers can be called upon to make in other directions. Indeed, one of the main arguments in favour of industrial maintenance is that, if it is adopted in the form which is suggested in this pamphlet, so far from retarding the development of workers' control in industry, it will be a very material help towards it. It will aid greatly in the decasualisation of labour, and every worker knows that casual labour is one of the great obstacles in the way, both of any improvement of the immediate economic position of the workers, and of the pushing of the demand for effective control in industry. Industrial maintenance will compel a re-organisation of the various industries, which will eliminate casual labour. The Labour Movement has long recognised that decasualisation is an essential step towards any improvement in the status of the worker; and the close connection between the decasualisation of industry and industrial maintenance must be fully recognised.

A Step Towards Better Organisation.

Moreover, industrial maintenance, in bringing about decasualisation and a better organisation of the various industries, should also give a powerful stimulus to the movement for improved Trade Union organisation. It will drive all the workers engaged in the various industries together, and will in that way give a new impetus to the movement for Union by industry. At the same time, it will necessitate close working arrangements between industries, and will in that way stimulate closer combination among the various industrial Unions which it will help to create. Guild Socialists have always recognised that Union by industry, in so far as it can be brought about in face of the present chaos of Trade Union organisation, is a necessary step towards control; and this furnishes another instance of the close connection between the propaganda of control and industrial maintenance. All these points will have to be borne in mind by the workers in any particular industry, when they are drawing up a scheme to suit their own particular case.

One or All?

But will industrial maintenance come about through separate schemes, forced by the workers upon the employers in the various industries, or, in a more comprehensive way, through legislation, imposing the obligation of maintenance upon every industry? It will be far better if it comes about in the latter way; for what is wanted is not that the workers in a few particular industries should establish the right for themselves, while leaving the workers in other industries in their present position of economic insecurity, but that the obligation of maintenance should be imposed immediately throughout the whole range of industries and services. The workers, however, will have to take things as they find them, and, if one industry is able to establish the principle of maintenance before the workers as a whole are able to enforce a universal scheme for all industries, it should by all means do so, provided that the scheme which it adopts is one which will fit in with a general system when the time comes for the universal application of the principle. The adoption, under such conditions, of industrial maintenance in one or two industries would, indeed, probably serve as a very material help in securing its further extension throughout the whole range of industry.

The Simple Right of the Worker.

The workers are sick of doles and charity, by whatever name they may be called. They are sick of going cap in hand to the State in order that it may protect them from starvation; for they know that the Government is a faithful servant of capitalism, and will succour them only enough to prevent them from revolting and to preserve their lives for future exploitation. They are seeking, not a charity, but the recognition of a right, and, if capitalism cannot, or will not, concede that right, it is not the workers, but capitalism itself, that must give way. The right of which the workers demand the recognition is simple: it is merely that, when a man is willing to work at his trade for the public service, that trade shall be so organised as to find for him work to do, or, if it fails in this, shall pay him the income to which he is entitled as a willing worker. The State bond-holder gets his interest regularly, though he does no service for it. Shall not the worker, who is prepared to do his day's work, get his income regularly too? To deny him this is to treat him, not simply as an inferior being, but as a mere commodity, a thing without rights—in fact, a slave. Chattel-slavery has been abolished: now it is wage slavery's turn to go. And a necessary step towards its destruction is the recognition for all workers of the right to continuous maintenance out of the product of their common service.

S.S.I.P. STUDY GUIDES.
No. 6.

THE PRINCIPLES OF SOCIALISM

BY

G. D. H. COLE

ISSUED BY
THE SOCIETY FOR SOCIALIST INQUIRY
AND PROPAGANDA

PRICE TWOPENCE

The Society for Socialist Inquiry and Propaganda

Chairman : E. BEVIN

Extract from the Rules.

"The Society consists of Socialists, *who are individual members of the Labour Party, or of such members of bodies affiliated to or associated with it as are not members of any other political party;* the object is the development and advocacy of a constructive Socialist Policy. With that object it may

(a) Promote and carry on research, discussion and propaganda.

(b) Undertake, promote and support the preparation and publication of pamphlets, books, reports, newspapers and the like.

(c) Organise and carry on conferences, meetings, lectures and schools.

(d) Promote and support any Socialist activity.

(e) Constitute and appoint sub-groups, local branches and committees.

Each member shall pay annually such subscription as he or she can reasonably afford. The minimum subscription shall be five shillings annually."

It is believed that a really practical Socialist policy, which is intended to cover the next ten or twenty years of development, cannot be worked out unless the keen Socialists in the country give their brains and time to thinking it out in co-operation. With this object in view, local branches are being founded throughout the country both to investigate local problems, and also to criticise and work out wider lines of policy.

The Society states emphatically that it has no intention of forming a rival influence within the party: indeed its supporters include members of the late Labour Government who realise the necessity for fresh and constructive thinking.

Applications for membership are invited, and further information can be obtained from the Secretary, **E. A. Radice, 23, Abingdon Street, London, S.W.1.**

THE PRINCIPLES OF SOCIALISM

The Principles of Socialism

By G. D. H. COLE.

NOTE.—This Study-Guide is only intended as a very general introduction. It should be supplemented by other Guides dealing in more detail with particular points, *e.g.*, Number 4, *The Socialisation of Banking*; Number 5, *How Capitalism Works*. See full list of Study Guides obtainable from the Society for Socialist Inquiry and Propaganda, 23, Abingdon Street, London, S.W.1.

I

WHAT IS SOCIALISM?

Questions for discussion: 1. *Is Socialism only an economic doctrine, or is it based on notions of human rights and duties?*

2. *Should labour be compulsory under Socialism, and, if so, in what sense?*

Socialism is not only a method of organising production and distribution, but also an attitude to life. It is based on a deeply rooted belief in economic and social equality, both for its own sake and as the necessary condition of a stable and prosperous economic system. Socialists set out to abolish class-distinctions, and to reorganise production and distribution so as to secure the use of the common resources of Society for the benefit of each and all. They see that class-distinctions are founded on the present methods of organising the production and distribution of wealth; and therefore they want to alter these methods. They believe that this can be done, at the present stage of social development, so as greatly to increase production, as well as to secure better distribution; for they hold that the capitalist system is acting as a clog on the production of wealth, and that this is shown by its inability to solve the problem of unemployment. Every citizen, they say, should labour, in one way or another, for the benefit of Society, and not for the profit of an individual. Social rights and the will to serve go together; and every one has both an obligation to serve to the best of his powers, and to share in the social product according to his needs. This idea is the basis of Socialist economic policy; and the conception of equality therefore lies at the very foundation of Socialism.

II

WHAT IS CAPITALISM?

Questions for discussion : 1. *Is it sensible to produce goods only when a profit can be made by their production?*

2. *What is meant by saying that the workers are exploited under Capitalism?*

We cannot go further with our discussion of Socialism until we have contrasted it with the present system. The outstanding features of Capitalism are : (1) that the means of producing wealth are owned, not by the whole community, but by a limited class ; (2) that this class lives by exploiting the labourer, who cannot work unless he can get access to the means of production ; (3) that capitalists will employ labourers only when they see a prospect of profit from doing so, and that in consequence unemployment is widespread in capitalist societies ; (4) that the capitalist is at a great advantage in bargaining with the labourers for a share in the product, because they will suffer more than he if they refuse to work on his terms, and because, unless they allow him to make a profit, he will throw them out of work. These are the general characteristics of Capitalism ; but modern Capitalism tends further (*a*) to restrict competition in its search for profit, so that the effective control of production passes into the hands of great combines ; (*b*) by means of these combines to restrict production in order to keep up prices to a profitable level, because it is unable to sell at a profit nearly as much as the world is equipped to produce ; (*c*) in its search for markets, concessions and supplies of materials to foment economic rivalries between nations, to exploit the less developed peoples, and make them politically subject.

It is true that there are many small capitalists as well as great ; for modern joint stock organisation, with shares of small amount, has helped in diffusing industrial ownership. This has increased the number of persons who seem to have an interest in Capitalism and its survival, and has strengthened its hold. But the small employers and, still more, the small shareholders have practically no control over industrial policy, which is dominated by a quite small class of big employers and financiers at the head of great business concerns. The general body of middle-class shareholders are only pawns in the game. Moreover, just as Capitalism keeps them in subjection, it also subjects the technicians and experts, who can use their knowledge for the benefit of mankind only if its use offers a prospect of capitalist profit. The heads of the capitalist world are not technicians, but financiers, who employ experts at a salary much as they employ manual workers at a wage. It is the root defect of capitalism that it fails to secure maximum production of wealth, because it treats production as a means to private profit, and not to the satisfaction of human needs.

III

SOCIALIST OBJECTIVES

Questions for discussion : 1. *Does Socialism aim at equality of incomes, and, if so, will men work hard enough under a Socialist system ?*

2. *What should be the Socialist attitude towards inheritance, and towards the receipt of incomes from property ?*

The economic objective of Socialism is to get as much wealth as possible produced (up to the limits set by men's preference for more leisure to more wealth), and to get this wealth distributed as nearly as possible in accordance with needs. Needs tend to be equal for adults—apart from the special needs of invalids—and for children. The Socialist objective in distribution is therefore *equality of income*, with public provision for special needs. But it is held that this would lower production, because men will not work hard without a monetary incentive. At present, probably many of them would not, if they had an assured income from Society ; for Capitalism has accustomed them to think in terms of monetary incentives. But a Socialist system would be able to call far more effectively on the spirit of service, and to create a powerful public opinion in favour of doing a fair day's work. Money incentives would become less necessary ; but it is agreed that they cannot be wholly abolished at once. Some inequalities of income must remain for a time ; but they should be confined to necessary incentives to service, and lessened as the need for them grows less. Equality remains the objective, though it must be approached by stages.

But inequality is now a matter, not only of unequal earnings, but still more of the receipt of incomes from property (rent, interest, and profits), including the inheritance of wealth. Socialists wish to transfer ownership of the means of production to the community, and accordingly to make rent, interest and profits, as far as they continue, a common possession. This does not exclude compensation to the owners of property, where industries are being socialised piecemeal. But it does mean that in the end the object is to abolish all private incomes from property. When this has been done, inheritance will be restricted to purely personal possessions, and allowed to continue, as it does now in Russia. But in the meantime an excellent method of transferring property to the community is the drastic taxation of inheritance. This is indeed by far the easiest way of taxing the rich heavily, under capitalism, without upsetting the productive system.

IV

PRODUCTION AND DISTRIBUTION

Questions for discussion : 1. *How does national economic planning work in Russia, and how could it be made to work here?*

2. *How is new capital for industry provided now, and how would it be provided under Socialism?*

The aim of Socialists is to secure the fullest and best use of the available productive resources. This is a matter, on the one hand, of getting industry run and developed with the greatest technical competence, and on the other of securing that incomes shall be distributed so as to create a demand for all that the community is able to produce. It involves, in the first place, a planned system of production, in order to ensure that the right goods are produced in the right quantities, the right provision made for the application of labour to making capital goods, *i.e.*, instruments of further production, and all available labour and other resources used to the fullest extent. When production is carried on for use, and not for private profit, it will be possible to arrange this, by means of a National Planning Commission, or similar body, which will decide upon (*a*) the proportions in which goods and services of different sorts are to be made available ; (*b*) the provision it is desirable to make, at the cost of present consumption, for increased production in the future. Each industry will have its own planning organisation, and these will be co-ordinated under the central body, which will review and pass judgment on the separate plans. Under this system new capital will no longer be provided out of private " savings " : it will be set aside out of the total productive power of industry before individual incomes are distributed. After this has been done, enough income will be distributed to ensure a market for all that can be produced. There will be no need for private " saving," and no means of using it to make profits or interest. Everyone capable of work will be employed ; and the only limit to the distribution of incomes will be the productive power of the community and its desire to provide for the future.

In the transition to this system, it is desirable to foster the collective direction of new capital by means of a National Investment Board empowered to borrow funds from the public for re-investment in industries which need to be developed in the public interest. But this is only a transitional measure. Under Socialism, "investment" will be not a private but a public affair, because the sources of new capital will be in the hands of the community.

V

SOCIALISATION

Questions for discussion : 1. *How should socialised services be administered, and what say should the workers employed have in their policy and control ?*

2. *Should compensation be paid to the present owners of industry, and if so on what terms ?*

Socialisation means the transference of industries and services from private to public control. But it does not mean their management by Civil Service departments, as the Post Office is managed to-day. Under Socialism, each industry will have its own largely autonomous administration ; and the various industries will be co-ordinated under the control of a National Planning Commission, or some similar body. This does not mean that each industry will have power to settle what prices it is to charge for its products, or what wages it is to pay. Prices will have to be subject to public control, and the distribution of incomes will be a matter for the community as a whole. But in managing its affairs within the conditions laid down on grounds of public policy, the best plan will be to leave each industry largely autonomous, under competent technical directors approved by the Planning Commission, and with proper provision for ensuring that the workers employed have an effective say in the management. There are likely to be many different forms of organisation for socialised industries, according to the special characteristics of each. You cannot run the building industry and the railways in the same way.

If the approach to Socialism is gradual, socialisation is bound to be gradual too. Some industries will be socialised before others. But as long as the key industries (and especially banking) remain under capitalist control, with profit as the condition of production, it will not be possible to socialise any industry in a complete sense, or to run socialised industries very differently from those still under capitalist management. Real socialisation involves socialising industry (and finance) as a whole, and not merely an industry here and there.

If industries are at first socialised piecemeal, it will be necessary to compensate their owners; for it is not really practicable to confiscate one sort of property while leaving other sorts in private hands. But compensation should be paid in State bonds or shares in the socialised industry, and not in money, should be terminable (either by sinking fund or directly), should be limited in amount, and should be secured only against the future earnings of the socialised undertaking, and not against the whole revenue of the State. It should, moreover, be speedily wiped out by taxes (*e.g.*, on inheritance), so as to leave the socialised undertakings free of all claims from private persons.

If Socialism is introduced suddenly, over the whole field of industry, compensation is unnecessary; for there is no injustice in confiscating all capitalist property at once.

VI

SOCIAL SERVICES

Questions for discussion : 1. *How far can the development of social reforms be carried without socialising production ?*

2. *Should women be " economically independent," and should there be children's allowances ?*

Socialism involves a great development of the social services in some directions, and a curtailment in others. It will make " doles " unnecessary; for each able-bodied producer will get an income from Society in return for his readiness to serve. But (*a*) all education will be free, and every citizen will receive secondary as well as primary education, while entry to the higher branches of education will depend on ability to profit by them, and not on the parents' means; (*b*) hospital and medical services will be free, and paid for by the community; (*c*) much more will be spent, nationally and locally, on the amenities of life—parks and open spaces, playing-grounds, theatres and concert halls, libraries and museums, etc.; (*d*) it may be decided to supply free to all certain essential things, such as water, bread, milk for children, and anything of which it is desired to increase consumption in the public interest; (*e*) there will be certainly separate incomes, publicly provided, for married women not working in industry, and probably children's allowances.

There will be, then, a big *social* budget of expenditure. Socialists have always tried, under Capitalism, to get more spent on the social services. But this policy cannot, under Capitalism, be pursued very far, because after a point higher taxation reduces profits, and this causes employers to contract employment, and imposes new burdens on the State for maintaining the unemployed. It is impossible to have a satisfactory development of the social services as long as profit remains the sole inducement to production. Social Reform involves Socialism; for in order to be free to distribute income in the form of services the State must control the production of wealth.

VII

THE TRANSITION TO SOCIALISM

Questions for discussion : 1. *Can Socialism be established suddenly in Great Britain? Compare the Russian situation in 1917 with the British situation to-day.*

2. *What are the first steps a Socialist Government in Great Britain ought to take, and what changes in political structure do they involve?*

In Russia, the transition to Socialism was made by revolution; and as a result the Soviet Government have now full power to organise production and distribution. Russia has a Five Years Plan, and no unemployment problem. In Great Britain, we have been trying to approach Socialism by very gradual stages; and the chief results so far have been some increases in the Social Services at the cost of aggravating the unemployment problem by upsetting capitalists' confidence in their power to earn profits. Obviously the policy of gradual transition to Socialism is in danger of meaning no transition at all, but the turning out of Labour Governments, which seem only to make the situation worse.

On the other hand, in Great Britain the possibility of a sudden change-over to Socialism simply does not exist at present. British Capitalism is far stronger than Russian ever was; and far more people in Great Britain have small amounts of capital or some security that makes them dread revolution or the sudden collapse of Capitalism. Russia only got Socialism because Russian Capitalism had completely broken down. But even so she would not have got it unless Russian Socialists had been ready to assume power.

The *present* policy of British Socialists has to be framed in the light of the *present* attitude of the British people. This, *for the present*, rules out a sudden transition, though circumstances may change so as to make such a transition possible (*e.g.*, chaos in Europe and the collapse of the credit system). For the present, Socialists here have to try to build up Socialism without an intervening period of chaos and misery, such as Russia underwent. This can be done only by a far more advanced Socialist policy than Labour Governments have so far pursued; for it involves an immediate frontal attack on the key positions of Capitalism. The essentials of such a policy seem to include :—

1. *The Socialisation of Banking*, including both the Bank of England and the Joint Stock Banks, in order to get the price system and the supply of credit effectively under public control. (See Study Guides 1 to 4, which deal with banking and financial questions.)
2. *The Reform of Parliament*, in order to make it a more effective and speedy instrument for the carrying of Socialist measures. This includes, of course, the entire abolition of the House of Lords, as well as the devising of speedier legislative methods and the reform of the Cabinet system.
3. *The Taxation of Inheritance*, and the use of the proceeds as capital for the development of publicly owned industries and services.
4. *National Economic Planning*, including the creation of a National Investment Board and the speedy socialisation of the leading industries, such as mines, railways, and iron and steel.

VIII

SOCIALISM AND INTERNATIONALISM

Questions for discussion : 1. *How far can Socialism be securely established in one country alone? Discuss this in special relation to* (a) *Russia,* (b) *Great Britain.*
2. *Will Socialism lead to a World-Government?*

Socialism is essentially an international movement. Socialists believe in the brotherhood of man across national frontiers as well as within them. Their ultimate aim is to secure the use of all the world's productive resources for the benefit of all the world's inhabitants. Socialism established in one country alone is bound to be incomplete and defective, as Socialism is now in Russia; for it cannot govern the terms of international intercourse.

Nevertheless, this Guide has been written mainly in national terms, because the approach to Socialism is bound to be made mainly by national action. Socialists in each country have to work out their own policy for getting Socialism, while helping one another whenever they can, and trying always to foster international co-operation on lines leading towards Socialism, and to check the exploitation of the less developed peoples by their own capitalist groups.

Under Socialism, there will be no wars; for the peoples of Socialist countries will be in control, and will not regard one another as enemies. But wars might arise between Socialist and non-Socialist countries; and therefore Socialists should help on any movement that seems likely to make wars more difficult, provided only that such movements are not turned into instruments for international action to uphold the capitalist system.

Under Socialism, foreign trade will be a real and mutual exchange of goods, collectively organised, and largely of the nature of barter. The more developed countries will doubtless continue to lend capital to the less-developed, in order to foster their economic growth. But probably they will lend either without interest, or on terms which will allow the interest to be paid in goods. They will avoid piling up huge burdens of money-debt, such as are weighing down the world to-day.

Probably Socialism will lead to some form of World-Government of a federal kind—an International Planning Organisation to co-ordinate the National Plans of the different countries. But the only possible basis for Socialism as a form of world organisation is the secure establishment of Socialism in the leading countries.

WHAT TO READ.

The number of books on Socialism is enormous; but there is a great dearth of good short books that will serve as an introduction. H. N. Brailsford's *Socialism for To-day* (1/–) is the best of the very short works. *Fabian Essays*, first published in 1890, and Robert Blatchford's *Merrie England* are both still worth reading. See also the Fabian tract on *Socialism* by Bernard Shaw and two smallish books by Sidney and Beatrice Webb, *The Decay of Capitalist Civilisation* and *A Constitution for the Socialist Commonwealth*.

For Communism, see H. J. Laski's *Communism* in the Home University Library, and for the Russian Five Years Plan *Social*

Economic Planning in the U.S.S.R. (Martin Lawrence, 2/-). Larger books on Russian developments are C. T. Hoover's *Economic Life of Soviet Russia* and M. H. Dobb's *Russian Economic Development*. See also, for Communist principles, N. Lenin's *The State and Revolution* (1/-).

The best book on the principles of Socialism is Bernard Shaw's *Intelligent Women's Guide to Capitalism and Socialism*. R. H. Tawney's *The Acquisitive Society* and *Equality*, Bertrand Russell's *Roads to Freedom* and *The Prospects of Industrial Civilisation*, and H. W. Laidler's *History of Socialism* are all useful and readable. For the recent developments of British Socialist Policy see G. D. H. Cole's *The Next Ten Years in British Social and Economic Policy*, and for the foundation of Socialist economic doctrines *The Communist Manifesto*, by K. Marx and F. Engels, of which there are many editions, and Marx's *Capital* (in Everyman's Library, edited by G. D. H. Cole).

Printed by The Hereford Times Ltd. (T.U.),
London and Hereford.

THE BANK
OF
ENGLAND

The Bank of England

I

WHAT IS THE BANK OF ENGLAND?

Questions for discussion : (a) *What is the Treasury, and what are its relations to the Cabinet and to the Bank of England?*

(b) *How did the Bank of England come to get its present powers and privileges? (Get someone inside or outside the group to give you an account of the Bank's history.)*

The Bank of England[1] is a private corporation, and is the property not of the State, but of a body of private shareholders, who are mostly financiers in the City of London. The Governor of the Bank is appointed by the representatives of these shareholders, and not by the Government.

The Bank's powers and duties are, however, largely defined and laid down by Act of Parliament, in as far as they relate to the regulation of the supply of money, that is to say of bank notes.

In its other activities, except when it is acting directly on behalf of the Government, the Bank is, broadly, not under any form of State control; but it acts almost always in very close consultation with the public officials at the Treasury,[2] so that it is hard to say whether the Treasury has more control over the Bank, or the Bank over the Treasury.

The Treasury is, of course, under the control of the Chancellor of the Exchequer and the Cabinet; but in fact the permanent officials at the Treasury have a great deal of power, especially when they are in close agreement with the Bank of England and can use its authority to bring pressure to bear upon the Government.

---

[1] The Bank of England was founded in 1694, in the reign of William III, with Government support. It obtained its privileges by making a loan to the Government. Since then its powers have been gradually enlarged by a series of Acts, and especially by the concentration of the issue of bank notes in its hands, and its position as banker to the State.

[2] The Treasury is a Civil Service department, of which the Chancellor of the Exchequer is the effective head. The permanent head of the Treasury is the chief of the Civil Service. The Treasury exercises a large amount of control over the expenditure of all other Government departments.

The Bank, moreover, has the weight of City financial opinion behind it, and is able by this means to put strong pressure on the Government, which depends on the City for short-term loans (Treasury Bills).[1]

[1] Treasury Bills are promises to pay issued by the Government when it wants to borrow for a short period. The Bank manages the issue of Treasury Bills, which are sold by tender to the banks and financiers in the City of London. There are since the war always hundreds of million pounds' worth of Treasury Bills outstanding; for the Government borrowed a considerable amount of the War Debt in this form. This is called the Floating Debt, as opposed to long-term debt such as Consols and War Loan. This Floating Debt has constantly to be renewed, by the issue of new Treasury Bills as old ones expire. The rate of interest which the Government has to pay on these Bills is always changing, as conditions vary in the money market.

II

WHAT THE BANK OF ENGLAND DOES

Questions for discussion : (a) *What are the three main functions of the Bank of England, and how do they affect the public welfare ?*

(b) *What are the chief differences between the Bank of England and other British banks ?*

The Bank of England has *three* main functions. (a) It manages the issue of currency[1] (*i.e.*, bank notes) and the gold stock[2] held as a reserve against currency and for making payments abroad. (b) It acts as the Government's banker, and manages the National Debt on the Government's behalf. (c) It is the banker of the other banks, including both the Joint Stock Banks and the important financial houses of the City of London.[3]

The combination of these three functions, which is the result of a long process of historical development, gives the Bank of

[1] Currency, *i.e.*, money which passes current, or circulates, in cash payment for goods and services. It consists of Bank Notes, which are the Bank of England's promises to pay, and of silver and copper coins, which are manufactured by the State at the Mint, but issued through the Bank of England. There used to be gold coins as well, but they were withdrawn in 1914.

[2] Gold. Before the war, gold was mainly circulating in the hands of the public in sovereigns, and the Bank had only a comparatively small stock. Now that paper money is used instead of gold coin, most of the supply of gold in the world (except what is used for industrial purposes or hoarded in the Far East) is concentrated in the hands of the great Central Banks.

[3] Financial houses. These include the great merchant banks, such as Rothschilds, whose operations are mainly international, the houses which specialise in the floating of new capital issues, and the special houses which deal in accepting and discounting trade bills (*i.e.*, promises to pay which are used largely for settling international trade debts).

England very great power. It occupies the key position of the entire British financial system.

The Bank of England has also many secondary functions of great importance arising out of its three main functions. Among these may be mentioned : (a) the regulation of rates of interest for many kinds of short-term borrowing, through the fixing and variation of Bank Rate ; (b) acting as banker and agent for foreign Governments and for Central Banks of other countries and other foreign institutions in their dealings in the London money market ; (c) collaborating with the Central Banks of other countries in the Bank of International Settlements and in other ways in the handling of international problems of currency and finance ; (d) advancing money for special schemes of industrial reorganisation, either directly or through its subsidiary organisations. The last two functions are largely developments of recent years.

III

BANK NOTES

Questions for discussion : (a) *Why use paper-money instead of gold ? And why limit the amount of paper-money that may be issued ?*

(b) *What purposes do gold reserves serve ? Is their present regulation satisfactory ?*

The entire issue of paper-money in Great Britain (except to a small extent in Scotland)[1] is now in the hands of the Bank of England. The Treasury Notes issued directly by the Government during the war have, since 1928, been replaced by Bank of England Notes.

The issue of Bank Notes is regulated by Act of Parliament. The Bank of England is allowed to issue up to £260,000,000 worth of paper money without gold backing. This is called the *fiduciary issue*.[2] The amount thus issued may be increased in emergency by Parliament on the application of the Bank. It has been so increased in the crisis of 1931. For all notes issued beyond the fiduciary limit the Bank must have a pound for pound backing in gold.

The object of limiting the number of notes issued is to maintain their value in purchasing power. If notes could be issued without limit, and their supply were increased without a corresponding increase in the supply of goods and services, each note

---
[1] Several Scottish banks still issue notes of their own, but only in small amounts. Their issues do not affect the general position.
[2] Fiduciary, *i.e.*, on trust, without gold backing.

would necessarily buy less. Such an over-issue of paper money is called *inflation*. It occurred in many countries during and after the war, and was accompanied by a huge rise in prices.

The object of keeping a reserve of gold is to have gold available as required for making payments abroad. For clearly paper money is valid only within the country of issue, and cannot be used for foreign payments.

While we were on the Gold Standard, the Bank of England was compelled by law to buy and sell gold at a fixed price in bank notes. Bank notes could thus always be exchanged for gold bullion at a fixed rate at the Bank. So could the notes of other countries fully on the Gold Standard, at their Central Banks. This sufficed, within narrow limits, to fix the exchange value of the pound with other gold standard currencies.

Our departure from the Gold Standard took the form of suspending the Bank's obligation to sell gold at a fixed rate. This meant that holders of Bank Notes could no longer change them into gold for export. It destroyed the fixity of the pound's value in relation to other national currencies.

(See further on this subject, STUDY GUIDE NUMBER I.—THE GOLD STANDARD.)

It used to be supposed that it was necessary to keep a reserve of gold against notes used for circulation within the country. But it is now recognised that gold is needed, even under the Gold Standard, only to meet possible demands for export. The important matter as regards the note issue is not the amount of gold held against it, but that it should be large enough to meet the needs of production and consumption, and not so large as to cause a rise in prices. The attempt to secure this is called *currency management*, and a currency so controlled is called *a managed currency*.[1]

---

[1] Managed, as opposed to automatic. Currency management is an attempt to regulate the quantity of currency in accordance with national needs, instead of leaving it to be governed automatically by the available supply of gold, which depends mainly on international conditions.

IV

THE GOVERNMENT'S BANKER

Questions for discussion : (a) *What are Treasury Bills ? Why are they issued, and how ?*

(b) *Ought the Government to bank with an independent body, or to act as its own banker ?*

The Bank of England is the Government's banker. That is to say, the Government pays the proceeds of taxation and other revenue into the Bank, and makes payments by writing cheques on the Bank. Sometimes the Government has a balance at the Bank; sometimes it needs an overdraft, and has to borrow from the Bank.[1] This depends largely on the time of year; for receipts from taxes come in irregularly,[2] whereas expenditure goes on all the year round. Further, at certain dates huge payments fall due for interest on the National Debt.

The Government sometimes borrows directly from the Bank; but more often it sells Treasury Bills through the Bank, and so borrows from the financiers of the City. (See Section I above.)

The Bank manages the National Debt for the Government, and is paid for doing this. It pays out interest to the holders of the debt, including the debt to the United States. In effect, it acts as the Government's agent in all major financial transactions. This gives it a position of great influence as the Government's financial adviser.

[1] Such Government borrowings are called Ways and Means Advances.

[2] Thus Income Tax becomes payable in January and July, except when it is deducted at source.

V

THE BANKER'S BANK

Questions for discussion: (a) What is Bank Credit?
(b) What are " open market operations,"
and how do they work?

The Bank of England is the bankers' bank. The Joint Stock Banks (and the other great City financial houses which are not dealt with in this Study Guide, but will be dealt with in a later issue) keep accounts at the Bank of England. The Joint Stock Banks have always large amounts standing to their credit at the Bank of England. They do not borrow from it, as the banks do in some other countries from their Central Banks.

The Joint Stock Banks regard their deposits in the Bank of England as the equivalent of actual cash, as they can always get notes and coin from the Bank by drawing on their accounts. The holdings of the Joint Stock Banks at the Bank of England are thus the primary cash foundation on which they build up the structure of *bank credit*.[1] A fall in their holdings at the Bank of England usually means a restriction of credit.

The Bank of England is not without influence on the size of the balances standing to the account of the Joint Stock Banks.

[1] Bank credit, *i.e.*, advances granted by the Joint Stock Banks to their customers by way of overdrafts and other loans.

It can affect them by what are known as *open market operations*, that is, by buying or selling securities such as Government loans.[1] For, if the Bank of England sells some of the securities it holds, the buyers have to pay it for them. They do this by writing cheques on their own accounts at the Joint Stock Banks, which have to pay the Bank of England. This reduces their balances at the Bank, and so decreases their available cash basis for credits to their clients. On the other hand, if the Bank of England buys securities, it pays for them, and the sellers pay the money into their accounts at the Joint Stock Banks, which thus find their balances at the Bank of England increased. The Bank of England uses this method when it wants to make bank credit temporarily scarcer or more abundant. By this and other methods, the Bank of England practically controls the total amount of credit which the Joint Stock Banks are able to grant.

[1] The Bank of England always keeps a considerable part of its assets in the form of gilt-edged securities, such as Government stock.

VI
BANK RATE

Questions for discussion : (a) *What is Bank Rate, and how does it affect other interest rates ?*

(b) *What are the effects of high and low interest rates, in good and bad times ?*

The Bank of England's chief method of controlling credit conditions is by means of *Bank Rate.* This is the rate at which the Bank of England is prepared to discount Trade Bills of good standing,[1] *i.e.*, to pay cash down for a bill payable at some future date, usually three months or less. But the influence of Bank Rate extends far beyond Trade Bills. Its real importance lies in the fact that the Joint Stock Banks and other City houses base upon it the interest rates they grant upon deposits[2] and charge for short-term loans and overdrafts of every sort. The other Banks are under no legal compulsion to do this ; but they do it as a matter of policy, and in effect the Bank of England, by open market operations and in other ways, could compel them to do it even if they were unwilling.

Bank Rate, which is fixed weekly by the Bank of England, thus governs the rates of interest charged for practically all types of

[1] Trade Bills. See Study-Guide Number I.—The Gold Standard.

[2] Deposits, *i.e.*, that part of their customers' accounts which is withdrawable only upon notice, as distinct from current accounts, which can be drawn upon at any moment. The word " deposits " is unfortunately used in two senses : (a) as above, and (b) in a wider sense, including both current and deposit accounts. Interest is paid on the latter, but usually not on the former, by the Joint Stock Banks.

short-term loans. It thus largely governs the plenty or scarcity of credit ; for high rates of interest check borrowing and low rates encourage it. (Note, however, that it is not the absolute height of the interest rate that determines the desire of borrowers to borrow, but the relation between the interest they have to pay and the profit they hope to make. Thus, more money is borrowed at high interest rates in prosperous times than at low rates in bad times.)

When the Bank of England wants to increase the supply of credit, it lowers Bank Rate. When it wants to restrict credit, it raises Bank Rate. Its action then becomes effective because the other Banks raise or lower their rates correspondingly.

VII

THE BANK'S INTERNATIONAL POSITION

Questions for discussion : (a) *What are Central Banks, and how far do they work together ?*

(b) *What is the Bank of International Settlements, and how does it work ?*

There is no space to deal adequately with this subject in the present Guide. It will be dealt with more fully in a later issue.

The Central Banks of the leading countries work closely together. They must do this, because what each does affects the others. Thus, if interest rates are higher in New York than in London, financiers will tend to remove their balances from London to New York. This will set up a drain on London, affecting the rates of exchange and perhaps causing, under the Gold Standard, an export of gold. The different Central Banks have therefore to counteract the movement of money from country to country by raising and lowering interest rates. Interest rates all over the world are not the same ; but they react greatly on one another.

In recent years, collaboration between Central Banks has greatly increased, and their representatives now meet regularly together for discussion. In addition, they jointly control the Bank of International Settlements, which may prove to be the nucleus for a World Bank.

VIII

SOCIALISATION

Questions for discussion : (a) *Should the Bank of England be socialised, and with what objects ?*

(b) *If it should be socialised, how should it be run under socialisation ?*

The powers of the Bank of England are clearly too great to be properly left in the hands of a purely private body, even if it does work in very close connection with the Treasury. The Bank of England ought to be socialised,[1] and to become a public institution controlled by the State.

Objection is taken to this on the ground that it would make the highly technical work of the Bank subject to inexpert political interference. But the work of the Bank so vitally affects the welfare of industry and the community that it must be managed in the public interest, and the public must learn how to control a body so vital to its well-being.

Actually, the Bank of England is not in effect now run mainly for the profit of its shareholders. It pays a fixed dividend, in fact though not in theory, and does not try to make the largest profit it can. But it is managed in the interest of the general body of financiers in the City of London, who control it by holding its shares and appointing its directors; and it is run in the interests of finance rather than industry.

It is necessary to work out the right constitution for a socialised Bank of England, so as to secure that it shall hold a right balance between the various groups and interests concerned in banking policy, and advance the public welfare as a whole. The Labour Party's proposal[2] is to make it a Statutory Corporation, with a governing body appointed by the State to represent labour and industry and the consumers, as well as financial and Government interests. The detailed form of socialisation is discussed in a later Study Guide dealing with Banking Socialisation as a whole.

[1] Socialised, that is, brought under public ownership and under the final control of the State in matters of policy.
[2] See *Labour and the Nation*.

WHAT TO READ

Withers. " Money " (Benn). 6d. ⎫ All fairly easy reading.
Lehfeldt. " Money " (Oxford Manuals). 2s. 0d.
Leaf. " Banking " (Home Univ. Library). 2s. 6d.
McKenna. " Post-War Banking Policy ". 7s. 6d.
Robertson. " Money " (Cambridge Manuals). 5s. 0d. ⎭

Keynes. " Monetary Reform ". 7s. 6d. ⎫ Rather more advanced.
Hawtrey. " The Gold Standard ". 3s. 6d.
Andreades. " History of the Bank of England ". 15s. 0d.
Einzig. " The Bank for International Settlements ". 10s. 6d. ⎭

Printed by The Hereford Times Ltd. (T.U.),
London and Hereford.

MONETARY SYSTEMS
AND
THEORIES

by

G. D. H. Cole

Fellow of University College, and
Sub-Warden of Nuffield College, Oxford

Published by
ROTARY INTERNATIONAL
in Great Britain and Ireland
TAVISTOCK HOUSE (SOUTH)
TAVISTOCK SQUARE, LONDON
W.C.1

R.I.B.I. Pamphlet No. 14. Price 6d.
Published January 1943, 10,000

FOREWORD

The R.I.B.I. Reconstruction Committee is issuing this pamphlet on 'Monetary Systems and Theories' because of the evidence it has received both of the widespread interest in the subject among Rotarians and also of the desirability of a clear and objective exposition of some of the most important facts and arguments about what is a matter of considerable controversy.

No one pretends, least of all Mr. Cole, that this brief survey is exhaustive. It is merely intended as a foundation on which a further study can be built. It is essential, in fairness to Mr. Cole and to the reader himself, that the author's short preface should be read.

On behalf of the Reconstruction Committee of R.I.B.I. I wish to express to Mr. Cole our appreciation of his effective response to our request for a brief and impartial presentation of the problem.

J. A. ROSE, *Chairman*,
Reconstruction Committee, 1942-43

December, 1942.

PREFACE

I should like it to be understood that, while the following pamphlet was written at the request of Rotary International in Great Britain and Ireland, any opinions expressed in it are entirely my own and in no way commit the Rotary Movement.

I have tried to be as objective as possible in describing both the existing monetary systems and the views of the various schools of monetary reformers, and have kept my own opinions in the background wherever their expression would have interfered with my main purpose, which was to sum up the views held by competent thinkers on monetary questions rather than to put forward my own solutions. I mention this because it may be thought that, in presenting the subject in this way, I have failed to make as forthright a statement of what I think ought to be done as might be expected of me. I did not feel that the two jobs—which are essentially different—could both be satisfactorily done within the length of a short pamphlet.

G. D. H. COLE

Oxford, November, 1942.

Monetary Systems and Theories
By G. D. H. Cole

I.

Here are six simple sentences, each perfectly intelligible in its context, but each using the key word, *money*, in a different sense.

'*I came out today without any* money *in my pocket: so I had to borrow half-a-crown.*'
'*How much* money *have you in the bank?*'
'*I suppose old ——— must be worth a pot of* money.'
'*Money has been very tight all this week.*'
'*Hot* money *was at the root of the trouble.*'
'*Each country has its own* money; *but gold is international* money.'

Let us look at each of these sentences, and try to see what the key word means in each of them.

'I came out today without any *money* in my pocket; so I had to borrow half-a-crown.'

'Money' here means *cash* or *currency*—paper notes, silver or copper coins. Cash is the kind of money that is used for settling small day-to-day payments; the kind of money in which wages (but not the larger salaries) are usually paid; the kind of money people carry some of in their pockets. There are some notes for large amounts, which are used in settling certain business debts; but they are unimportant in Great Britain, and need not concern us here.

At one time some of this cash-money was made of gold, and the gold was worth as much, or nearly as much, as the things it could be used to buy. It could not for long be worth more, or it would have been worth while to melt it down, and it would have vanished from circulation, even despite laws against melting. In most countries gold-money was worth a little less than what it would buy, because a small charge was made to meet the cost of coinage. But the British sovereign was not subject to such a charge. That was why it was acceptable almost anywhere in the world.

Other cash-money is seldom of an *intrinsic* value equal to its purchasing power, though silver money sometimes used to be. Cash-money which is not intrinsically worth what it will buy is called 'token-money'. It may have some intrinsic value (e.g. silver), or practically none (e.g. paper money). It makes no practical difference whether 'token money' has any intrinsic value or not.

'Token money' gets its purchasing value from being issued by some authority—either the State's, or that of a bank or other agency authorized by the State. In this country, coins are issued from the Mint, which is a State department, whereas notes are issued by the Bank of England (and in small numbers by Scottish Banks). During the last war, the State issued its own notes (Treasury Notes); but in this war the whole issue is managed by the Bank of England under arrangements with the Treasury.

'Token-money' usually circulates only within the country which has authorized its issue. You cannot as a rule use a British bank note to buy things abroad. But you can in normal times usually take any kind of 'token-money' to a bank or foreign exchange office and get it changed into the kind of money you want. You will be charged a commission for this service; and how much of the one money you will get for so much of the other will depend on the current rate of exchange, which is a matter involving considerations we must leave over for the moment.

Some countries make much more use of 'token-money' than others; and in general as countries advance economically they make relatively less use of it in business transactions, finding other means of settlement more convenient. The decreased use of 'token-money' and of currency generally in business transactions is closely associated with the growth of banking and of the use of cheques.

'How much *money* have you in the bank?'

This question assumes the possession of a bank account in some sort of bank. It may be the Post Office Savings Bank, or a Trustee Savings Bank, or an ordinary joint-stock commercial bank, such as Barclays or the Midland. In this sense, money does not mean coins or cash: it means a book-entry in the bank showing so many pounds, shillings and pence to your credit. The bank has not nearly enough cash to pay out to all those who have money in the bank; but you can always, unless something has gone badly wrong, get cash for your own cheque against any credit standing in your name. Indeed, you can get more, if the bank is prepared to grant you a loan or overdraft. A loan is paid straight into your account: an overdraft is there to be paid in as you want it, up to the amount the bank is prepared to allow.

This is possible because most people do not want to draw out more than a small proportion of their bank-money in the form of cash. If some of them do draw large weekly amounts for paying wages, most of it soon flows back into the banks, being paid in by the tradesmen, property-agents, insurance companies and others to whom the wage-earners pay it over. Industrial areas, where large sums are regularly paid out as wages in cash, have a much larger relative cash turnover than middle-class residential areas, where most incomes are received and paid out by cheque. Bankers soon get to know what relation the cash demand in any particular place is likely to bear to the total of customers' deposits. Naturally, the amount needed fluctuates greatly between periods of boom and slump, and any rise in working-class incomes means a bigger demand for cash. It follows that there is no fixed ratio between the total of bank-money and the total of cash that is needed. A boom on the Stock Exchange will not cause the same increase in demand for cash as a rise in wages, because most of the transactions will be settled by cheque.

The demand for cash depends on the amount of bank-money in circulation, and on the uses to which this bank-money is being put. Nowadays, the State and the banking system see to it that enough cash is available to meet all demands. How much demand there is for cash depends on the policy of the banking system in supplying *credit*, in the form of bank-money. In order to understand how the financial system works, it is necessary to fix attention on the ways in which the supply of bank-money is regulated.

Bankers still sometimes deny indignantly that they ever 'create credit' or bank-money, and maintain that they only lend out what their customers leave with them on deposit. This is nonsense. It is admitted that the supply of bank-money varies greatly from time to time. But the banks' customers have clearly no power to make it vary. They cannot create money. Someone must be responsible for varying the supply; and this someone can be only a bank (or of course the State, when the State creates money directly, instead of handing over its powers to a bank).

The truth behind what the bankers say is that the power of the ordinary commercial banks to vary the supply of money is limited, under modern conditions. There are two main limiting factors. First, if one such bank were to create credit (by granting loans or overdrafts) faster than the others, it would soon find that it was getting into debt to the other banks, into which many of the cheques drawn by its customers would be paid. The commercial banks have a clearing house for cancelling their mutual debts; and, as long as they all march in step, their clearing accounts will tend to balance.

This, however, would not of itself stop the commercial banks from creating as much credit as they pleased, provided they all followed the same policy. The really effective check on their power to create credit is the Central Bank—in this country the Bank of England. The commercial banks all keep accounts at the Bank of England, and treat the sums standing to their credit at the Bank of England as the equivalent of cash, because they can always be drawn upon in cash up to any amount. By tradition, the commercial banks keep a fairly regular ratio between their cash holdings (including their credit at the Bank of England) and their total deposits (which include the amounts lent to their customers). This ratio is not absolutely fixed, nor is the matter nearly so simple as I am making it appear; but the complications do not affect my general point. This is that the amount of credit the commercial banks are prepared to give is limited by the amount of their cash holdings, and mainly by the size of their balances at the Bank of England.

Now comes the vital point. The Bank of England can alter the size of the balances standing to the credit of the commercial banks. It can do this by what are called 'open market operations'—that is, by buying or selling securities in the open market. Whenever the Bank of England buys a security and pays for it with its own cheque, it is creating bank-money. It is doing so, because usually its cheque will be paid in by a customer to a commercial bank, which will thus find its own balance at the Bank of England increased. The exact opposite will happen when the Bank of England sells securities. It will then be paid for them mainly by cheques on the commercial banks, whose balances at the Bank of England will therefore fall. In this way, the Bank of England can make bank-money scarce or plentiful at will. There are in practice forces which restrict the Bank of England's use of this power within limits; but we will come to these later, as they affect foreign exchange.

The Bank of England can always reduce the supply of bank-money by selling securities. But its power to increase the supply by buying securities is less complete; for it can become effective only if the commercial banks co-operate by increasing their loans. Usually they will do this; for they get interest on what they lend and therefore have an incentive to lend as much as they feel they safely can. But they clearly will not lend except to customers on whom they feel they can rely to repay the money in due course. In times of depression, the bankers' confidence in their customers' solvency is apt to be low; and they may accordingly refuse to expand their loans even if their balances at the Bank of England are increased. This is a very important point; for it means that, whereas the Bank of England can always reduce the supply of bank-money, and so force a contraction of business, it cannot always bring about an expansion, even if it tries.

It is sometimes said that what brings about an expansion or contraction of the supply of bank-money is the moving up or down of Bank Rate—that is, the rate of interest charged by the Bank of England for rediscounting bills of exchange or other approved commercial instruments. This view is incorrect. A change in Bank Rate does not of itself affect the supply of bank-money. It is, however, true that when the Bank of England wishes to restrict the supply of money it does often raise Bank Rate, or *vice versa*, and that commercial bankers normally regard a change in Bank Rate as a signal to expand or contract their credits. It is also true that they normally alter the rates of interest they charge to borrowers in step with changes in Bank Rate, and that *to a limited extent* other interest rates tend to react to such changes. To the extent to which potential borrowers are encouraged or discouraged by changes in the interest rates they will have to pay, changes in Bank Rate may affect their willingness to borrow, and therewith the amounts which commercial bankers are able to lend. But it is common to exaggerate the importance of this factor. Open market operations are, in these days, much more influential than Bank Rate in determining the supply of bank-money.

Let me try to sum up. Bank-money is created by a double process. The Central Bank is in a position to determine the total amount available, and to create the *cash-basis* needed for this amount. Within the maximum thus set, the commercial banks can create money, to the extent to which they can find borrowers to whom they deem it reasonably safe to lend. This is the mechanism of credit-creation, and it has no relation to the notion that bankers merely re-lend what their customers deposit with them. How can it have, when every loan the banker makes becomes a deposit as soon as it is used? Banker A. lends me £1,000. I pay it over to someone, who puts it into his bank—Banker B.'s. Banker B., when he makes his next loan, may think he is merely re-lending the money; but it is in fact merely money which was created by Banker A. There is, and can be, no distinction between the money paid in by depositors and the money created by bankers in making loans.

Presumably, the reason why such a fuss is made about the question whether banks create money is that many bankers regard the admission that they do so as somehow either discreditable or dangerous to their prospects. If banks are mere lenders of money already in being, no one can charge them with being responsible, by their action in making or destroying money, for the ups and downs of business: whereas, if money is of their making, they can be blamed for making too much or too little of it, and thus engendering booms and slumps. Moreover, if the banks create the money which they lend out at interest, it may be asked why the State should delegate this profitable art of money-making to the banks, instead of reaping the profit of it for the taxpayers' benefit. The bankers still in some cases like pretending that they do not create or destroy money; but there is no getting away from the fact that they do.

'I suppose old —— must be worth a pot of *money*.'

When old —— dies, and death duties have to be paid on his property, his assets will have to be valued. There will be a little loose cash in the house, and probably a much larger sum in bank-money—his balance at the bank. But most of his 'pot of money' will be found to consist not of 'money' in either of these forms, but of investments and holdings of land or houses or other forms of physical property, or perhaps of debts due to him from others. The 'money' referred to in the sentence we are discussing is not really money at all, but mainly things of which the value is expressed in money terms. For 'money' serves not only as a means of exchange—the sense in which we have so far dealt with it—but also as a unit of accounting and valuation. If we wish to add up in a common sum a number of valuable things of quite different kinds, there is usually no way open to us except that of expressing their values in money terms. What we are in effect doing in the case of old ——'s possessions—his investments and his land and house property—is to value them at so many years' purchase of the income they are expected to bring in, or rather at what we could expect a purchaser to be willing to give for them in view of this expected income.

'Money' in this sense does not need to exist in any form separate from that of the things which we value in terms of money. In certain times of emergency, certain countries have issued 'token money' against the security of the land and property of the nation. *Assignats* during the French Revolution and the *Rentenmark* in Germany after the last war are examples. It has been supposed that issuing money against such real things gives some guarantee of security, corresponding to that which is supposed to be given by issue against a reserve of gold. But the two cases are really quite different because at a pinch the gold can commonly be used to pay debts outside the country, whereas the land and other physical property cannot, unless a foreigner can be found willing to buy them. Moreover, the amount of land or other physical property existing, and the money value set upon it, give no clue at all to the amount of cash or bank-money the community needs to effect the circulation of its current output, or to cover the volume of its current financial transactions. The amount of these kinds of money that is needed depends on the current volume of transactions and on the level of prices, and not on the amount of a nation's assets in land and property which are not necessarily up for sale.

It may be said that the amount of a country's gold stock is also a very bad basis for settling its supply of cash and bank-money. I agree that it is; but may I leave that point over for the present?

Some financial reformers argue (and have been arguing for a very long time past*) that, even though the amount of land and capital in existence may be a bad basis for settling the supply of cash and bank-money, the amount of current production is a good one, and should be the criterion of banking policy in the supply of credit. Or rather, what is often argued is that credit—that is, bank-money—should be made available *in proportion to productive power*, so that no one equipped with the means of producing useful things should be prevented by lack of credit from producing them. This idea has a great deal of truth in it; but the matter is not so simple as may at first sight appear. 'Power to produce' is not unqualified: it is power to produce some things, but not others, and it is power to produce these things at not less than a certain minimum cost But power to produce things at a price which no one is prepared to pay for them, even if he has the money, is not real productive power; and power to produce more of certain things than people want, even at reasonable prices, is hardly more real. The supplies of different kinds of goods have to be balanced so as to meet the demands for them. These demands are, of course, affected by the size of the incomes people have to spend; but no imaginable increase in the incomes of the British people would cause them to buy all the cotton goods Lancashire could produce for them, supposing its export markets to disappear. Thus, in such circumstances, a large part of Lancashire's apparent power to produce would not be a real power, and it would be useless to issue credits in order to make possible an output that would greatly exceed the demand.

What people really mean, or should mean, when they urge that credit ought to be based on productive power is that there ought to be enough bank-money available to keep total production at the highest possible level, up to the limits set by shortage of man-power or other instruments of production, or by lack of balance in the supply of such instruments— and of course they also imply that, if there is a lack of balance, steps ought to be taken to correct it as speedily as possible. I believe the doctrine, in this form, to be sound sense.

But, it is objected, any amount of money, however large or small, can be used to circulate any quantity of goods, or to finance any volume of transactions, if only prices are allowed to adjust themselves freely to the available supply of money. This is true; but it is a barren truth. For the process of price-adjustment to large changes in the supply of bank-money is so painful that it is never allowed to happen 'freely'. Some prices are held up because they are governed by long-term contracts (e.g. long-term interest rates), or by successful monopoly action, or by superior bargaining power. Other prices have to fall all the more in order to make up for these hindrances to free adjustment. There is always a very strong presumption that any action which forces price-alteration by altering the supply of money will do much more harm and injustice than good.

This does not mean that prices ought not to alter. Of course they should. Technical invention is continually lowering the costs of pro-

---

* Thomas Attwood, for example, adduced the argument during the depression after the Napoleonic Wars.

ducing things in many instances, and sometimes other forces are pushing costs upwards—for example, when it is decided, as a matter of policy, to try to allow the agriculturist a standard of life nearer to that of the industrial producer. The prices of particular things should alter in response to such changes; and as prices in general are simply an average of particular prices, it follows that the general level of prices should alter too. There is no magic reason why upward and downward changes should cancel out, so as to leave the general level stable. Nor is there, so far as I can see, any valid reason why States or banks should deliberately interfere in order to make this happen, by manipulating the supply of money. Price-changes are not bad in themselves. They are bad when they arise from irrational causes. But men tend to think them bad because they have suffered so much from irrational forces in recent years.

'*Money* has been very tight all this week.'

Here we are faced with yet another kind of 'money', or rather with a particular species of the genus, bank-money, with which we have dealt already. The 'money' that is 'tight' turns up usually in the City columns of the newspapers, in discussions of what is called 'the money market'. The money market is, very broadly speaking, the set of agencies through which business men, as distinct from ordinary people, borrow bank-money for use, not directly in production, but in financial transactions, including the financing of foreign trade. Generally, the phrase is used to describe the agencies concerned with lending for short terms, as distinct from the 'capital market' for long-term investments; but the two cannot be entirely separated. Under war conditions, the Government is the chief short-term borrower, and always Government short-term borrowing is important. But in time of peace the chief functions of the money market are to provide the funds for financing foreign trade and, rather more deviously, the funds for stock market and other forms of speculation.

The 'money' which is available in 'the money market' consists chiefly of funds seeking short-term investment and belonging either to the British commercial banks or to the numerous foreign and colonial banks and other financial agencies with offices in London. The ordinary commercial banks so regulate their total lending as to keep a part of it outstanding only for very short terms ('money at call or at short notice'). They lend this money largely to bill-brokers who in turn use it for making advances on trade bills; and they also buy for themselves both trade bills and Treasury Bills. The foreign and colonial banks in London have often large balances accruing to them which they can lend out only for a short time—for example, until they are needed for paying interest or dividends to British holders of overseas securities. They, and various other financial agencies, also lend to bill-brokers or themselves buy trade or Treasury Bills; and some of these agencies also lend money for stock speculation.

The plenty or scarcity of money of this kind in relation to the demand for it is the main determinant of the short-term rate of interest, or rather of the group of rates that goes by that name. The rate of discount on commercial bills and that on Treasury Bills are closely connected; and

'Bank Rate' is, as we have seen, the rate at which the Bank of England will rediscount certain bills. The rate of 'discount', of course, is simply the rate of interest seen from the other end in point of time. £1 due in three months is worth £1 − x_1; whereas for £1 lent now it will be necessary in three months' time to repay £1 + x_2. x_1 is the discount: x_2 is the interest.

Writers on economic questions used often to write as if the movements of these short-term rates of interest or discount determined the rates charged for long-term borrowing. I do not deny that the two groups of rates interact; but the relation is certainly not one of simple determination. They interact because certain borrowers—notably the State—can shift between the two groups—for example, by raising a funding loan to pay off floating debt, or by increasing the floating debt to pay off a long-term loan at maturity. They also interact because ordinary commercial bank advances occupy an intermediate position; and in some cases borrowers can shift from bank loans either to short-term borrowing in the bill market or to long-term capital issues. But movements in short-term rates do not necessarily bring about corresponding changes in long-term rates. To suppose that they do is a fallacy which underlies the belief that a low Bank Rate is an infallible means of stimulating industrial activity.

Short-term rates for 'money' are usually much lower than either long-term rates or the rates charged on ordinary bank advances. This is partly because money subject to recall at very short notice is less desirable than money of which the loan is assured for a longer period. But it is mainly due to the existence in great financial centres of large masses of bank-money which those who control it are only prepared to lend for very short periods and must therefore lend for what borrowers are ready to pay for it.

'Hot *money* was at the root of the trouble.'

The 'money' we have just been talking about, the 'money' that is lent and borrowed in the short-term 'money market', includes as we have seen a good deal of money that belongs to foreigners. It also includes a good deal that belongs to persons or institutions whose dealings are essentially international and whose 'money' moves about from country to country. The owners of this money are actuated, under normal conditions, by the desire to get the best available return on its short-term use; and they therefore send it to the international money centre in which short-term rates are highest for the time being. But under abnormal conditions fear replaces hope of gain as the main incentive; and then 'hot money' is sent where it is felt likely to be safest, even if the interest obtainable on it is low or *nil*. This occurs mainly when the rates of exchange between different national moneys are unstable, as they were for most of the time between the wars.

Movements of 'hot money' were the cause of important money market disturbances, by causing money to become alternately scarce and plentiful to a remarkable extent as the 'hot money' was brought in or withdrawn. To some extent, Central Banks learnt the practice of sterilizing 'hot money' by buying gold and thus locking it up out of use until its owners wanted to remove it, when the gold could be exported to meet the claim. This was part of the purpose served by the British Exchange Equalization Fund and by similar funds elsewhere.

'Hot money' is thus only a kind of bank-money; but it brings us right up against the problem of international exchange, or 'foreign exchange', as it is usually called.

'Each country has its own *money*; but gold is international *money*.'

Each country has its own *money*—that is, its own money units in which values are measured. Ours are pounds, shillings and pence; or, more particularly, our unit is the pound sterling, of which the others are subdivisions. Other countries use the pound, for example Australia; but an Australian or Egyptian pound is not necessarily or in fact the equivalent of a British pound. Nor is a French franc the same as a Swiss franc, or a Mexican dollar as a United States dollar, or a Swedish as a Czech crown. Each nation's money standard is different from each other's; and yet somehow, for purposes of trade and investment, all these money's have to be exchangeable one for another.

The idea which found much favour in the past, and still finds favour in some quarters, is that of making them exchangeable at nearly fixed rates by making each pound, dollar, franc, mark, or what-not exchangeable for a fixed amount of gold at the Central Bank of the country concerned. Where this is done, and the cash-money can be actually exchanged for so much gold, the rates of exchange between national moneys can fluctuate only between limits set by the cost of transporting gold, and insuring it in transit, or at most only a very little beyond these limits, which are known as the 'gold points'. For if the relative values moved beyond these points, it would pay to transport gold instead of changing the one kind of money directly for the other. The 'gold standard', in the full sense of the term, involves that the national money shall be freely exchangeable for gold at a fixed rate, and that there shall be freedom to export gold. It also involves that gold shall be exchangeable for the national money at a fixed rate, or in other words that the Central Bank or the Government shall be always prepared to give the national money in exchange for gold at a fixed rate, which need not, however, be the same as the rate at which the same bank sells gold, but must not be far apart from it.

Very few countries have ever in practice worked a completely unrestricted gold standard. Great Britain did, up to 1914; and the United States did, up to the world crisis of the early 'thirties. But most countries which worked the standard did so with some qualifications. There were great efforts by international bankers to get the gold standard universally adopted after the last war; and it was widely accepted in various modified forms. But scarcely had this been achieved when the world crisis of the 'thirties drove one country after another off gold. Great Britain gave up the gold standard in 1931, and has never returned to it. The United States lowered the gold value of the dollar as a result of the crisis, but continued to buy all the gold offered to it. In practice, the United States was, during the period before the war, practically the sole buyer of the world's new gold; and an enormous proportion of the world's total gold stock found its way to the United States.

This was not because the United States wanted the gold, which was for the most part a source of dead loss. It was because the United States was (a) a creditor nation, entitled to receive interest and dividends from abroad, (b) an exporter more than an importer, the volume of imports being severely restricted by the high American tariff, and (c) a country to which 'hot money' flowed for safety out of Europe. The United States had to accept the gold, because there was no other way of getting paid what was owing to its citizens; but it then had to sterilize most of it, because if it had been used as a basis for issuing credit, there would have been a great rise in prices and an entire upset of the American economy. Moreover, the Americans knew that, if they were to stop buying gold, there would be an immediate world crisis even worse than that of 1931-32.

The situation which existed in the world was quite absurd; but no one could see how to deal with it. The effect of the high American price for gold in terms of dollars was to stimulate an immense increase in gold production all over the world, though the world needed not more gold but less. But however much gold was produced, it nearly all found its way to the United States, because no other country could afford to buy it. In order to buy gold, a country must have something to spare after paying for its imports of commodities and meeting any other external charges on its national income; and most countries were having a hard struggle to balance their international accounts even without buying gold.

The case for the gold standard is that, by fixing within narrow limits the value of one national money in terms of another, it facilitates trade and investment across national frontiers. The trader knows that, if he sells a thing for so many dollars or marks, he will get so many pounds sterling when he is paid—that is, if both the countries concerned are on the gold standard. The investor in fixed-interest securities has a similar knowledge, and the investor who buys equities (i.e. shares bearing a variable dividend) has one source the less of uncertainty to face. These are great advantages; but they can be bought at too high a price. They may, moreover, be unattainable advantages; for it may be quite impossible for a country to be or to remain on the gold standard, even if it would wish to.

The disadvantage of the gold standard, from the standpoint of a particular country, is that it makes the supply of bank-money depend, not on its need for credit, but on the amount of its gold holdings. Under the gold standard, the issue of currency is based on the stock of gold. Usually there is a 'fiduciary issue'—that is, a supply of currency (or cash) not backed up to 100 per cent. by gold. The system may be either that a minimum percentage of the currency issued shall have gold backing, or, as in Great Britain, that there shall be a fixed, or nearly fixed, fiduciary issue, and that all currency beyond the fiduciary limit shall be backed 100 per cent. by gold. Silver also is sometimes brought in as a subsidiary source; but we can neglect that complication here.

Now, the amount of currency issued does not in practice determine the amount of bank-money, as we have seen. But it does set limits to it;

for there must be enough currency to meet the demands for it to which the supply of bank-money gives rise. Moreover, the Central Bank under the gold standard in practice regulates the amount of bank-money largely in accordance with its supply of gold. The idea is that it must do this, because if it does not there will arise a divergence between the fixed gold value of its money and its real value in internal purchasing power, and this will lead to its money being either too cheap or too dear. If it issues so much bank-money that internal prices rise, it will be unable to sell its exports to foreigners, who will refuse to pay the higher gold prices demanded for them. If it issues too little bank-money, its internal prices will fall, and this, while stimulating its exports, will make it a bad place for foreigners to sell in, and will also create all sorts of domestic difficulties, by making production unprofitable to many producers, and thus causing widespread unemployment.

Thus, a country which is on the gold standard cannot regulate its issue of bank-money according to its own needs, but must follow the course dictated by its gold supply and by the movements of credit and prices in other gold-standard countries, so as to keep the value of its money in goods and services running parallel with theirs. This has meant in recent years that any country on the gold standard is largely compelled to follow the actual movements of money and credit in the United States, which is by far the most powerful economic influence. It means also that a gold-standard country cannot, save within narrow limits, attempt to meet a depression by enlarging the supply of credit or by large loan expenditure on public works, for fear of being unable to maintain the exchange value of its currency, as Great Britain found itself unable in 1931.

In recent years, opinion has swung strongly in favour of attempting to maintain prosperity in face of threatened trade depression by easier credit and by the institution of public works or other measures designed to stimulate investment. The extent to which this can be done under the gold standard depends on other gold-standard countries simultaneously doing the same thing, and apart from this is limited to what can be done without affecting prices—which is, in practice, under a 'free capitalist' economy, very little.

When countries are not on the gold standard, their moneys have still to be exchanged. But they no longer exchange at fixed, or nearly fixed, rates. The limits set by the 'gold points' being removed, the exchanges can fluctuate to any extent, though over short periods their fluctuations may be limited or prevented by various expedients, including Exchange Equalization Funds. But no fund can stand out against a long-term tendency for the values of two national moneys to diverge.

What determines these relative values in the absence of a fixed standard, such as gold? The full answer is very complicated, and I cannot attempt to give it here. Very broadly, the relative values depend on the supply of and demand for the currencies in question; and the supply and demand depend mainly on the course of trade and investment. If a country's products are cheap, foreigners will buy more of them than if they are dear, in relation to prices elsewhere; and accordingly the country will get more or less foreign exchange by selling its exports. Its imports, on the other hand, have to be paid for in foreign currency, for which they therefore represent a demand. If these two forces fail to balance at the current rate of exchange, the rate will alter until they do balance. In the last resort, accordingly, exchange rates depend, where there is no fixed standard, on relative prices, or what economists call 'purchasing power parity'.

This is a gross over-simplification; but I cannot avoid it without taking up too much space. The essential point is that, in the absence of a fixed exchange standard, exchange rates can fluctuate without limit, and are governed by forces of international supply and demand.

II.

We have now, with the aid of our six sentences, done what can be done in a short space to lay bare the principal variant meanings of the word 'money', and incidentally to throw some light on a number of monetary problems. Let us next look at a very few of the criticisms which are flung, as the basis of various reform projects, at the entire monetary system, and try to see which parts of them are indisputably sense or nonsense, and which are open to reasonable doubt. Again I shall use the method of citing certain sentences, and then trying to elucidate their meaning.

'Stabilize exchange rates, and everything will go smoothly.'
'Stabilize prices, and everything will go smoothly.'
'Stabilize the supply of money, and everything will go smoothly.'
'The function of creating money ought not to be in the hands of private persons: it ought to be performed by the State, and the profit accruing from it ought to accrue to the community as a whole.'
'The faster money circulates, the more work it does: therefore faster circulation means fuller employment.'
'It is an inevitable outcome of the present monetary system to cause a deficiency of purchasing power.'
'The great evil of today is under-consumption: the remedy is for the State to place additional purchasing power in the consumers' hands.'
'The great cause of depressions is under-investment: the remedy is for the State either to invest more extensively in public works, or to devise means of stimulating private investment, or both.'
'The State, like the individual, must cut its coat according to its cloth. An unbalanced budget destroys business confidence.'

Let us now discuss each of these sentences, behind each of which lies a general theory of monetary reform.

'Stabilize exchange rates, and everything will go smoothly.'

This is the old orthodoxy, in its extreme form; and much effort was spent in endeavouring to act on this precept between the wars. It means, in effect, going back to the gold standard, though not necessarily in quite the traditional form. Many countries did this between 1918 and 1931. Great Britain did in 1925. But, so far from things going smoothly thereafter, they went very bumpily indeed. I am not blaming the gold standard for all the bumpiness; but it is pretty clear, in the light of experience, that a return to gold is not a cure-all. The gold standard might work reasonably well if (*a*) all the leading countries were on it, at reasonable levels of parity; (*b*) all the countries on it pursued in common a policy of 'full employment', avoiding both deflation and inflation; (*c*) the Americans abolished their tariff, or lowered it so much as to make it harmless; (*d*) countries with a tendency to a 'favourable' balance of payments (i.e. having more owed to them than they had to pay) would regularly invest the surplus overseas; (*e*) provision were made for revising the 'parities' (i.e. the relative values of the different currencies) from time to time, so as to offset changes in their real internal purchasing power.

This is an enormous 'if'; but unless these conditions are satisfied, I do not believe the gold standard can be made to work, or any stable system of exchanges be put in its place. Stable conditions of foreign exchange can exist only within a stable economic system, resting on a fair balance of real economic forces and a workable international division of labour. Short of this, fluctuations in exchange rates can be kept in check by various devices and tolerable stability over short periods can be secured without a return to a fixed standard; and that is all we can reasonably expect in the near future. An attempt to achieve more would most likely lead to breakdown, and a return to chaos. This was what happened after 1931; and we cannot afford, in deference to financial orthodoxy, to let it happen again.

'Stabilize prices, and everything will go smoothly.'

Why should it? Prices should surely change as costs of production change, and be related to the costs of producing particular kinds of goods. Would it have been a good idea to stabilize the price of motor-cars thirty years ago? But, it is said, we ought to stabilize, not the prices of particular things, but the price level. What is the price level but an average of particular prices? Why stabilize an average? If some prices fall because technique improves, is that a reason for raising others where it is stationary? The germ of truth in this notion of price-stabilization is that prices ought to be guarded against fluctuations which have nothing to do with changes in production costs, but arise out of monetary mismanagement or the ups and downs of the trade cycle. It is sound sense so to manage money as to keep monetary influences on the price-level as small as possible; and it is sound sense to do everything possible to eliminate the trade cycle—a point to which I shall come back later. But absolute stabilization of the price-level is just nonsensical. Let us agree that price-fluctuations are bad, except when they arise from changes in costs, or, I would add, temporarily from such causes as a decline in the demand for a commodity due to changes in consumers' desires. Let us agree that price-fluctuations have been hitherto unreasonably and disastrously great, and that they ought to be reduced within much narrower limits. But let us refrain from erecting a statistical average into a standard of policy.

'Stabilize the supply of money, and everything will go smoothly.'

Again, why? Different communities, at different stages of development, have different monetary needs. The amount of money a country requires depends not only on the size of its population, but also on its habits and the nature of its economic pursuits. A peasant country, where the producers live largely off the produce of their own farms, with relatively few money exchanges, obviously needs less money to sustain any given level of production than a country in which most goods are exchanged by means of money; and in this matter there are many gradations between one country and another, both in the proportion of output which is exchanged and in the number of exchanges needed for getting goods into the hands of the final consumers. Moreover, what kind of 'money' do those who advocate this form of stabilization wish to stabilize? Currency? But the demand for this depends largely on the extent to which wages and salaries are paid in cash, or by cheque. Bank-money? But the demand for this depends largely on the degree of integration between the successive stages of production, on the extent of such activities as Stock Exchange speculation, and on the monetary habits of the people. Such things change; and there is no reason to suppose that stabilization of the quantity of money, in either sense, would conduce to economic stability.

It is, however, true that the supply of money ought not to fluctuate nearly so much as it does. It fluctuates, both because it is controlled by banks which follow no clear or constant principle in regulating its amount, and because the level of economic activity fluctuates in accordance with the changing expectations of profits entertained by business men, the changing attitude of the bankers, and the changing economic condition of the world as a whole. Remedies for these causes of fluctuation are much to be desired; but stabilization of the total supply of money would be no remedy. It would operate, in practice, to prevent an increased supply, even when more was needed, but not to prevent a decrease in the effective supply in times of depression; for the mere availability of money, as experience shows, is by no means a guarantee that what is available will be actually used. The supply of money should be made to respond to the need for it; and the main objective of economic policy should be to ensure that the real resources available are fully used and then to supply the money lubricant to the required extent. Money produces nothing: it is a lubricant, and not a motive power. Monetary policy should second productive policy: it cannot be erected into an independent factor without jamming the productive machine.

'The function of creating money ought not to be in the hands of private persons: it ought to be performed by the State, and the profit accruing from it ought to accrue to the community as a whole.'

I agree with this view; but it has to be remembered that the function of creating money is not without cost. The banks have to meet the expenses of their establishment, and a part of the gain which accrues from their creation of money is absorbed by these costs—for salaries, bank premises, and other necessary expenses. It is doubtless true that banks make very high profits on their capital, and that their power to create money contributes to these profits. But the capital of the banks is very small in relation to their turnover, and the appropriation of bank profits by the State would not make very much difference. This is no argument against appropriating it, and I do not doubt that economies in banking costs could be achieved under unified control; but it is an argument against the view that the nationalization of banking would of itself make credit very much cheaper than it is by eliminating the bankers' profit.

The really cogent arguments in favour of nationalization of the banks rest on a different foundation. The case for nationalizing the Bank of England rests on the fact that the Central Bank controls the total amount of bank-money, and that this control is too vital a matter, for the whole community, to be left in private hands. The Bank of England, though the basis of its directorate has been widened in recent years, is still predominantly representative of 'City' finance. It represents even capitalist industry very imperfectly, and the main body of the producers and consumers not at all. It is often a moot point whether, under existing conditions, the Treasury controls the Bank of England, or the Bank the Treasury. There ought surely to be no doubt. The volume of bank-money ought to be settled as a matter of public policy; for on it depends the level of employment and the entire working of the financial machine in relation to the production and distribution of goods and services.

Those who oppose this view do so mainly on the ground that the State cannot be trusted to behave sensibly in financial affairs, and that it is better to trust in such matters to an expert corporation than to the politicians. I agree that politicians are often foolish; but has anyone yet solved the problem of finding an expert corporation capable of acting with enlightenment solely for the public good? The Bank of England represents too much financial and big business interests, and too little the main body of the people, or even the smaller employers. It may be that the directors of a Central Bank ought to be given a large degree of independence of day-to-day political interference. But surely they ought to be finally responsible to the people, and not to a body of private shareholders or to a group of powerful financial interests.

The case for nationalizing the commercial banks rests on rather different grounds. The commercial banks regulate in the main, not the total amount of bank-money, but its distribution among would-be borrowers. The banks lend to those in whom they feel 'confidence', and refuse to lend to those in whom they feel none. In this discrimination, they are guided mainly by expectations of the profitability of the enterprises to which they lend. But is this, from the standpoint of the public, the best test? If the State decides after the war to play a part in planning production, it will have to see that bank credit is apportioned to productive concerns in accordance with their several parts in the national plan of production. For this purpose it will need, through the appropriate agencies, to control the distribution of credit, and therefore to control the commercial banks.

Of course, those who are opposed to the planning of production are free to oppose public control of the banks, and to affirm their continued faith in private financial, as well as industrial, enterprise, and in *laissez-faire* as the right principle of economic policy. But we cannot have planned production (or, in my view, 'full employment') without planned finance, or without public control of the commercial banks.

It is often suggested that State Banking would make it harder for the small producers to get credit. I believe the opposite to be the case. Bank credit is at present much easier for big business than for the small producer or trader. The State in planning production will certainly not want to take over small-scale business, but will want it to work with the fullest efficiency; for otherwise 'full employment' will be impossible. Therefore State banks would advance credit liberally to the small man.

It is also sometimes alleged that private deposits would be less safe under a State banking system than they are today. But why? The State's credit is better than any banker's; and it is inconceivable that the State would repudiate its liability to the depositors. Moreover, the best guarantee of profitability for the banks is a condition of 'full employment'. Bank nationalization would not, of itself, guarantee any improvement in monetary policy; for the State *might* manage the banks on the same principles as the private bankers do now. But publicly owned banks are indispensable as the financial instruments of a planned policy of 'full employment'; and the pursuit of such a policy implies a liberal supply of credit. Bank nationalization is needed, not for its own sake, but as the instrument of a policy of 'full employment'.

These paragraphs are not meant to convince opponents of economic planning and 'full employment'. They are quite right in opposing bank nationalization on individualist grounds, granted their fundamental point of view. I am only trying to show that those who favour economic planning and 'full employment' must favour public ownership of the banks as one of the essential elements.

'The faster money circulates, the more work it does: therefore faster circulation means fuller employment.'

The first part of this sentence states a truth. The faster money circulates, the more transactions it can be used to finance at a given price level, over a period of time; and accordingly, the faster money circulates, the less of it will the community need. It is also true that in times of depression the circulation of money slows up because those who possess it tend to hoard it instead of spending it quickly on either consumption or investment, and the effect of such hoarding is plainly to make depression worse. Anything that would cause people to spend or invest money in a depression instead of hoarding it would be an indubitable advantage.

On this truth, certain writers have based a theory that the best means of ensuring prosperity is to speed up the circulation of money. There have been proposals to institute a kind of money that goes bad unless it is promptly spent—for example, a kind of money that depreciates by so much per cent. every week, and has to have its value kept up by affixing stamps to it to offset this depreciation. In other words, some people advocate a kind of money bearing a *negative* rate of interest, so that every holder of it would wish to turn it into real goods as speedily as possible, and thus pass it on to someone else. I can see no valid argument against such money, and much to be said for it wherever hoarding is prevalent. It would be, in my view, preferable to the existing kind of money, which can be held indefinitely in cash or at the bank without deterioration. I believe that unspent money should forfeit its purchasing power, either gradually, as has been suggested, or altogether after a certain lapse of time. This, of course, does not mean that there would be any penalty on *saving*, but only that saving would have to take the form of investment, and not of mere abstention from buying anything at all. A person could still save as much as he pleased, provided he lent his money to someone who would use it, or invested it himself in the purchase of some real asset. Not saving, but only hoarding, would be penalized.

I cannot, however, agree that the institution of 'vanishing money' would cure most of our economic ills. For the hoarding of money is only one among a number of our present monetary troubles, and a speeding up of the velocity of circulation is of much more importance if the total supply of money is limited narrowly, as it is under the gold standard, than if the supply can be adjusted readily to changing needs. If we accept the gold standard, there is a strong case for 'vanishing money', or at all events for subjecting the holding of money to a special tax during periods of economic depression. If we reject the gold standard, and any other system which arbitrarily fixes the total supply of money, the case for 'vanishing money' is not invalidated; but it becomes much less strong.

'It is an inevitable outcome of the present monetary system to cause a deficiency of purchasing power.'

This opinion, in the forms in which it is most often advanced, I regard as untrue. But I have considerable sympathy with what lies behind it. The classical economists, in what is called 'Say's Law', used to maintain that there could never be any deficiency of purchasing power, because every act of production necessarily generated the income required for buying what was produced. This view is patently wrong. Even if all costs of production are also incomes for those to whom they are paid, or at all events represent an equivalent purchasing power, it by no means follows either that all the purchasing power thus generated will be spent in buying what is produced (for some of it may be hoarded), or that total production will be pushed to the limit set by total capacity to produce. If everybody were unemployed, and nothing at all were produced, income at zero would balance zero output, just as much as maximum income would balance maximum output if productive resources were stretched to the full; and the same truism (bar hoarding) would hold good for any intermediate level of production.

But, if Say's Law is a barren truism at best, the contentions of those who argue that the present system engenders inevitably a deficiency of purchasing power rest on a fallacy. The argument takes many forms; but its commonest form is what is called 'the A + B theorem', associated with the name of Major Douglas. According to this theorem, the total purchasing power distributed to the citizens may suffice to buy all the finished goods that are produced, but does not provide anything for the purchase of intermediate goods at the various stages of production. In practice, however, part of the available money goes in buying these intermediate goods, so that there is not enough left over to buy all the finished goods.

This is sheer fallacy. Intermediate goods are not, in general, bought out of incomes, but out of credits which are repaid as the goods pass on to a later stage of production. The purchase of intermediate goods does not use up purchasing power: it merely transfers it. The gross prices of all goods at all stages of production far exceed the value of the national output, because the same goods are sold several times over at different stages. If the incomes of the people were equal to the gross prices in this sense there would be an immense redundance of purchasing power over the goods available for purchase, and either prices would have to rise immensely, or much purchasing power would have to remain unused. Incomes ought to equal not gross but net output—that is, they ought to balance the output of *finished* goods and services; and so, on the whole, they do.

It is, however, quite true that, when the same sort of money can be used to buy either finished or intermediate goods, as it can be under the existing system, money can be diverted from the market for finished goods to that for intermediate goods, so as to create a deficiency of demand for finished goods. This is most likely to occur during a boom, when rising prices lead to speculation in intermediate goods, and when incomes are very unequally distributed, so that the recipients of big incomes do not want to spend them on consumption. It is least likely to happen during a slump, when there are many inducements to hoard money, but few to speculate in the purchase of intermediate goods. It may be that this diversion of purchasing power is a factor in bringing booms to an end and in causing financial crises. But it is quite certain that it does not occur during slumps, and that it is not a permanent factor in the existing economic system. Disinvestment in intermediate goods is, indeed, a marked feature of periods of depression; but, so far from curing depression, it contributes to make it worse.

My own belief is that the use of the same sort of bank-money for final and for intermediate purchases is a cause of instability in the economic system, and that credits to producers ought to be kept entirely separate from money used for making final purchases of either capital goods or consumers' goods. But this opinion lends no support to the 'A + B theorem', which is simply not correct.

'The great evil of today is under-consumption: the remedy is for the State to place additional purchasing power in the consumers' hands.'

Under-consumption is in truth a great evil; and J. A. Hobson, who traced it to the maldistribution of incomes, made it the central point in his account of the causes of underproduction and unemployment. We ought not to rest satisfied while our actual production falls short of what we are able to produce without working so hard that the extra product is worth less to us than the leisure we forgo in producing it. We ought to base our consuming power on our power to produce, within this limit, and also within the limit set by the need to use a part of our producing power in making capital goods to increase our producing power for the future. In other words, consumption *plus* investment ought to equal producing power, whereas endemic unemployment is evidence that they fall a long way below it.

But are subsidies to consuming power the best remedy? Certainly they are greatly preferable to no remedy at all. But, if what has been said earlier is accepted, it will be agreed that purchasing power does tend, except under abnormal conditions, to equal actual production; and it would seem reasonable to conclude that the best course is to ensure that production shall be increased up to the level of productive capacity rather than to pay out additional money to consumers without ensuring that production shall increase to a corresponding extent. If we employ the unemployed in producing useful things, and pay them for doing so, up to the point of 'full employment', there will be enough purchasing power to buy all that is produced—unless part of the purchasing power is withheld as a result of hoarding, a possibility which I shall return to a little later. On the other hand, if purchasing power is handed out to consumers without any service being exacted from them in the form of production, there is a clear prospect of total purchasing power exceeding total production at the prevailing prices, or in other words of inflation. If we wish to ensure adequate consuming power, it is much better to ensure that every available worker is employed, and thus produces something to balance his consumption, than to pay out doles which may increase consuming power without a corresponding rise in output.

This argument, however, does not apply if the owners of purchasing power choose to hoard it, instead of spending it on consumers' or on finished capital goods or intermediate goods. If this occurs, subsidies to consumption may stimulate production which would not be undertaken without it, and may therefore have good results. But, even so, it would be greatly preferable to prevent the hoarding, and to pay out incomes in return for production rather than for doing nothing. This, of course, is not meant as an objection to paying out living incomes to those who are not in a position to produce—to the aged, or the disabled, or to children in the form of family allowances, or to the sick or the temporarily unemployed who will exist under any system. But the incomes paid out to such recipients ought to be paid out of the proceeds of taxation, and not by the creation of additional money; for otherwise there will be a redundancy, instead of a deficiency, of purchasing power in the community as a whole. If men are paid for producing all they can produce, there is no source from which additional incomes can be paid out, except taxation of the producers' incomes. The only qualification of this statement is that, if hoarding is not prevented, its effects in causing a deficiency of demand may need to be offset by a creation of additional purchasing power credited directly to consumers.

Hoarding, as we have seen, can be prevented by causing money to depreciate if it is not used; and this is probably the best way of dealing with it. But we have not yet done with the under-consumption argument. It is often urged that the very unequal distribution of purchasing power in the community leads to a deficiency of demand for consumers' goods, and to an attempt to save an undue proportion of the national income. As long as the saved income is invested in capital goods, no deficiency of purchasing power in relation to total production arises; for spending on capital goods is also spending, and takes goods off the market. But the use of capital goods is to make consumers' goods; and therefore finally the demand for capital goods depends on the demand for consumers' goods. If more capital goods are bought than can find an outlet for their products in the consumers' market, investment will slow down for lack of profitable outlets, and hoarding will take its place. Instead of saving by investing in real things, men will try to save without investing—a process which is possible for the individual, but impossible for the community as a whole. Under-consumption will thus cause under-investment, by making investment unprofitable; and hoarding will add to one man's riches only by destroying another's, because it will inflict losses on all those who have goods to sell and find less purchasing power ready to buy them. Under-consumption and under-investment are now seen as two aspects of the same fault in the working of the economic system; and it appears that over-saving may lead directly to under-investment, because the profitability of investment depends on the maintenance of a high level of consumers' demand.

'The great cause of depressions is under-investment: the remedy is for the State either to invest more extensively in public works, or to devise means of stimulating private investment, or both.'

Our forefathers were generally concerned to encourage thrift by all means, lest too little should be saved and invested: we are more concerned lest people attempt to save too much, and lest a gap appear between money savings and real investment, and between total producing power and the sum of consumption and investment in terms of real goods. This change has come about largely because of the decline in foreign trade and overseas investment, which is itself a phenomenon of the changed character of the economic world since the great epoch of imperialist expansion came to an end. Our forefathers were never for long at a loss for new fields for the investment of capital; and the opening up of undeveloped areas all over the world was continually enlarging the scale of production in the advanced countries. But nowadays, in face of the closing of the 'frontier', competition steadily gives place to monopoly, and the great monopolies are as keen on preventing additional investment as their forerunners were in encouraging it. This change has totally altered the face of the economic system, and has tended to open up a dangerous gap between what individuals try to save out of their incomes and what business men are prepared to use by way of investment. Hence the growth of endemic unemployment in many countries; and hence the resort to large-scale public works when monetary 'reflation' fails to give the needed stimulus to industry.

For the time being, these processes are in suspense because war needs all the man-power of the nations. Even for some time before 1939 re-armament was a powerful factor in keeping unemployment in check. But there is no assurance that, when the war is over, the conditions of unemployment and under-investment will not return. Whether this is likely to happen or not depends on the nature of the post-war settlement, especially on the economic side. If the settlement is such as to lay secure foundations for the rapid economic development of the poorer countries —Eastern Europe, India, China, and most of Africa—there is every reason to expect a large-scale expansion of overseas investment, and therewith a closing of the gap. On the other hand, if the world reverts to economic nationalism after the war, the gap will almost certainly become much wider, and it will be possible to stave off mass-unemployment only by resort to public works on a prodigious scale.

The nature of the 'gap' I have spoken of needs a little explanation. 'Saving' is one process, and 'investment' another. 'Saving' in itself is merely abstention from consumption; and it needs someone who is prepared to put the saved money to real productive use to turn 'saving' into real 'investment'. Investment in existing securities is not real 'investment' in this sense: it merely transfers the money to someone else, without calling any additional productive power into being. 'Investment', from the standpoint of the community, involves the creation of new productive assets.

Now, the individual can 'save' as much of his income as he pleases; but the amount of real 'investment' depends on the willingness of businessmen to create productive assets. When they fail to do this to the required extent, and the 'saved' money remains unused, the consequence is that the total money demand for goods and services (including capital goods) adds up to less than the cost of producing these goods and services (including normal profits). If this occurs, some business men are bound to make losses, or go without profits, to the extent that will offset the withheld purchasing power. Consequently, from the standpoint of the community, 'savings' that do not lead to 'investment'—that is, to the spending of the saved money on capital goods—are not real savings at all. They are cancelled by the losses made by those who cannot sell their goods at remunerative prices. This is the gist of Lord Keynes's theory of 'savings' and 'investment'; and most economists are now agreed that this part of his theory is true.

If it is true, it follows that whenever 'investment' fails to take up the whole of what the recipients of income do not spend on consumers' goods and services, a 'gap' in employment is bound to appear; and prosperity is impossible unless this 'gap' can be filled either by State public works or by measures which bring ordinary 'investment' up to the required level. One weapon for achieving an increase of investment is the deliberate lowering of interest rates. But it is quite ineffective to lower short-term rates of interest unless long-term rates can be lowered as well; for it is the long-term and not the short-term rate that affects the worthwhileness of capital investment. It is even doubtful how far business men react in most industries to changes in the long-term rate; but they certainly do react to it in building and other constructional activities in which interest on capital is a big factor in total cost.

It is, however, pretty clear that in periods of general economic depression no practicable lowering of interest rates will avail to bring 'investment' up to the required level. Even zero interest will not attract a business man if he sees more prospect of actually losing part of his capital than of making even a small profit. Accordingly, in periods of severe depression, monetary manipulation is apt to be ineffective, and the only form of 'investment' that can be successfully stimulated is apt to be 'investment' by the State and other public authorities in public works.

'The State, like the individual, must cut its coat according to its cloth. An unbalanced budget destroys business confidence.'

Much evil has been done under the guidance of this maxim; for it has caused Governments, in times of business depression, to impose additional taxation in order to balance the budget, just when what is needed is more and not less purchasing power. Of course, if the State uses the proceeds of the taxation for *additional* expenditure of such a kind as to increase the total of economic activity, the resulting situation may be an improvement on what would have happened if the taxation had not been imposed. If, however, the proceeds are used, as they usually have been, not for additional creative expenditure, but for meeting existing obligations in order to avoid a budget deficit, the effects are bound to be bad; for people will have less money to spend, and the depression will be made more severe.

There is in truth nothing necessarily bad about an unbalanced budget in times of depression, provided only that the business world can be persuaded not to be scared by it. State creation of additional money for productive spending at such times stimulates economic activity and, by making enterprise profitable, increases the yield of taxation and so helps to bring the budget back into balance. It is, I think, in such circumstances better for the State to add to the supply of money than to remit existing taxation; for if it creates *and spends* the additional money the good effect is certain, whereas if it merely remits taxation the result may be increased hoarding by the recipients of the relief, rather than additional consumption or investment, and if that happens depression will continue and the budget will have been unbalanced to no purpose. It is of the greatest importance to disabuse the public of the notion that an unbalanced budget is necessarily an evil. There is, when one comes to consider it, no fundamental reason why State receipts and expenditure should balance over twelve months rather than over one month or one day. Many economists hold that there ought to be, in addition to the ordinary budget, a State budget of *capital* expenditure, which would not need to balance against tax receipts, any more than a company has to cover its whole capital out of its receipts within a single year.

III.

We have now examined our second set of sentences, and therewith the main lines of attack upon the existing financial system and its working. Let me try to sum up.

(*a*) It is generally agreed that stable exchange rates are an advantage; but it may be doubted whether a system of stable exchanges is practicable except under world conditions of expansion and encouragement of international trade accepted and operated by the leading countries. Even under these conditions, it would probably be wise to leave the door open to changes in relative currency values corresponding to real changes in the condition of the various countries.

(*b*) It is generally agreed that steps ought to be taken to reduce the amplitude of price fluctuations; but it is by no means agreed that complete stabilization of the price level is a desirable objective.

(*c*) It is generally agreed that the supply of money has been liable to irrational and harmful fluctuations, and that greater stability is desirable; but it is not agreed that the supply of money ought to be fixed, either absolutely, or in proportion to population.

(*d*) There is no general agreement on the question of bank nationalization, which raises political as well as economic issues; but there is a widespread opinion that the issue of currency and the determination of the amount of bank-money ought to be functions of the State, and accordingly that Central Banks ought to be public concerns, as they already are in many countries. Advocates of State planning of economic development commonly favour public ownership of commercial banks as well, whereas this is usually opposed by those who are hostile to such planning.

(*e*) It is generally agreed that money circulates too slowly in periods of depression; and some writers (notably Gesell) have favoured a kind of vanishing or depreciating money designed to speed up circulation. There is something to be said for this; but it would hardly produce the effects claimed for it, and there may be better alternative methods of dealing with the problem.

(*f*) It is not true that the present monetary system necessarily leads to a permanent deficiency of purchasing power (as Major Douglas contends). But neither is it true that every act of production automatically creates a market for what is produced (Say's Law). Deficiencies of purchasing power can and do arise, either from hoarding ('saving' without 'investment') or from maladjustment of the distribution of purchasing power in relation to the structure of production, or from certain other causes.

(*g*) Under-consumption, i.e. consumption of less than could be produced after due allowance for depreciation and capital accumulation, is a manifest evil, to which persistent unemployment bears witness. The granting of consumers' credits could be effective at certain times in calling unused productive capacity into play; but it is generally preferable to pay out money in return for work than with no economic return.

(This of course is not meant as a denial of the desirability of consumers' incomes financed out of taxation, such as family allowances: it refers only to proposals to institute consumers' credits financed out of specially created bank-money.)

(*h*) There is no doubt that, between the wars, there was a 'gap' between 'savings' and 'investment', i.e. that a part of current income tended to be used neither on consumption nor in purchases of capital goods. There is no doubt that this 'gap' involved heavy unemployment, or that it is necessary to close it. Nor is it in doubt that the effect of the 'gap' was that 'savings' which were not invested were cancelled, from the social standpoint, by business losses, and were thus not really saved at all. If active international investment revives after the war, the 'gap' may disappear: if not, it will have to be closed either by extensive State investment in public works, or by some method of stimulating ordinary investment. Measures designed to stimulate investment by lowering interest rates are unlikely to be effective by themselves.

These eight points are not intended to cover the whole of the ground, or to summarize all the questions which have been discussed in the previous pages. They have been chosen not with this purpose, but as representing the broad state of contemporary opinion on a few of the proposals which are most often put forward in the course of controversies about monetary policy. These controversies can be divided very roughly into two groups—one dealing with the institutions by means of which monetary matters are handled, and the other with the policies which these institutions should be called upon to follow. The question whether banks should be private or public bodies falls into the first group, whereas most of the remaining points fall into the second. To the first group belong also certain related questions which for lack of space I have been compelled to leave unconsidered—for example, whether investment should be left to be carried on by means of an unregulated system of private appeals for capital or should be brought under some form of public control through a National Investment Board, or again, whether stock market speculation should be left in the hands of stock exchanges as they now exist, or subjected to forms of public regulation designed to reduce the effect of speculative influences. In the second group I have had to leave aside any full discussion of the problems of inflation and deflation, and also of the issues involved in proposals for price-regulation designed to promote economic stability, and of the many highly technical problems connected with the working of foreign exchange. On these and many other questions I can only refer readers to the list of books which I have appended to this brief essay.

HOW TO OBTAIN FULL EMPLOYMENT

G. D. H. COLE

POST WAR DISCUSSION PAMPHLETS   No. 4   Price 3d.

FOREWORD

By Percy Cudlipp

Editor of the DAILY HERALD

THE phrase "full employment" is heard more and more often in public discussion.

It has all the perils, as well as the attraction, of a popular phrase.

Just as, say, "Homes for Heroes" proved a treacherous slogan, so too we should beware of thoughtlessly reiterating "full employment" as if the mere utterence of the words could bring full employment into being.

The avoidance of mass unemployment after the war will require radical departures in policy, both national and international.

There will have to be, stimulating and criticising the Government, an informed electorate.

And since the time is already at hand for planning the "full employment" measures which will be put into effect after the war, it follows that the process of stimulation and criticism should already be active.

Mr. Cole has written this booklet as an aid to the ordinary citizen whose duty it has now become to examine the theories of the economist and the policies of the statesman.

His gift of making plain a complicated subject has rarely been better displayed.

HOW TO OBTAIN FULL EMPLOYMENT

by G. D. H. COLE

CHAPTER ONE
WHAT IS MEANT BY FULL EMPLOYMENT?

THE maintenance of a high level of employment was laid down by Sir William Beveridge as one of the assumptions underlying his social security plan. This does not mean, as seems to be widely supposed, that the Beveridge Plan is unworkable unless a high level of employment is secured. The Plan is workable at any level of employment; but if unemployment is severe the cost will be much greater than he has allowed for, and the standard of living of the population as a whole will be much lower than there is any need for it to be. We want a high level of employment in order that we may all be able to enjoy a good standard of living, and that the burden of maintaining in reasonable comfort those who for any reason are unable to work may be as light as possible. The less unemployment we have, the more we shall be able to produce; and the higher the total national income the smaller will be the burden of affording really good conditions for the children, the sick, the disabled and the old. That is the sense, the only sense, in which the Beveridge Plan depends on Full Employment being achieved. We must not allow the enemies of the Plan to get away with the argument that it cannot be adopted until we have made sure of Full Employment.

What is 'Full Employment'? It does not mean a situation in which there is no unemployment at all. As long as men are free to change from one job to another, or as jobs themselves are in many cases temporary, there will be some unemployment; for men will spend some time out of work between one job and the next. Again, as long as the demand for labour is liable in some occupations to seasonal or casual fluctuations, some people will be less than fully employed. There will be some underemployment, which is a form of unemployment. Of course, if workers in these seasonal or casual occupations were paid a regular wage, even when there was no work for them to do, they would cease to be counted as unemployed. But if industry continued to be wastefully organised, so as to keep workers standing about with no jobs on hand, there would still be unemployment from the national standpoint, even if no individual were counted as out of work. There would be waste of productive resources, causing the real national income to be smaller than it ought to be.

The kinds of unemployment described in the preceding paragraph are usually called *frictional*. They are due to friction in the working of the economic machine. We ought to aim at reducing such friction to the lowest point that can be made compatible with the worker's freedom to change his job. We must no longer allow employers to keep what they call a 'reserve of labour' hanging around unpaid to be taken on when they want it in order to meet a peak demand. 'Standing-off' without wages is a thing we must get rid of; and even 'standing-off' with wages is a thing we shall not be able to afford to tolerate as soon as we get our industries rightly organised for the service of the people. For as soon as we do that we shall need all the labour that can be made available for increasing the total wealth produced.

It is implied in what I have just written that there ought not, after the war, to be any unemployment at all, beyond the necessary minimum of *frictional* unemployment which must remain in any free economic system. So much unemployment and no more would not constitute any social problem : it would be perfectly easy to deal with in such a way as to avoid any hardship to the unemployed. In order, however, to reduce unemployment to this level we need to get rid of two other kinds of unemployment which are much more devastating in their social effects than the *frictional* kind, bad as that can sometimes be. These other kinds of unemployment are usually called *cyclical* and *structural*.

Cyclical unemployment is the sort that comes in waves or cycles of depression. It is the sort that hit this country in 1921 and again in 1931, and has been hitting it at intervals of from seven to a dozen years for the past two centuries at least. It is the sort of unemployment that hits nearly all industries and occupations simultaneously, though it hits some of them very much harder than others. Such depressions have been to a large extent international, in the sense that most countries have suffered from them nearly at the same time. Probably about half of the unemployment that exists at the bottom of a bad depression is of this *cyclical* kind ; but, as we shall see, it is not always easy to distinguish clearly between it and other kinds of unemployment.

Structural unemployment is the sort that exists because there is something wrong with the structure of industry. The commonest cause of *structural* unemployment is a decline in demand for a product or class of products which a country has equipped itself to produce. Such a decline may occur either because consumers' tastes or needs change—*e.g.* if lace curtains go out of fashion the demand for Nottingham lace falls off, or when people take to motor-cars they give up buying horse-drawn carriages—or because the country in question can no longer make a particular type of goods as cheaply or efficiently as they can be made elsewhere—*e.g.* cheap Japanese cotton goods and bicycles and electric bulbs compete with more expensive British products—or because other countries put up tariff or other barriers in the way of imports which they used to take from the country in question —*e.g.* the high tariffs erected in many countries against British textile goods.

"Depressed Areas" of Capitalism

Whatever the cause may be, the decline of an industry is bound to lead to unemployment ; for at best not all the labour which is flung out of work can be transferred to other occupations. The difficulty of transfer is greatest with the older workers ; and the problem is most serious where an area has depended to a very great extent on a single industry, which then falls into decay. The 'depressed areas' which were found in Great Britain between the wars were mainly areas which depended very largely on coal, or the heavy metal industries, or on textiles. Obviously, their plight would have been much less evil if, as soon as it could be seen that the industries on which they depended were falling away, steps could have been taken both to re-train the surplus workers for alternative occupations and wherever possible to establish new industries in the same areas in order to avoid the need for mass movement of their populations elsewhere. That nothing of this sort was done, save late in the day and even then on an almost insignificant scale, is one of the main charges that can be laid at the door of the pre-war economic system.

War tends almost always to aggravate structural faults in the economic system. It swells up certain industries to a huge size, and then leaves them to face a collapse of markets when peace returns. Moreover, it upsets normal export trades. Countries at war are unable to go on supplying their regular customers; and these customers are driven either to seek other suppliers or to set up in manufacture for themselves. Consequently, when manufacturers seek to regain their pre-war foreign markets, they find some of them already occupied either by other exporting countries (*e.g.* Japan's industrial expansion after the last war) or by home manufactures usually protected by high tariff barriers against foreign competition.

Post-War Prospects

We must expect both these causes of *structural* unemployment to be powerfully at work after the present war. There has been in all the belligerent countries an immense growth of the armament industries; and there will come a drastic scaling-down where they are not capable of conversion to rapidly expansible peace-time uses. How drastic this scaling-down will have to be will depend partly on the extent to which a policy of full employment at home creates a brisk demand for capital goods to keep the heavy industries busy, and partly on the extent to which the world follows an active policy of building up productive power in the more backward parts of the world (*e.g.* China, India, Eastern Europe) by supplying them with capital goods (where necessary, on Lease-Lend terms). It is sometimes suggested that to do this will in the long run cause, instead of preventing, unemployment in the already industrialised countries, by equipping the less advanced countries to make for themselves goods such as they have hitherto purchased abroad. But (*a*) the greater part of the capital goods needed by the backward countries are not competitive in this way—they consist of railway plant, power plant, agricultural machinery, and other transport and public utility capital equipment; and (*b*) the effect of raising productive standards in the backward countries will be to make them not worse but better markets for the more advanced; for as their standards rise they will need many more of the diversified and high-quality products which only the advanced countries can supply. Nations prosper when other nations are prosperous, not when they are poor.

The second form of *structural* unemployment, due to the growth of industries abroad displacing exports from the advanced countries which have specialised in particular kinds of goods for the world market, will probably not manifest itself immediately after the war. There will be, owing to the wartime diversion of energy to making war products, a worldwide scarcity of most sorts of consumers' goods ; and as the industries which make these goods gradually get back their factories and their labour which have been diverted to war uses, they will for some time be able easily to sell all they can produce. The testing time for these industries will come later, when the immediate needs for replenishing consumers' supplies have been met and the industries making such goods have to adjust themselves to a normalised post-war market. How much *structural* maladjustment will then appear to exist will depend largely on the success with which the world as a whole settles down to operate a policy of Full Employment on a basis of national plans co-ordinated internationally.

What "Full Employment" Means

In the preceding paragraphs I have distinguished three kinds of unemployment—*frictional, cyclical,* and *structural.* Some economists prefer to relate the term ' full employment ' exclusively to the second of these types. They would describe a country as being in a state of ' full employment ' if it had succeeded in eliminating *cyclical* unemployment, no matter how much it might still be suffering from either or both of the others. Of course, such economists recognise that all three kinds of unemployment need dealing with ; but they prefer to use the term ' full employment ' in a restricted sense, meaning by it the highest level of employment attainable without altering the structure of industry, or its habits in engaging or discharging labour. On this showing Great Britain was in a condition approaching ' full employment,' say, in 1929, when there were about a million workers registered as unemployed ; for this million consisted, as to about one-half of the *frictionally* unemployed and as to the other half of those out of work in the specially depressed industries which were suffering from structural maladjustment.

This is, of course, a question of terminology. I prefer, and propose in this booklet, to use the phrase ' full employment ' in a wider sense, to imply the best possible use of all the available labour that can be brought about, without labour conscription, by concerted national planning. In this sense, ' full employment ' cannot be reached without measures both to eradicate *structural* defects and to reduce *frictional* waste, as well as to eliminate *cyclical* variations in the demand for labour. It is, however, clear that the measures needed for these different purposes may be to a considerable extent of different kinds, and can therefore best be discussed separately. The elimination of *cyclical* unemployment is in the main a matter of sustaining by general measures the *total* demand for labour ; whereas the measures needed for combating *structural* and *frictional* unemployment are largely *particular*, applying to this or that industry rather than to industry as a whole.

Before we proceed to consider these measures, both general and particular, it is necessary to add a word more by way of definition. In time of war a large number of persons work for wages or salaries who under normal conditions would not so work at all ; and a large number more work much longer hours than they would work under the stimulus of ordinary economic incentives. It needs to be plainly stated that ' full employment ' does not mean the continuance of these conditions. It does not mean compelling to work for wages persons who prefer not to do so and can support themselves without (*e.g.* persons past normal retiring age, or housewives with families to look after) : nor does it mean forcing people to work longer hours than they are prepared to accept as reasonable under the terms of collective bargains made by Trade Unions or of laws regulating the duration of the working day. It is for the community to decide how much work it is prepared to do, and whom it will allow or encourage to work for hire. It is for the community to settle at what age children shall enter the labour market, at what age retiring pensions shall be made available, what the permitted daily or weekly hours of employment are to be, and to what extent married women are to be encouraged to work for wages. In other words, it is for the community to decide at what point it values additional leisure for its citizens above more output of material wealth, and what classes of persons it wishes to exclude from, or include in, the labour market. 'Full employment' does not mean everyone working as hard and as long as they possibly can : it means not wasting any of the labour that is available inside the rules and conventions which society lays down. We can afford to dispense with the labour of the young and the old and to reduce the hours of those who do work in proportion as we make efficient use of the labour which is available for employment and adjust our economic arrangements so as to produce what we really need with the least possible expenditure of effort.

CHAPTER TWO

THE OUTLOOK FOR EMPLOYMENT AFTER THE WAR

IT seems reasonable to expect that there will be immediately after the war a short period of dislocation as war factories close down and firms need time to get factories diverted to war uses ready for peace-time production. To this will succeed a period of brisk activity in meeting demands which have had to be set aside during the war, including overseas as well as home demands. This second period will last until the more urgent arrears of peace-time demand have been overtaken, and will then be succeeded by—what ? By a slump such as occurred after the last war ? Or by a period of sustained full employment ? Who can say ? The answer from this point depends not on foreseeable facts and tendencies, but on the *policies* followed by Governments in this and in other countries throughout the world.

Let us call these three periods the period of *industrial demobilisation*, the period of *re-stocking and relief*, and the period of *long-term reconstruction*. They will not of course be sharply distinct : they will run one into another, and before one is over the next will have begun. But the distinction between them is useful. Clearly we should aim at passing as quickly as possible from the first to the second, and at laying the foundations for the third even before we have entered upon the first. That is to say, we ought to *plan* now, not only for the transition from war to peace, but also for the further process of building up a satisfactory post-war economic system.

Some unemployment is bound to occur in the first period as the munition factories close down. In many cases the factories will have to be cleared of workers before they can be adapted to the new work which they are to undertake in time of peace. This applies both to war factories proper and to other factories which have been diverted for war purposes from their normal lines. It will not be possible in many cases to pass over at once from producing war goods to making what will be needed after the war. Therefore, the workers who are discharged from the war factories, as well as those who are demobilised from the armed forces and the civil defence services, will have to be maintained until work is ready for them, and will have, where necessary, to be trained for the types of work for which new recruits will be wanted. For this purpose, the requisite parts of the Beveridge Plan ought to be in full operation well before the end of the war. If they are not, emergency arrangements will have to be made, as they were made in 1918; but this is a much less satisfactory way of going about the matter.

It is important that factories equipped to make peace-time goods which have been converted into war factories or used for storage during the war shall be evacuated as speedily as possible and re-equipped at once for peace-time production. It is hardly less important that plans be made in advance for converting as many as are suitable of the great Ordnance and other war factories to the production of peace-time goods, and that no opposition of private employers' associations to such conversion shall be allowed to stand in the way. Workers now in the war factories who are prepared to remain and are of suitable types should be assured in advance of jobs in these converted factories, and should be paid retaining salaries while they are being got ready. One large use will be to make fittings and furniture of all sorts for the millions of houses which will have to be built. Another will be to arrange for the standardised mass-production of many types of consumers' goods which could be greatly cheapened if they were made after simple designs by modern standardised methods.

Probable Demands of the Building Industry

I do not propose to discuss here the many difficult problems of demobilisation, as these are being dealt with in a separate booklet. I must, however, point out the very great importance of ensuring early release both from the forces and from the war factories of skilled men who will be urgently needed to deal with the re-equipment and restarting of peace-time industry. This is especially important in the case of skilled building craftsmen, of whom there is bound to be an acute shortage. There will be huge arrears of house-building and repairs to be made up, war damage to houses to be made good, and a competitive demand for building labour to help in the reconstruction and re-equipment of factories of all kinds. Not even the most forthright measures will prevent a really serious shortage of skilled builders; and plans for training large numbers of additional skilled men ought to be put into operation at the earliest possible moment. The Government has already promised to do this; but I am not convinced that the task is being handled energetically enough, or on a sufficient scale.

Building of all sorts will make very large and immediate demands on the supply of labour after the war. There will be openings in the building and allied trades for great numbers of returning soldiers and disbanded munition workers. This demand, however, will be mainly for men, and for relatively young men at that ; and young men will be scarce, even if the scarcity is not greatly increased by heavy war casualties. It will be necessary to train for the building trades men who are already in middle age, if these trades are not to absorb more young workers than the country can afford to assign to them. The shortage of young men will evidently be a factor making for the continued employment of a large proportion of young women in the post-war factories. It is to be anticipated that many of those who have entered the factories under war conditions will wish to leave them when the war ends. Many are married already, and many will be marrying and having children. No doubt, a substantial number will remain in the factories after marriage ; but I think it will become much commoner than it has been hitherto for women who have left the factory on marriage to return to it later, when their children no longer make so heavy demands on their time. It is also likely that arrangements for enabling women to undertake part-time factory work have come to stay.

Women in the Labour Market.

There are some who will dislike these notions on the ground that the increased employment of women will mean more competition in the labour market, and threaten to " do the men out of their jobs." I do not take this view. I am sure that, if we manage our affairs sensibly, we shall be facing not a surplus but a shortage of labour after the war, and that we shall need all the help with production that women can give without neglecting their family responsibilities. Why I think this will appear more clearly in the next chapter, when I go on to discuss the forces that determine the demand for labour.

In the first period immediately after the war, the essential things will be (*a*) to provide adequate maintenance and, where necessary, training for those who are thrown out of work ; (*b*) to carry through as quickly as possible the re-equipment of the factories for peace-time production ; and (*c*) to get the building industry going quickly on the largest possible scale. In the second period, which I have called the period of *re-stocking and relief*, the most urgent tasks will be to expand as rapidly as possible the output of all kinds of consumers' goods both for the home market and for export, in order that consumers and traders may replenish their stocks, and goods be made available for relieving the more pressing needs of the peoples of Europe, Asia and North Africa. During this period it will be indispensable to keep a large amount of control over what is made and how it is distributed, both in order to avoid wasteful use of materials (many of which will continue scarce for some time) and to ensure that sufficient supplies are made available for export, both for relieving pressing needs abroad, and for giving in payment for necessary imports. It seems probable that rationing will have to be retained for many kinds of consumers' goods until, throughout the world, the more pressing needs have been met. There will be in this second period no question of unemployment owing to shortage of demand in the trades producing consumers' goods : in fact it seems probable that the only sources of unemployment in these trades will be either shortage of re-equipped factory space, or of the necessary nuclei of *skilled* workers, or of raw materials necessary to particular industries.

This second period will merge into the third—that of *long-term reconstruction*. Long-term reconstruction should, indeed, be proceeding from the very beginning; but unavoidably, during the first and second periods, the largest amount of attention will have to be given to short-term problems. For us in Great Britain the chief economic problems of long-term reconstruction are the abolition of *structural* unemployment and the construction of an economic and financial system which will ensure that the general demand for labour will be maintained continuously at a high level. The measures needed for abolishing structural unemployment will make large demands on the industries which produce capital goods; for it will be necessary, while scaling down some branches of production, to expand others with much new capital equipment and to modernise many more by introducing more efficient plant and better planned factory buildings. We shall need also to bring thoroughly up to date our transport system, to amplify greatly our public utility services for the supply of power (including the coal industry), gas and water, to build many new and well-equipped schools, hospitals and other public buildings—to say nothing of the thorough re-designing and rebuilding of our cities, blitzed and unblitzed alike. These essential tasks may be supplemented by other needs which may arise in the years of peace.

Controlling Capital Investment

These tasks of capital construction will rise to a position of predominance during the third period, and will, as they fructify in improved productive and human efficiency, make possible a rapid rise in the supply of consumers' goods and services—that is, in the standard of living of the people. During this period, it is to be hoped, acute shortages of consumers' goods will disappear, and personal and household rationing will vanish with them. It will, however, be imperative in this period to keep a tight control over the processes of capital investment, in order to ensure that the capital goods industries produce the goods that are needed for dealing with structural defects in our productive equipment, for modernising obsolete plant, and for raising the standard of life for the whole population. The nature of the required controls I shall discuss later. What must be grasped now is that when it becomes possible to dispense with the rationing of consumers' goods this will not mean that the time has arrived for giving up public control altogether. Public control over the key industries is, as we shall see, indispensable for the maintenance of full employment. It is not a thing which we can afford to give up gradually, in the passage from war to peace. This control must become a permanent feature of the new industrial order if we are to avoid the mistakes which were committed after the First World War, with their aftermath of large-scale unemployment.

CHAPTER THREE

ON WHAT DOES THE GENERAL LEVEL OF EMPLOYMENT DEPEND?

FULL employment does not come of itself, as we have ample reason for knowing. Under the profit-seeking system, employers employ labour up to the point to which they think they will add to their profits by employing it, and no further. This need not mean that employers take on all the labour which they could employ and make a profit; for sometimes they can make a higher profit by using less labour rather than more. If the economic system were entirely competitive, no doubt employers would be forced by competition to employ all the labour they could use at a profit; but when, as is always the case under modern conditions, many industries are under the control of trusts or cartels or other kinds of business association which are able to regulate output or prices, it often pays a group of employers to sell less at a higher, rather than more at a lower, price, and this means that they employ fewer workers than would be set to work under purely competitive conditions. Monopoly thus becomes a cause of unemployment—a more and more important cause as the scale of production increases and combination is made easier by the difficulties in the way of the entry of additional competitors into a trade.

To this special cause of unemployment we shall come back; but first of all let us consider what, given the prevailing conditions of monopoly or competition, determines the fluctuation in the amount of employment offered in good and bad times. In Great Britain between 1929 and 1932 the percentage of registered workers out of work rose from 10·3 per cent. to 21·9 per cent.; and in the United States over the same period the index of workers in industrial employment fell much more sharply from 100 to 63 (employment in 1929 = 100). What was the cause of such prodigious fluctuation—a cause which must clearly be removed or offset if we are to enjoy secure conditions of full employment?

Reasons for the Slumps

A study of the figures in either country will show that the fall in employment was very much more severe in the industries making capital goods than in those making consumers' goods, and that there was also an exceptionally sharp fall in exports. The reasons for both these phenomena are quite clear. If there is any fall in consumers' demand, it is almost bound to react heavily on the industries which make capital goods. Suppose in year A the output of consumers' goods is 100, and that in year B this demand falls to 90. Suppose that the rate of depreciation and obsolescence of capital goods used in making consumers' goods is 10 per cent. per annum. If no new capital goods at all are ordered to replace those which wear out in year A, there will be still enough capital goods left to produce 90 units of consumers' goods in year B. Thus, a fall of 10 per cent. in consumers' demand could apparently produce a fall of 100 per cent. in the demand for capital goods. Of course, in practice, the fall is not quite so severe as this; for some new capital goods will be ordered even in bad times. But enough has been said to show why the demand for capital goods usually falls off in bad times very much more than the demand for consumers' goods and services.

The export trades are also for the most part hit harder in a depression than the trades which cater mainly for the home market. This is because countries which find themselves suffering from economic distress are apt to impose barriers in the way of imports both in order to protect home industries from foreign competition and to reduce the pressure on their foreign exchanges—especially when they are debtor countries. Depression is apt to be most severe of all where an export trade is also an industry producing capital goods or dependent largely on the capital goods industries (*e.g.* steel and coal), or where a home industry depends largely on foreign trade (*e.g.* shipbuilding, or work at the docks).

Purchasing Power and Demand

A part of what has been said in the foregoing paragraphs can be summed up, and put in a rather different way, by saying that in times of depression *investment* usually falls off much more than *consumption*. The national income flows at any time into two streams, one, the larger, supplying directly the consumers' needs, and the other going to the making of instruments of production for the replacement of plant which is wearing out or for the supply of additional instruments for the increase of productive power. Of course, this classification ignores exports ; for capital goods may be exported in exchange for imported consumers' goods or *vice versa*. Equally of course instruments of production are of no use unless they result in an increased flow of consumers' goods and services later on ; for the use of all production is to be consumed either at once or over a period of time. A country can go on producing more than it consumes only if it lends or gives away some of its production by exporting capital, as Great Britain did in the nineteenth century and as the United States did after the last war, and is doing now. We can, however, for the moment ignore these complications, and discuss the position of a country which is using up all its product at home.

The national output of such a country will consist partly of consumers' goods and services and partly of capital goods. When all is going well, the entire national income will be spent either on consumers' goods and services (consumption) or on capital goods (investment). There is, however, a difference between the motives which lead persons to expend their incomes in these two ways. The purpose of consumption is directly to satisfy wants ; whereas the purpose of investment, when it is made by private persons, is usually the making of a money profit. If for any reason those who are in the habit of investing become pessimistic about their prospects of profit, and fear that investment is more likely to result in loss, they refuse to invest, and thus throw producers of capital goods out of employment. In doing this, they destroy the purchasing power of those who are thrown out of work (employers and shareholders as well as workers in the industries producing capital goods), and thus help to make their pessimism come true by reducing consumers' demand. That is why any slump, once started, tends to get worse ; for every person who loses his purchasing power tends to throw others out of employment, and unemployment is worsened by this accumulative effect. Let us now consider the same point in yet another way. In a healthily working economic system, the sums spent in buying the current output constitute the incomes of the producers, and as long as the whole income paid to the people is spent on some part of the output production can continue unchecked. If, however, the owners of incomes keep back a part of their incomes, and do not spend this part on either consumption or investment, the total sum offered for the current output will be less than the cost of producing it, including the normal profits of the owners of the capital in use. If this occurs, some or all of the producers will be bound to make losses, which will deter them from producing as much as before. They will discharge workers, and thus make the situation still worse.

The way in which this happens can be made clearer by introducing a further distinction. The older economists used to say that all incomes were either *spent* or *saved*, equating spending with consumption and saving with investment. But in fact, from the standpoint of the individual, saving and investment are two quite different things. To *save* is merely to abstain from consuming a part of one's income; and saving turns into investment only if the money saved is thereafter used in buying new capital goods. There is no real investment if the money is merely left lying in a bank, or locked away at home, or if it is used in buying second-hand capital goods in the form of stocks and shares representing existing capital assets. In order to keep the producers of capital goods employed, someone must order new capital goods from them. In the capitalistic societies of to-day this ordering of new capital goods is done only in part by those who save out of their incomes. It is done mainly by a limited class of business men who either float new companies or expand the capital resources of companies which already exist. It is done either out of reserved profits built up by existing firms, or out of money borrowed by business men from the public or from the banks. Thus, the flow of money into investment depends mainly on the willingness of this limited class of business men to risk their own money or to borrow other people's money at interest and use it for the purchase of capital goods, *i.e.* buildings, machinery, and other instruments of production.* If these business men fail to see a prospect of satisfactory profit from doing these things, investment will not occur, no matter how much of their incomes the public as a whole may have ' saved ' by abstaining from consumption. When this situation arises, the more the public ' saves ' the worse unemployment becomes; for their ' saving ' means that the demand for goods for consumption is further depressed. Finally, the reader must be reminded that business men may refuse to invest, not only because they fear loss, but also because they think scarcity will yield them higher profits than plenty. The more industry is in the hands of monopolists, the more likely is it that business men will refuse to invest as much as the members of the public are attempting to ' save.'

The position is further complicated because the total supply of money is not fixed, but can be varied at any time by the action of the banking system.

---

* Economists distinguish between ' consumers' goods,' that is, goods which are bought for immediate use, such as food, clothing, and other current supplies, and ' capital goods,' that is, things which are used in making other things, such as factory buildings, machinery, power stations, and so on. There is a third category of ' durable consumers' goods,' such as houses, which are used up only over a long period. For the purposes of the present argument, these should be classed with ' capital goods,' under the wider heading of ' investment goods.'

In Great Britain, the power to vary the supply of money is mainly in the hands of the Bank of England, which can make or destroy money practically at will by what are known as 'open market operations'—that is, by buying or selling securities from or to the public. I have no space to explain this process fully here.* It is enough to say that, whenever the Bank buys securities, it pays the public for them. The recipients of the money pay it into their banks, which thus find their cash resources enlarged, and are in a position to lend more money to business men. As the banks by convention lend up to about ten times the amount of cash (including balances in the books of the Bank of England) in their possession, every £100 spent by the Bank of England in buying securities enlarges the supply of bank money by about £1,000. When the Bank of England sells securities this process is reversed, and the supply of bank money—which is the kind of money chiefly in use—is correspondingly reduced.

Essentials of Economic Prosperity

The relevance of this to the question of employment is that an addition to the supply of money increases, whereas a subtraction from the supply reduces, purchasing power, and thus affects the incentives to employ labour. A withdrawal of money by the banking system has much the same effect on employment as a refusal to invest, and an effusion of additional money will, under most conditions, stimulate employment. There are, however, conditions under which the latter effect may not develop. An addition to the supply of money is only potential until someone actually borrows it from the banks. If the business world is pessimistic, it may refuse to borrow, and the additional money may fail to come into actual circulation. On the other hand, a reduction in the amount of money in circulation will always depress employment.

We are now in a position to answer, in general terms, the question which stands at the head of this chapter. The volume of employment depends on the level of active purchasing power. This level must be high enough to induce employers to engage all the available labour, or unemployment is bound to exist. Moreover, as neither labour nor plant is homogeneous, the purchasing power must be used in such ways as will ensure a rightly balanced demand for different kinds of goods and services, corresponding to the productive powers available, or unemployment will exist in some occupations even when there is an acute shortage of workers in others. In very general terms, we may say that in order to reduce unemployment to a low level the demand for both consumers' goods and services and capital goods must be high. Any serious unemployment in particular industries or areas which persists even when the total demand for both classes of products is high is a sign of *structural* maladjustment, and needs to be put right by the expansion of forms of production which are in good demand by means of new capital investment and re-training of labour for alternative jobs.

In general, if the demand for consumers' goods and services is high, business men will expect good profits from responding to it, and will be ready to invest in capital goods. A high level of consumers' demand is therefore

---

* For a fuller explanation, see *The Means to Full Employment*, by G. D. H. Cole (Gollancz).

the first essential for economic prosperity under the capitalist system. But where the system is dominated by monopolies, investment may remain low even when consumers' demand is high. The remedy in such a situation is to destroy the monopolies, either by outlawing restrictive practices and controlling prices and profits, or by taking them over into the hands of the public and thus abolishing the restrictive influence of the profit-motive. In the absence of monopoly, a high level of consumers' demand is enough, without special measures, to ensure activity in the industries making capital goods.

In periods of depression, both consumers' demand and investment fall to a low level, but, as we have seen, the fall is usually much the greater in the industries making investment goods. Accordingly, the most obvious way of stimulating a revival is to create an additional demand for such goods by increasing the amount of investment. How this can be done we shall see in the next chapter. It is, however, also possible to stimulate consumption instead of investment, leaving the increase in consuming power to act in turn on the business world's willingness to invest. Either policy can be so managed as to achieve the desired result—or, of course, the two can be applied together. The essential thing is, by the one means or the other, or by both, to raise purchasing power to a level at which the total volume of employment will be as high as is required.

In the foregoing argument, it has been assumed that investment is undertaken by business men in pursuit of profit. In practice, however, *some* investment in all societies is undertaken by the State or other public bodies, and profit is not the end in view. This applies most obviously to armaments, schools and other public buildings, roads and bridges; and it can apply to other things of which the State makes itself responsible for some or all of the supply. Houses are an outstanding example, and transport services, where they are publicly administered, are another. Naturally, public investment has just the same effects as private investment in stimulating employment. What counts is the total level of demand for labour, irrespective of the sources from which it comes.

POINTS FOR DISCUSSION
(*see also p.* 22)

1. Should future Governments assume responsibility for maintaining employment at a satisfactory level?
2. What do you expect to be the situation in relation to the demand for labour
    (*a*) immediately after the termination of hostilities?
    (*b*) during the following two or three years?
    (*c*) subsequently?
   To what extent is it necessary to have these three periods in mind in planning *now*?
3. How do you distinguish between cyclical, structural and frictional unemployment? To what extent are different methods needed for dealing with these three kinds of unemployment?
4. How are the amount and character of labour supply after the war likely to differ from those which existed in 1939 in respect of
    (*a*) age distribution?

(b) sex ?
(c) employment of juvenile labour ?
(d) age of retirement ?

Do you consider that there is likely to be a shortage or a surplus of labour after the war ?

5. On what does the general level of unemployment in a capitalist society depend ? Discuss this question in relation to the demand for
   (a) capital and investment goods ;
   (b) consumption goods and services.

   Why are the trades producing capital goods usually more depressed in bad times than those producing consumers' goods and services ?
6. Discuss the relations between saving and investment.

CHAPTER FOUR
PUBLIC WORKS AND EMPLOYMENT

IF business men, acting under the stimulus of profit, are unwilling to employ the available supply of labour, what can be done ? Either the State must step in to create an additional demand for labour, or the effective supply of purchasing power in the hands of the people must be increased, so as to make business men willing to expand production and employment. In this chapter, we shall discuss the first of these alternatives.

Action by the State to increase the demand for labour commonly takes the form of *Public Works*. The State, by building, or arranging for the building of, more houses, schools, hospitals, other public buildings, waterworks, power stations, roads, bridges, harbour works, and so on, or by buying more armaments, causes more workers to be employed in the capital goods trades either by itself or its agents, such as the local authorities or public corporations, or by contractors working on public orders. The workers thus employed (and the contractors) then spend their money on goods and services of every sort and kind, and the additional employment induced is much greater than that provided directly on the Public. Works. This indirect effect of Public Works on the general level of employment is called by economists " the Multiplier."

In the past the State in times of depression has usually cut down its own expenditure on capital goods, thus making the depression worse. It has done this under the mistaken impression held until lately by orthodox politicians and economists that it is a virtuous act to make the annual Budget balance. Why it should be necessary for the State's Budget to balance each year no one has ever explained—much less why the State should insist on trying to meet capital expenditure out of current revenue. It is now pretty generally agreed that such views are wrong, and that the State should expand, instead of contracting, its capital expenditure when the total demand for labour looks like falling off. It is further agreed that the cost of capital works should not be charged against the ordinary Budget, and that the State should keep a separate capital account, meeting out of revenue only interest and sinking fund charges, and not necessarily covering even these in the ordinary Budget in bad years. The money for State capital expenditure could be raised either by borrowing in the open market the money which business men are unwilling to use (see p. 12), or by borrowing on special terms from the banks, or by the State itself creating the money in the same way as the banking system can create it now. I have no space here to discuss the respective merits of these alternatives :* the point is that the State must provide the money in such a way as not to reduce proportionately what the public would otherwise spend, as it would do if it raised it by taxation of the ordinary kind. The demand created by the State's action in starting Public Works must be *additional* demand, increasing the volume of employment.

Clearly, Public Works will exert their effect on the economic situation most smoothly and to the best advantage if they employ unused resources of plant and labour with the least possible disturbance to the structure of industry. If resources have to be largely transferred from one industry to another, and if labour has to be used in ways that will not take advantage of existing skills, there will be serious loss and friction. Moreover, profit-seeking capitalists will want the State to confine itself to types of Public Works out of which there is no profit to be made, and to avoid competing with their own businesses in the works it undertakes. The result of this capitalist opposition is apt to be that State Public Works are limited to a narrow field, so that the things produced to the State's orders are not those which the public most wants, and there is a large diversion of labour from industries in which the capitalists object to State activity into industries in which less opposition is aroused. Public Works are apt to be concentrated very largely on building and road-making, because these are industries in which private contractors are accustomed to working on public contracts. There is accordingly no *direct* stimulus to industries such as merchant shipbuilding or heavy engineering, in which depression may be much more severe.

Key Industries for State Control

The wider the sphere of *public ownership* of industry is, the greater is the State's power to carry out a balanced programme of Public Works. The demand for capital goods is quite highly concentrated in a limited number of industries and services. If the State owns and operates these services, either directly or through Public Corporations such as the Central Electricity Board, it is in a position to carry out a policy of public investment far more smoothly and efficiently than it can be where these great *capital-using* industries are in private hands.

The key industries from this point of view—the industries which the State needs to own and operate in order to carry through a really effective policy of Public Works—include the following :—

1. *Housing*, i.e. the State or its agents should be the chief suppliers of new houses, through municipal building of houses to let at reasonable rents, and should thus be in a position to determine the level of employment in house-building. It is a secondary matter whether the public bodies arrange for the actual building to be done through private contractors or undertake it themselves by Direct Labour. House-building will need to be at a very high level after the war, in order to overtake arrears, replace

---

* For a discussion of them, see *The Means to Full Employment*, by G. D. H. Cole (Gollancz).

bomb-destroyed dwellings, and provide for replanning and a larger number of separate families. It occupies a key position in the provision of employment.
2. *Public Utilities*—Electricity, Gas, Water. These services are at present partly in the hands of public and partly of private bodies. The most important single step is to bring the entire business of *generating* electricity under full public ownership. The 'Grid' at present owns the main transmission lines, but not the power stations or the distributing centres.
3. *Inland Transport*—Railways, Canals, main Road Services for both passengers and goods. Public ownership of roads and bridges is assumed. The railways are great customers of the heavy engineering and steel industries, and road services of lighter branches of engineering. Inland transport plainly needs an investment policy co-ordinated for all branches under a common public control.
4. *Sea Transport*, together with *Docks and Harbours*. The public ownership of shipping services would enable the State to determine the level of employment in ship-building, which is of all industries the most liable to cyclical unemployment.
5. *Air Transport*. All airports ought to be publicly owned, and all air transport services brought under public ownership, subject to international arrangements designed to make the air free to the services of all nations and to the running of some of the main long-distance services by fully international agencies.
6. *Land*. British agriculture stands in need of a big plan of capital development, which cannot be carried through except with the aid of public money. There is also a recognised need for a big programme of afforestation. Moreover, urban land and land needed for new development must be brought under effective public control, in order to avoid land speculation and the appropriation of unearned increment by the landlords. The best way would be to nationalise the land outright: failing this, the State should at least acquire the 'development rights' in all land, and public acquisition of land needed for development should be made easy at prices not exceeding those of 1939. Both these things are proposed in the Uthwatt Reports.

State Administration

I am by no means suggesting that these are the only industries which ought to be brought under public ownership. What I am saying is that these are the key industries to socialise *for the purpose of giving the State the means of carrying through a really effective policy of Full Employment* by the method of Public Works. In control of these industries, the State could scale up or down its investment in such a way as to keep the demand for capital goods at a satisfactory level, with the minimum of disturbance to the structure of industry and with the best assurance of getting good value for the money spent.

From the standpoint of achieving Full Employment, it would not matter whether the State operated these industries directly, or through Public Corporations, or through local or regional authorities, provided that it kept in its own hands the determination of the level of investment in them. It would, however, matter if they were handed over to Corporations or local authorities in such a way that it was left to these bodies and not to the State to settle the level of investment. The policy of Public Works outlined in this chapter implies the existence of a National Economic Plan, administered by an Economic Planning Authority armed with wide powers. It falls beyond the scope of this booklet to discuss how such an authority should be constituted, or precisely what its functions should be. The essence of it, from the standpoint of employment policy, is that the State must be in a position to alter the total level of its demand for capital goods in such a way as to offset fluctuations in private demand and to keep the capital goods industries adequately and regularly employed. No doubt, it may be necessary from time to time for the community to alter the proportions of its total productive capacity used respectively in providing capital goods and consumers' goods and services. After the war, there will be a period during which a high level of investment will be required. Thereafter, the proportion needed may fall, and it will become necessary to transfer resources from the industries making capital goods to those supplying consumers' goods and services. But this in no way conflicts with what has been said in this chapter. I shall come back to it later, when I have discussed the question of maintaining the demand for consumers' goods and services.

CHAPTER FIVE

THE MAINTENANCE OF CONSUMPTION

IT is in general true that, the less equally incomes are distributed, the larger will be the proportion of total income saved instead of being spent on consumers' goods and services. What economists call the " propensity to consume " is lower among well-to-do people than among the poor. This may result in ' over-saving,' in the sense of an attempt to *save* more than business men are prepared to *invest ;* for what they are prepared to invest depends on their expectation of what will be consumed, and the more people save out of their incomes the less they consume.

We have seen how the State can raise the level of investment by Public Works. It can also raise the propensity to consume by taking income from the richer classes and giving it to the poor, either by taxation or by insisting on high minimum wages. The Social Services are partly financed by taxing the better-off ; but they are very largely paid for by contributions which fall heavily on the poor. Their effect in re-distributing incomes is therefore very limited ; and there is everything to be said for developing Social Services financed out of general taxation. It is generally agreed that Family Allowances, which will have an excellent effect in increasing the consuming power of the poorer households, ought to be financed in this way.

It is, however, often argued that heavy taxation of the richer classes, designed to bring about a redistribution of incomes in favour of the poor, will react on the profit-expectations of business men and make them less willing to invest. This is in the main a fallacy, at any rate where taxation is so arranged as to fall upon incomes and not on the costs of production.

High taxation as such does not discourage investment or production, if the proceeds are applied to increasing the consumption of the poorer classes. It is, however, undesirable to increase taxation in bad times, upon whomsoever it falls; for at such times it is bad to do anything that will decrease private expenditure. It is better in bad times to lower taxation, so as to give private citizens more money to spend, and to meet some part of public expenditure by incurring budget deficits, financed by borrowing or by the creation of additional money by the State. Such deficits can be wiped off by increased taxation of the larger incomes in times of prosperity, to the extent to which it is desirable to wipe them off at all.

Avoiding Inflation

It may not be desirable to wipe them off. There ought always to be enough money in circulation to provide for the exchanging of all that can be produced at prices corresponding to the costs of production. As productive efficiency increases, and more goods and services can be produced, it may be preferable to increase the supply of money rather than to enforce a fall in prices by restricting the amount of money available. But this is desirable only if there is an effective control over prices, in order to prevent the making of excessive profits as the costs of production fall. There ought always to be just enough money available to buy all that can be produced at prices which will cover the necessary costs of production, including only such profits as are regarded as affording a reasonable incentive to keep the means of production well employed.

There is accordingly a limit to the extent to which the State or the banks should go in making more money available. When Full Employment has been reached, further emission of money can result only in inflating prices, without a corresponding addition to the output of goods and services. Inflation is best defined as emission of money beyond what is needed to finance production under conditions of Full Employment.

We have seen that the State can stimulate employment, not only by promoting Public Works, but also by putting additional purchasing power at the disposal of the consuming public. For example, the distribution of the war veterans' bonus in the United States stimulated consumption and employment at a time when there were large productive resources unused; and after this war the paying out to consumers of the sums which have been withheld during the war as deferred pay can be used as a means of stimulating consumption when it shows signs of flagging towards the end of the post-war replacement boom. The introduction of Family Allowances would have a similar effect; and so would any arrangement for making presents of purchasing power to the poorer sections of the public. The effectiveness of such measures would, however, depend on their being financed in such a way as not merely to transfer purchasing power from one section of the public to another. What is needed in times of depression is mainly a real addition to the amount of purchasing power, not a mere transference from one section of the public to another.

Money expended on Public Works and money granted directly to consumers have precisely the same effect in stimulating consumption. The difference is that, in the case of Public Works, the State acquires capital assets to offset its expenditure, whereas in the case of direct grants of purchasing power no assets are acquired in return. It is in general better for the State to pay out money in return for services rendered—the more so because such expenditure directly stimulates activity in the industries which are most seriously depressed. But it may well be desirable to accompany a policy of Public Works, designed to stimulate investment, by a secondary programme of direct stimulus to consumption, meant to increase activity in the industries producing consumers' goods and services. The need for such a programme is greater where the tendency is for incomes to be very unevenly distributed. The more the State enforces a policy of high minimum wages and extensive Social Services in normal times, the less necessary will it be to resort in bad times to exceptional measures for the direct stimulation of consumption.

When the State accepts responsibility for maintaining a condition of Full Employment, it acquires therewith a power to regulate the level of wages, and can enforce good conditions of employment without adverse effects on the level of production. The State can, moreover, by control of the supply of money and of the banking system, regulate the level of interest rates and, therewith, of the profits normally expected on invested capital. It can thus influence the distribution of incomes, so as to reduce economic inequality. To the extent to which it does this, it will also increase the 'propensity to consume,' and thus diminish the tendency of the economic system to generate crises of under-consumption. A high 'propensity to consume' is essential to the successful working of the profit system ; but such a 'propensity' can be secured, under the conditions of modern capitalism, only by extensive State intervention in industry, including the socialisation of those key industries which must be publicly controlled if a policy of 'Public Works' is to be successfully applied.

Employment in the U.S.S.R.

The general conclusion to be derived from the foregoing argument is that the direct stimulation of consumption should, in a mainly capitalistic system, play a secondary part to a policy of Public Works designed to maintain investment at a satisfactory level. In a completely socialised system, such as exists in the Soviet Union, different conditions apply. Where the State is in complete control of economic activity, the problem of unemployment disappears, though a certain amount of *frictional* unemployment may of course still exist. The only problem in such an economic system is to secure the best possible distribution of the available economic resources among the alternative uses to which they can be applied—that is, between investment and consumption and, in each of these fields, between the various forms of production which are possible with the available economic resources. There is for such a country as the Soviet Union no problem of maintaining employment : there is only the problem of ensuring that the available resources of production are put to the best possible use in the interests of the whole people. It may be decided, in the Soviet Union, either to devote more resources to immediate improvement in the standard of living or, at the cost of lower standards in the immediate future, to produce more capital goods so as to raise living standards later on. There is no fixed rule by which such a society can decide how much to consume at once, and how much to invest with a view to increasing future consumption. The choice is open ; but, whatever choice is made, there is no reason why unemployment should arise, save in a purely frictional form. A capitalistic country, on the other hand, must always be faced by the danger of unemployment. It may be able to offset this danger by the right measures for stimulating either investment or consumption, or both at once ; but the danger remains inherent in any system which depends on the profit-motive to bring about the employment of any considerable proportion of the total available supply of labour. Unemployment is a disease of capitalism : it may be possible by a large extension of public enterprise and redistribution of incomes to reduce it to manageable dimensions without abolishing capitalism altogether ; but it cannot be entirely eradicated except under a system which makes need, instead of profit, the criterion of the worthwhileness of production and employment over the entire economic field.

CHAPTER SIX

INTERNATIONAL ASPECTS OF FULL EMPLOYMENT

A COUNTRY such as Great Britain, which depends largely on imports of both foodstuffs and raw materials, has to take special account of the reactions of Full Employment on its international position. If more people are in work and more is being produced and consumed, the demand for imports will tend to rise unless home production of goods which are normally imported can be considerably increased. If markets can be found for additional exports to exchange for the increased imports required, well and good. If, however, this cannot be done under the prevailing conditions of international trade, the country must either give up its full employment policy, or accept a lower standard of consumption in respect of the goods which have to be brought in from abroad, or set to work to produce at home more of the kinds of goods it has previously imported. Some of these goods —*e.g.* tropical products and raw materials which are not found at home—it cannot produce for itself. Some other things it can produce, but only at a higher cost than they could be bought at abroad if there were the means of paying for them. Yet others it may be possible by taking the right measures to produce at home as cheaply as they can be imported ; and for yet others it may be possible to find home-produced substitutes that are nearly or quite as good.

The extent to which it is practicable to expand exports so as to pay for larger imports is bound to depend on the economic prosperity of other countries. If they too are following policies of Full Employment their need for imports will be greater, and world trade as a whole will expand. It is of the greatest importance to each country that other countries shall follow expansionist economic policies ; and it will be much easier for each country to follow such policies if the others are doing the same.

Accordingly, there ought to be an endeavour to incorporate in the economic settlement which will follow the war an agreement to follow a common policy of expansion. This involves the establishment in each country of an elastic monetary system, in order that economic activity may not be pulled up short by monetary deflation. It involves also special measures to enable countries whose economic and monetary systems have been dislocated by the war to start out on expansionist lines. This is one aim of the Keynes Plan, which proposes to give to each country an international banking credit on which it will be able to draw while it is recovering from the effects of the war and setting its economic house in order. As against this, the 'Morgenthau Plan' prepared by the United States Treasury has the very serious disadvantage that, by forcing all countries back on the gold standard, it would put them all at the mercy of any deflationary tendencies that might manifest themselves in the United States.

I have no space in this booklet to discuss this problem at any length. It is dealt with in my companion booklet in this series on the subject of postwar international trade.* Here it is only necessary to observe that the power of Great Britain or of any other single country to follow a full employment policy will be undermined if the gold standard is put back without any guarantee that the United States, and indeed all the leading countries, will follow internal and international policies designed to maintain production and employment steadily at a high level. In the absence of such guarantees, any country which sets out to maintain Full Employment must retain control over its own monetary system and over the rates of exchange between its own money and the monies of other countries (or at any rate must retain the power to fix and vary the value of its own currency in terms of gold).

Development of the Backward Countries

The pursuit of Full Employment as an aim of international policy requires that measures be taken to plan world production so as to achieve a high level of international trade, and that active steps be set on foot to develop the productive systems of the more backward countries, most of which were before the war suffering heavily from what economists call 'concealed unemployment' on the land. This means that there were in these countries too many people engaged in agriculture : indeed, in many areas a substantial part of the agricultural population could have been withdrawn from the land without any adverse effect on output, and even with positive advantage to output as soon as there had been time for technical standards to be improved. These countries, in order to achieve a condition of Full Employment, need to develop substantial industries and services of their own, partly for the production of cheap, standardised consumers' goods, but even more for the provision of improved services of transport, power-supply, land drainage and higher capitalisation of agriculture, as well as for the fuller exploitation of their mineral wealth. For these purposes they will need supplies of capital goods from the more developed countries. Some of these they will no doubt be able to pay for by exporting their own products ; but with a considerable proportion they will have to be supplied on loan, or even on Lease-Lend terms, until there has been time for their productive capacity to be developed. The more advanced countries will find themselves at the end

---

* See *The Planning of World Trade*, by G. D. H. Cole (Odhams Press, 1944).

of the war possessed of an economic equipment well suited to supplying just the kinds of capital goods which are most needed by the more backward areas ; and it will be much easier for the countries which possess this equipment to maintain conditions of Full Employment if they can use it in forwarding the economic development of the rest of the world. The point also is more fully discussed in my companion booklet on the future of international trade.*

POINTS FOR DISCUSSION
(see also p. 13)

1. What do you understand by " public works policy ? "
2. Is it necessary for the State, in order to be in a position to pursue a satisfactory public works policy, to own and direct the principal capital-using industries ?
3. Which industries would you select as important to bring under public ownership and control from the standpoint of ensuring the maintenance of full employment ?
4. What steps are desirable to maintain the level of consumption ? To what extent should this be aimed at by means of redistributive taxation ? Under what conditions is it desirable for the State to incur budget deficits in bad times in order to maintain consumption ?
5. To what extent should the State regulate the level of wages in order to bring about a better distribution of consuming power ? What contribution would family allowances make towards this ?
6. What international policy should Great Britain aim at in order to ensure the success of a full employment policy in this country ? How far can a full employment policy be pursued in this country apart from what is done by other countries ? How would your answer to this question be affected by a decision to return to the Gold Standard ?
7. What contribution could a full employment policy in this country make to the improvement of the standard of life in the more backward countries ?

---

* See also *Europe, Russia and the Future* and *Great Britain in the Post-war World*, both published by G. D. H. Cole (Gollancz).

APPENDIX

A NOTE ON THE SUPPLY OF LABOUR AFTER THE WAR

[The following particulars are mainly based on figures prepared for the author by Mr. P. W. S. Andrews, Statistician to the Nuffield College Social Reconstruction Survey. They take no account of war casualties, as no estimate can be made of these at present. Accordingly, the numbers of young men likely to be available are to some extent overestimated.]

Post-War Population

If the war is over by 1945, total population in Great Britain, without allowing for war casualties, can be put at a little less than 47 millions, or about half-a-million more than in 1939. Population of pre-war working age (14-65) will have increased by about 250,000, apart from war casualties. This of course means that it may in fact not have increased at all, or may have fallen if casualties are heavy.

Post-War Occupied Population, under 45 and over 45

If there is no change in the proportions in the different age-groups at work, *occupied* population will be up by about 300,000, part from war casualties. But the occupied population *under* 45 will have *fallen* by about 250,000, whereas the occupied population *over* 45 will have increased by over 550,000. Of course, war casualties will tend to fall most on those under 45, and their effect will be to increase still more the *proportion* of working population over 45.

Effect of Raising School-Leaving Age

When school-leaving age is raised to 15, the effect will be to reduce the occupied population by about 400,000 ; and if it goes to 16, the total reduction will be nearly 900,000.

Reduction of Juvenile Labour Supply

When school-leaving age is raised to 15, and part-time education is made compulsory *for one day a week* up to 18, the additional reduction due to part-time continued education will be equivalent to the full-time employment of about 300,000 persons. If part-time education were on a *half-time* basis, the reduction would be nearer 800,000. Thus a *minimum* estimate of the probable reduction in juvenile labour supply is about 700,000, or much more than enough to cancel the entire increase in population.

Probable Reduction of Total Post-War Labour Supply

Thus total post-war labour supply, even apart from war casualties, is certain to be considerably smaller than the pre-war supply *unless there is a large increase in women's employment*. It is not possible to make any estimate of the number of women of types who were not in employment before the war who will wish to be in employment after the war. But it is clearly unlikely to be large enough to offset both the fall in juvenile employment and the loss due to war casualties. We can conclude safely that the total post-war labour supply will be smaller than before the war and that the average age will be considerably higher.

NOTE

The present booklet travels rapidly over much of the ground which I have covered much more fully in a book, entitled *The Means to Full Employment*, which I issued through Messrs. Gollancz Ltd. in December, 1943. Any reader who wants to go on from this necessarily brief presentation of the subject is advised to turn to the book, especially if he is interested in the monetary and banking aspects of the problem or in a fuller exposition of the underlying theory. For the convenience of any group which may be using the present booklet as the basis for a series of discussions, I here give a rough key to the arrangement of the book in relation to the somewhat different arrangement used in the shorter treatment.

Booklet	Book
1. What is Meant by Full Employment?	Chapters I and II.
2. The Outlook for Employment after the War	(Not separately covered).
3. On What Does the General Level of Employment Depend?	Chapters III, IV and V.
4. Public Works and Employment	Chapters VI, VII and XII.
5. The Maintenance of Consumption	Chapter IV (in part) and Chapter XI.
6. International Aspects of Full Employment	Chapter X.

The book has in addition special chapters on Structural Readjustment as a means of combating unemployment (Chapter VII), on Monetary Measures (Chapter VIII), and on the effects of Monopoly on employment (Chapter IX). These subjects are treated incidentally in the booklet.

G. D. H. C.

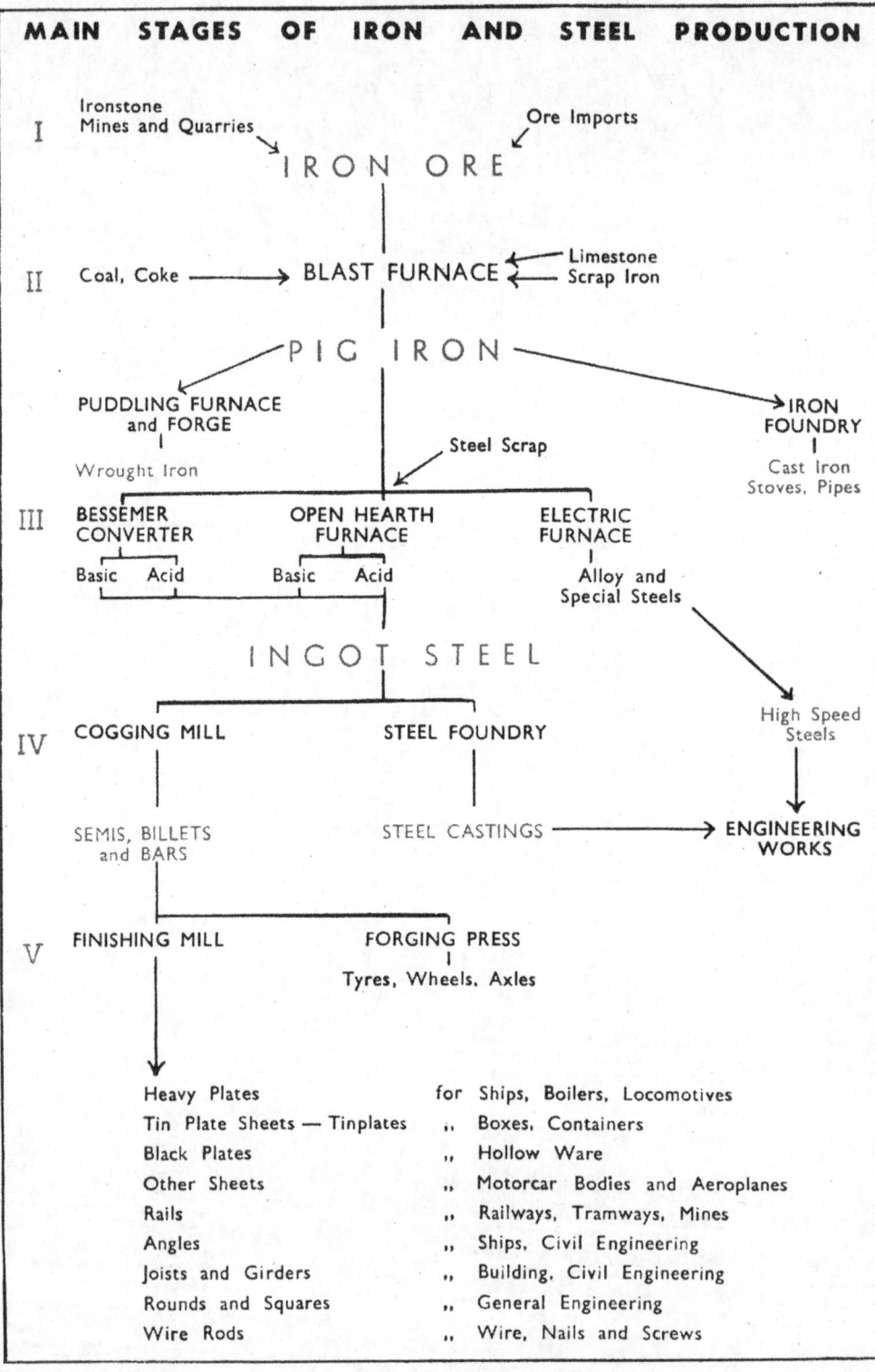

NEW STATESMAN PAMPHLET

WHY NATIONALISE STEEL?

by

G. D. H. COLE

June, 1948.
Reprinted July, 1948.
Revised Edition, July, 1948.

NEW STATESMAN AND NATION
10 Great Turnstile London W.C 1

CONTENTS

		PAGE
1.	**THE PROBLEM STATED**	3
	The Labour Party's Pledge.—When is Socialisation "Socialistic?"—Steel and Capitalism—Why "Disturb" the Steel Industry?	
2.	**THE STEEL INDUSTRY ANALYSED**	7
	The History of Steelmaking—Steel and Coal—Integration and Location—Where Does the Steel Industry Begin and End?—Pig-iron and Ore-mining—Scrap—The Non-Ferrous Metals—The Making of Ingot Steel—Alloy and Special Steels—Wrought Iron and Iron Founding—"Semis" and the Finishing Trades—Public and Private Sectors—The Federation and the Cartel—The Steel Problem in Western Europe—The State and the Federation.	
3.	**THE FEDERATION'S PLAN EXAMINED**	18
	The Federation's Plan—How Much Steel Do We Need?—Home and Export Targets—The Financial Aspect—Obsolete Plant and the Federation's Target—How Much Can We Afford to Scrap?—Costs and Prices.	
4.	**WHY NATIONALISATION?**	23
	The Case against Nationalisation—The Steel Industry's Record Considered—Steel Prices—The Fall in Exports—Why the Steel Industry Tends to Restrictive Monopoly—Steel and Armaments—The Fears of Excess Capacity—Steel and the Balance of Payments—The Problems of Centralisation.	
5.	**THE METHOD AND THE PROBLEMS**	34
	The Method of Acquisition—Re-grouping and Planning—The Shortage of Capacity—The Steel Firms under Public Ownership—A National Steel Board—Labour Relations—Consultation and Control—The Board and the Minister—Problems of Administration—Research and Development—Costs and Prices under Public Ownership—Export Policy.	
6.	**THE CASE CONCLUDED**	42
	The End of an Epoch—Steel and Economic Imperialism—The "Steel International"—Steel and the British People—Steel Policy under Public Ownership—The Problems of Quality and Location—The Coming Battle.	

DIAGRAMS AND TABLES

The Main Stages of Iron and Steel Production	Cover ii
Exports Depend on Steel	,, iii
Output of Steel Ingots in the United States and in Western Europe, 1937-9 and 1946-7	17
The Iron and Steel Federation's Plan for Building and Scrapping by 1953.	22
Steel Production in Great Britain, 1913 and 1924-1947	24
Imports of Steel into Great Britain, 1913 and 1929-1937	24
British Steel Prices after 1929	26
British Steel Exports, 1913 and 1929-1937	27
Principal British Exports of Iron and Steel, 1938 and 1947	31
Other British Exports Largely Dependent on Steel	31

WHY NATIONALISE STEEL?

I

THE PROBLEM STATED

When the Labour Party drew up its programme, defining the range of industries and services which a Labour Government would seek to transfer to public ownership during its first term of office, only one manufacturing industry was included in the list. This was the steel industry. All the other forms of private enterprise singled out for socialisation, with one exception, were services which can be regarded as falling broadly within the " public utilities " range. The Bank of England, the electricity supply industry, the gas industry, road, rail and inland water transport, civil aviation—all these belong to the " service " group, and have from the outset been subject to special forms of public regulation and control. Parliament has been passing Acts for the regulation of banking, gas, electricity, and the various branches of transport for a very long time past; and even in the heyday of *laissez-faire* the need for special regulation of these types of service was seldom denied. The Bank of England was already a Chartered Corporation, working under rules laid down by law and in close association with the Treasury: the railways and canals were set up by special Acts of Parliament and were always subject to special forms of public control. Private electricity and gas undertakings were also subject to special parliamentary regulation; and in these services a substantial section was already owned and operated by municipal bodies, side by side with the sections under private operation. In the case of electricity, a further step had been taken when the " Grid " was established and the entire system of main-line transmission brought under public ownership through the Central Electricity Board. Civil Aviation was also under regulation from the very beginning; and there had been in the decade before the war a large development of public control, through licensing, over road transport.

When is Socialisation " Socialistic ? "

Thus, there was nothing essentially " socialistic " in proposals to nationalise any one of these services. Indeed, in many countries, one or another of them has been transferred to, or established under, public ownership by Governments which no one could possibly regard as having any sympathy with Socialism. In Great Britain it was a Conservative Government that set up the "Grid" under national ownership and a predominantly Conservative Government that established the London Passenger Transport Board. No doubt, there was something "socialistic" in proposing to deal at once with so many services and to make public ownership complete in services in which it existed only in part; but all the same the proposal to socialise "public utilities" raised no real question of principle between Socialists and Anti-Socialists. The Conservatives could argue that the Labour Party was proposing too much socialisation, or that this or that particular proposal was inexpedient or badly drafted. They could not take any stand *on principle* against socialisation in this field, because, within limits, they had practised it themselves.

The only industries, as distinct from services, which the Labour Government marked down for immediate socialisation were coal-mining and iron and steel manufacture. The coal industry was recognised as occupying a special position, both as forming with gas and electricity a member of the "fuel and power" group and as manifestly needing a thorough reorganisation and re-equipment which could be brought about only under *unified* control. The choice, in this industry, lay between public ownership and the creation of a vast private monopoly; and it was clear that, if the second course were taken, it would be necessary for the State to provide or guarantee most of the large capital sums needed for bringing the coal industry up to date. In such a situation there was no real choice. If the Conservatives, instead of the Labour Party, had come to power in 1945, they would have had to nationalise the coal industry whether they wished to or not, just as before the war they had been driven by sheer necessity to nationalise the ownership of the coal itself. The Conservatives could not find any ground of principle for opposing the nationalisation of the coal-mining industry; and in practice their opposition in Parliament and outside was perfunctory and half-hearted, because they knew that the change to public ownership and operation had to come.

Steel and Capitalism

Steel stood in a different category, both because it was a manufacturing industry which ramified into many others and because it could be argued that it was advancing in efficiency under private enterprise, whereas the coal industry manifestly was not. Coal-mining could be treated as belonging in effect, as a "fuel and power" service, to the "public utilities" group, and could be treated as a special case. Steel, on the other hand, was so integrated and interconnected with the whole group of metal-working and engineering industries, and so much formed with them *the* key sector of modern large-scale capitalist enterprise, that its transference to public ownership and operation was bound to be felt as a blow right at the heart of capitalism. The capitalist system could maintain itself under conditions which required it to get its supplies of fuel and power from public sources, to use publicly owned transport agencies, and even to depend, in some degree, on a publicly operated Central Bank. But if Steel went the same way the position, it was felt, would become entirely different; for where, thereafter, would the citadel of capitalism be? Certainly not in the once preponderant textile industries, which had lost their leadership to the metal industries a long while ago. In the chemical and allied industries perhaps, for a time; but, if steel became a public service, how long would Imperial Chemical Industries be let alone? In the heavy engineering and vehicle trades, again perhaps; but how greatly would they be affected by the public ownership of their principal material—steel!

The battle over the issue of nationalising the steel industry was joined the very moment the Labour Government took office. It was widely felt in capitalist circles that none of its other socialisation measures would really matter, or would involve any real advance towards Socialism, if only it could be stopped from nationalising steel. Ever since 1945 this battle has been going on behind the scenes, and the public has got occasional glimpses of its vicissitudes. There have been two main lines of argument designed to induce the Government, in this matter, to depart from its election pledge. One is that it is in practice impossible to separate the steel industry proper from its finishing branches, which stretch out into engineering and into many other industries, and that accordingly the Government cannot carry out its pledge without going further than it has any mandate to go—for it has, the opponents argue, no mandate to nationalise any part of the engineering and metalworking industries. The other line, which is at present the more used, is that the steel industry is doing very well as it is, and that it would be disastrous to "upset" it just now, when all the output it can deliver is indispensable for the success of the export drive and for British internal recovery.

Why "Disturb" the Steel Industry?

This line is being plugged hard just now. The newspapers are continually telling the public about the great achievements of the iron and steel industry, its "record-breaking" output, and its drive for the highest efficiency under its present leadership. Public opinion, it is hoped, will react by concluding that it would be the height of folly to disturb an industry that is doing so well under its present ownership, and that anyone, from the Government downwards, who persists in pressing for nationalisation—above all during the present crisis of the national economy—must be actuated by "doctrinaire" motives, and cannot have the good of the country at heart.

"Doctrinaire!" It is a word that has a bad smell; and well those who use it are aware of its subtle effects. It means, I presume, pushing a theory, or a principle, into practice without a proper regard for expediency or common sense. I myself should regard as a doctrinaire anyone who proposed to socialise all industries in one fell swoop—for at least three good reasons. In the first place, I do not want to see *all* industries socialised, now or ever. Secondly, I do not believe it would be practicable to tackle efficiently all at once all the industries I do wish to see socialised. And thirdly, I recognise that the present Government has a mandate for only a limited socialisation programme. But this mandate does, plainly and unequivocally, extend to steel.

I do not, however, and I feel sure the British Government does not, wish to socialise the steel industry on "doctrinaire" grounds. If I were a "doctrinaire," or if *it* were, there would be no particular reason for singling out steel, in preference to a number of other industries, for early socialisation. Chemicals, for example, or tobacco, or flour-milling would do just as well. The reason for wishing to socialise steel is not a mere general preference for socialisation: it is a particular belief that in the national interest and in the cause of speedy industrial recovery the steel industry ought to be brought as soon as possible under public ownership and operation. Those who wish to take this course do not agree that the steel industry is doing very well as it is, or that it is making the contribution it should make to the national effort. What is more, they believe that there are inescapable reasons why the steel industry cannot be expected to make its proper contribution while it remains in private hands and continues to be conducted in the interests of private profit-making. This pamphlet is an attempt to explain why this is so, and also, in a broad way, to suggest *how*, as well as *why*, the steel industry should be converted without more delay into a public service.

But, before I take up the *why* or the *how*, it seems best to attempt to get a broad general picture of the steel industry and its main branches, and to attempt to answer the question of the scope of a sound and workable socialisation plan. *If* the steel industry, or a part of it, is to be socialised, over how wide a field should any immediate plan of socialisation extend? If we take this question first, before attempting to discuss the general merits of the case, or the methods to be adopted in any concrete scheme, we shall know a great deal better what precisely we are discussing than if we plunge straight away into the arguments for and against doing anything at all to transfer the industry, or some parts of it, from private to public ownership and operation.

II

THE STEEL INDUSTRY ANALYSED

When, in the 1850's, Henry Bessemer introduced " mild steel," a new industrial age began. The metallurgists wagged their heads and told one another that the new substance was not really steel at all, but merely " carbonised iron "; and it was indeed a very different material from what had till then been called " steel " and been made by processes so expensive as to prevent its use except for cutting tools and for a few other special purposes for which great strength and hardness were indispensable. Bessemer " steel " and the other new steels which soon followed it onto the market were not steel, in the old sense of the word; but, whatever they were, they changed the face of industry, driving out cast and wrought iron from one use after another, combining cheapness with durability, and presently showing themselves capable of being endlessly adapted and combined with other metals to yield materials possessing widely different properties and suitable for an immense range of uses. Siemens, a decade after Bessemer, introduced his new " open hearth " process for making mild steel; Gilchrist Thomas, Gilchrist, Martin and others added their improvements, which made it possible to use for " steel "-making ores with a high carbon content, such as those of Lorraine. As " steel " replaced iron, a great process of change and re-equipment set in. The old iron industry contracted, and new steelworks had to be built to replace its superseded plants. In the course of this great conversion, between the 1860's and the 1880's, the modern steel industry came to birth.

Of course, a great deal has happened to the industry since those pioneer decades; and throughout men have gone on making steel of the old high-quality types, and have been devising many new " special " steels for high-grade work. But ever since Bessemer and Siemens the steel industry has been primarily, in terms of output, a producer of *cheap* steel for widespread industrial use. " Special " steels of high quality are still too expensive to find more than a limited market in either peace or war. In war, as in peace, the emphasis is on mass-production; for vast quantities are needed, and much of it need not be of high quality. A biscuit tin, or even a motor-car body, need not be built like an " ironclad." Modern metallurgists, by mingling metals, have found ways of producing steels that are just as hard, just as tensile, just as strong as they need to be for each particular use to which they are to be put. Not much modern steel is " just iron with a dash of carbon " ; in the steel industry, iron and a wide and growing variety of other metals—manganese, tungsten, vanadium, chrome, and a great many more—are intimately linked together.

Where does the steel go ? Into ships, motor-cars, and aeroplanes. Into railway rails, locomotives, carriages, bridges, and stations. Into docks and dock plant. Into power stations and gasworks. Into buildings, as structural steel and also for fittings and equipment. Into factories, for machine-tools and engine-plant, as well as structurally. Into tanks and containers of every sort and size, down to household cans and tins of tobacco. Into tubes and into wire and nails, bolts and screws. Into railings and piers and gratings. Into cutlery and tools and agricultural implements. In short, into most things that are not made of some textile material or of wood or of paper—which nowadays *is* mostly wood. Steel, in a word, is everywhere ; it is the very basis of modern industrialism.

Steel and Coal

Steel depends on coal, as well as on iron ore and other metal deposits. It takes very different quantities of coal to make a ton of steel, according to the nature of the ores used, the processes of manufacture, and the type of steel required ; but, all round, technical progress is continually reducing the amount of coal used, directly or indirectly, in the making of a ton of steel. Part of the reduction is due to integration of successive processes, as when the waste gases generated in the blast-furnace are recovered, instead of being allowed to escape, uselessly or sometimes noxiously, and are employed to provide energy for a subsequent stage of production. But, in face of all economies in fuel, the link between coal and steel remains very close. The steel industry cannot flourish except on the foundation of a well-organised industry of coal-mining. Until British coal again becomes plentiful enough to afford supplies ample for the steel industry's needs, as well as for the requirements of other users at home and abroad, the development of steel production is bound to be held back. Even when the coal shortage has been thoroughly overcome, fuel economy in steel-making will continue to be a vital matter ; for we shall be in a position neither to waste coal nor to tolerate the high costs of production which too much consumption of fuel involves. It is indispensable, not only now, on account of the coal shortage, but also for the future, to make the greatest possible effort to keep down the steel industry's consumption of fuel.

Integration and Location

This is a question not only of continually improving the technical equipment of the industry, on foundations laid by steady and well directed research, but also of the correct siting of works and the fullest possible use of opportunities for continuous processing from stage to stage. It is necessary to take every chance of utilising waste gases as fuel for subsequent processes, as well as of avoiding the solidification and re-heating of the material wherever it can be used molten in the successive stages. Much of the steel industry grew up at a time when the need for such practices was not realised, or the opportunity for them did not yet exist; and the result is still seen in faulty location or in the divorce of processes which can best be carried on together in the same establishment. Besides, the exhaustion of some ore-fields, the change-over to imported ores, the increased use of scrap, and the changing proportions of coal or coke used in relation to other ingredients, have altered the economic conditions affecting location, and call for extensive re-designing of the industry. A good deal has been done already to recast some sections of the industry in the light of these new techniques; but much remains to be done, above all at the blast-furnace end and in the development of sheet steel production, and the necessary changes can be made much more easily under common than under divided ownership. The further this integration of successive processes is carried, the more marked is the tendency for the later processes of steel manufacture—or for a good number of them—to be best carried on under the same auspices as the earlier. That is why it is quite out of the question, if nationalisation is to occur at all, to stop short at the taking over of the primary processes of producing merely raw, or " ingot " steel. Already the firms which make raw steel in most cases carry on a number of subsequent processes in the same works as parts of a single, closely integrated concern; and it would be grossly uneconomical—and indeed mere folly—to break up these intimately connected operations. A steelworks which makes both raw and semi-finished, and very likely in addition some types of finished steel, must be nationalised as a whole, or not at all. It forms an essentially indivisible economic unit.

Where Does the Steel Industry Begin and End?

Nationalisation, then, cannot stop short at the stage of crude steel production. It must, however, stop somewhere, if it is not to spread out over iron-founding, engineering, and a host of other industries to an extent that the Government certainly does not have in mind. It must also begin somewhere; for the industry stretches far back as well as forward. Steel is made mainly of iron, nowadays with a good deal of admixture of other metals and, in the "open hearth" and electric process, with a large proportion of "scrap." The scrap comes partly from the steelworks themselves, partly from engineering and other factories, and partly from second-hand sources. The iron is made in blast-furnaces, which are sometimes integrated with the steelworks and sometimes separate. It is made with iron ore that is about two-thirds home-produced and about one-third imported from abroad. The making requires limestone as well as coal, and limestone quarrying as well as iron ore mining is therefore a preliminary process. The other metals that are blended with iron to make particular kinds of steel are largely imported, but are partly mined or produced at home. They require to be processed: this is mainly done in this country, and thus close connections exist between the steel industry and the importers, producers and processors of a number of the non-ferrous metals.

Pig-iron and Ore-mining

If there is to be nationalisation, where is it to begin? I am writing without any inside knowledge of what the Government will propose, but obviously it must include the production of pig-iron in the blast-furnace section of the industry; for, as we saw, this stage is considerably and increasingly integrated with the production of raw steel from the pig or directly from the molten metal as it emerges from the blast-furnace. It is no less clearly necessary to include the coke-ovens, which are largely carried on as part of the same establishments as produce pig-iron. Most of the limestone quarries which produce limestone for use in iron and steel making are already owned by the iron and steel concerns, and will naturally be included in any scheme of transference to public ownership. A considerable proportion of the mines and quarries which produce iron ore are also owned by the iron and steel makers, and in a number of cases, including the modern works based on mass-production of steel from low-grade home ores, are operated as sections of integrated concerns which cover every stage from the quarrying of the ore to the production of at least semi-finished steel. The whole business of iron-mining and quarrying obviously needs to be in the same hands as the production of pig-iron and steel.

The problem of the imported ores is rather different. Some British iron and steel concerns own, or hold shares in, iron-mines abroad, and import a proportion of their own supplies—subject of course at present to the "control" exercised by the Government. Other ores are bought from independent foreign companies or syndicates;

and there is, of course, also a small import of pig-iron and bar iron, especially of high-quality iron from Swedish and other sources. In recent years, increasing use has been made of British ores, despite the low quality of most of the remaining British supplies—for we have used up most of the high-grade deposits of Cleveland and Cumberland. The increasing use of British ores arises largely in connection with the home production of the cheaper, low-quality steels which we used to import mainly from Belgium and Germany. Imported ores, which are bulky, can naturally be used most economically in works near the ports; whereas most of the deposits of British low-grade ores lie well inland. Roughly, we now produce at home twice as much iron ore as we import; but the average metal content of the imported ores is considerably the higher.

It has to be decided, in any plan of nationalisation, whether the authority set up to conduct the iron and steel industry as a public service is to do its own buying of imported ore (and also of pig-iron) or is to buy from some other importing agency, perhaps based on and taking over the functions of the existing "control." The sensible course would surely be to let the new Iron and Steel Board, or Corporation, or whatever it is to be called, have its own buying department for imports, subject, of course, to any regulations the Government may have to impose in the interests of the balance of payments. The Iron and Steel Federation already handles pig-iron imports on behalf of the privately-owned industry; and this function would naturally pass to the new Board.

Scrap

In the past, the market for iron ores has been closely related to the market for scrap; for, within limits, it is possible to vary the proportions of ores and of scrap used in the blast-furnace as well as the proportion of pig and scrap used in later processes. The scrap used in steelworks is about half bought from outside sources and about half originates in the works which use it. An integrated steel industry would itself produce a high proportion of the scrap which it required. But it would also need to purchase from outside both second-hand scrap and scrap originating, say, in engineering and other works at home, or procurable from abroad. At present the question of getting supplies of scrap from Germany is a very big question, complicated by the necessity to pay in dollars for all German purchases since the Americans took over the main financing of the import requirements of the Western Zones. The open-hearth process by which most British steel has hitherto been produced requires a high proportion of scrap, whereas the Bessemer process involves relatively little scrap. The question is whether the buying of scrap from outside shall be organised directly in all cases through the nationalised industry, or whether there shall be still an intermediary class of scrap merchants, at any rate where sorting and treatment of second-hand scrap are required. Here again, it would seem to be best for the authority controlling the nationalised industry to take over the entire job.

The Non-Ferrous Metals

Non-ferrous metals raise a different problem; for many of them are linked to industries other than iron and steel, and even where the link with iron and steel is close, they may have other uses. Probably it will be best for the present to let the non-ferrous metal trades, including the importing merchants, carry on as they are, under government control, and to let the steel industry buy what it needs from them without taking over production or processing or importation. It will, however, be necessary to ensure adequate supplies, including home-produced supplies where they can be had; and there will evidently need to be closely co-ordinated policies of development in order to take full advantage of the growing possibilities of the various ferro-alloys, with their wide range of different properties adapted to different uses.

The Making of Ingot Steel

So far, then, we have in view, if nationalisation is to occur at all, a publicly owned industry beginning with iron-ore mining and quarrying, and including pig-iron (blast-furnace) production based partly on home-produced and partly on imported materials. Next in order comes the production of raw steel, which is itself a highly diversified product of widely varying cost and character. The main bulk of British production—in 1946 nearly five-sixths of the total—is " open-hearth " basic steel; about one-twelfth is " open-hearth acid " steel; about one-seventeenth is " basic Bessemer "—the cheapest kind; and a still smaller proportion, but of high average value, is " alloy " steel, largely produced by electrical processes. The quantity of " high-speed " tool steel, which alone is " steel " in the old, pre-Bessemer sense of the word, is smaller still.

This structure is quite different from that of the American and German steel industries, and the average quality is higher, even apart from the British reputation for producing high-grade alloy steels and high-speed special steels for cutting edges. The position of the British steel industry, in the mass-production as well as in the more specialised sections, depends greatly on quality. Open-hearth processes in general yield products of higher quality than the Bessemer converter, because they make possible better continuous control; and Great Britain as a producer of ships and machinery and other metal products which have to stand hard wear and strain uses a large proportion of high-quality steel. In the United States on the other hand a great deal of cheap steel goes into mass-produced motor-cars; and even in other uses many things are not made to last nearly so long as here. Our cheap steel goes largely into motor-cars or into various types of container or box, chiefly in the form of tinplate or plate of other types.

Alloy and Special Steels

Clearly any plan of nationalisation must embrace all forms of large-scale steel production, whatever the processes employed. Moreover, the production of alloy steels is already so closely integrated with the main branches that it cannot be severed from them. The only separable section is that which produces special steels, mainly for tool-making. This is largely in the hands of separate firms, including the larger tool-makers, and unless it is proposed to take over tool-making, which is really a separate industry, it may be best to leave the " special " steel-makers out of the nationalisation plan, or at all events, rather than take them over, allow them to continue private production under licence. There is enough that must be taken over to make it undesirable to extend the range of the new nationalised controlling agency over anything that it can do without, and not lose efficiency; and " special " steelmaking seems to be a case in point.

Wrought Iron and Ironfounding

There is another case falling within the range of "iron and steel," which are in many respects inseparable, but outside " steel " itself. The old wrought iron industry, which has been driven out of one activity after another by the development of steel, is really quite a separate business, which it seems unnecessary to include. The same can be said of the iron castings industry, which turns out stoves, grates, fenders, and similar products. Some ironfounding, which is carried on in close connection with blast furnaces, must be taken over if they are; but this is only a small proportion of the whole trade.

" Semis " and the Finishing Trades

We have now added all the main branches of crude steel production to the earlier branches of iron and steel that must be included in any workable plan. It is, however, entirely out of the question to stop at this point; for most steelworks do not stop at the production of crude steel. Some of their crude steel they sell to other firms to work up to further stages; but a large proportion they themselves use in producing what are called "semis" and also a number of kinds of finished steel goods. They do this sometimes in different works under the same ownership, but more often in the same or contiguous works, as parts of a closely integrated succession of processes. The main forms of "semis" are billets, blooms and slabs—that is, lumps of more or less refined steel conveniently shaped for use in subsequent processes—and bars designed for the production of various forms of sheet steel and tinned or other plates. These "semis" are "rolled" products; and there is no possible way of severing their production from that of the crude steel of which they are made. Moreover, apart from the "semis," the main steelworks turn out a large proportion of further finished products, such as sheet steel and plates for tinning or galvanising or for other forms of treatment, railway and other rails, joists, girders, and many kinds of steel used in structural work, tubes, especially heavy tubes, tyres, wheels and axles, and a fair range of other products.

In this wide field, it is clear that a great deal must be included in any plan of public ownership that can be expected to work. Where any of these processes are carried on either in the same works as the making of crude steel, or in contiguous or closely-connected establishments, it would be manifestly a source of inefficiency to attempt division. Where they are carried on in really separate works, two possibilities arise. These works may be independent, or they may be owned or controlled by firms which carry on the production of the crude steel. In the second case, *if firms as such are taken over* (we shall be coming to that later), they will be acquired together with the firms that own them; but it will be possible, if it is so decided, to reconstitute them as separate businesses under separate ownership. Where the finishing firms are already independent, they need not be taken over at all unless it is decided that they should be. If these firms are not taken over, or if some which are are handed back to private enterprise, a situation will arise in which products of the same type are being made partly by private enterprise and partly by a nationalised service.

Public and Private Sectors

Well, why not? Except in the case of a relatively small number of clearly defined industries and services, there is no practicable way of nationalising some industries and leaving others in private hands that does not involve overlapping at the edges, and therewith a terrain in which public and private enterprises producing the same, or closely similar, types of goods will exist side by side. I can see no good reason why they should not so exist, and compete with each other : indeed, the co-existence may help to keep both of them up to the mark. This, of course, implies that public services will be so conducted as to cover their costs—or that, if for any reason a particular product is to be sold below cost, any subsidy shall be made available to the private as well as to the public producer. This, however, is the basis on which, in normal cases, any plan of socialisation ought clearly to be based. There is no valid reason why finished steel products manufactured under public and under private enterprise should not compete : a public monopoly is necessary only where there is good cause for complete unification in the interests of efficiency—for example, in order to make possible mass-production based on a high degree of specialisation of works to the scientific manufacture of particular goods.

Thus, in the case of steel, it will be necessary for public ownership to extend over the whole of certain types of productive plant—e.g. large-scale steel production—over a high proportion of certain other types, which are mainly carried on in close connection with such production ; and over smaller proportions of other types, which are integrated in varying degrees with crude steel-making. In general, a nationalisation plan for steel can stop short of those types of finishing which are independent of the earlier processes ; and it may even be desirable to hand back to private enterprise—possibly with a continuing element of public shareholding—some of the factories which are at present under the ownership or control of the main steel-making firms or combines. Where exactly the line can best be drawn can be decided only by taking each case on its merits. In the majority of cases steel foundries, and in some steel forges, are more closely related to the engineering group of industries than to steel ; and, where this is so, they should obviously be left out of a steel plan, unless there are very cogent reasons on the other side in certain particular instances. What must not be done, however, is to break up inter-connected units which are economically sound, in pursuance of any theoretically conceived line of demarcation between the sectors that are and are not to come within the scope of the socialisation plan.

The Federation and the Cartel

At present the Iron and Steel Federation, with the various "product associations" that have been linked up with it, covers a very wide range of finishing processes as well as the whole body of producers of crude and semi-finished steels. In practice this has meant that the main influence has rested with the big firms, which produce both nearly all the crude steel and a considerable proportion of the more finished products, and that the interests of the independent finishers, who want crude steel to be cheap, have taken second place. This has been the position especially since the tariff introduced in 1931, and thereafter the arrangements made between the Federation and the foreign producers through the International Steel Cartel, prevented the finishers from getting cheap steel from Belgium or Germany. With the nationalisation of the big steel-making firms, the key position would pass to the body which was put in control of the public section; but there would be the essential difference that this body would be aiming not at maximum profit for itself, but only at covering its costs and, subject to this condition, supplying steel as cheaply as possible to its competitors equally with its own finishing plants. No doubt, even under the system which existed in the 1930s, it was open to the aggrieved finisher to complain to the Import Duties Advisory Committee if he felt that he was suffering from monopolistic practices on the part of the crude steel-makers. The I.D.A.C. was given the function of regulating the practices of the Federation, with the power, if it thought fit, of removing or reducing tariff protection. This power, however, even if the I.D.A.C. had been at all disposed to use it, would not have been of much effect in face of the close arrangements made between the British and foreign steel-makers through the International Steel Cartel. It was the Cartel's policy, and not the tariff, that in fact regulated the import of steel into Great Britain; and the prices charged in the British market were settled by the Federation pretty much as it pleased.

The Steel Problem in Western Europe

One big question that will have to be faced in the near future is that of the future organisation of steel production in Western Europe as a whole. The world is short of steel: the Americans are increasing their production fast, but their consumption fully keeps pace with it. Germany, which used to be by far the largest European producer, has had its capacity drastically cut down under the conditions imposed by the victors, and is still able to produce only a quantity much smaller than the revised "Potsdam" terms impose. French output is only at two-thirds of the pre-war level, Belgian output is above the level of 1938-9, but still well below that of 1937. On the following page, in *metric* tons, are the figures for the United States and for the leading Western countries:

OUTPUT OF STEEL INGOTS
Monthly Averages, 1937-9 and 1946-7 (in Thousands of Metric Tons)

	1937	1938	1939	1946	1947
United States	4,282	2,400	3,991	5,035	6,410
Great Britain	1,101	881	1,118	1,074	1,057
Germany	1,669	1,934	—	244*	324* (estimate)
France	660	518	662	367	479
Belgium	322	190	252	190	241
Luxembourg	209	120	146	108	143
Italy	175	194	190	96	142 (av. of 11 mths.)
Sweden	94	83	99	101	99

* Three Western Zones only.

In face of the West European shortage, and above all of the decline in the German production, there will obviously be for some time to come a market for all the steel Great Britain can spare. Under the Marshall Plan the countries of the West have now agreed to work together in planning their economic recovery; and an important part of their planning will relate to the extent and character of the redevelopment of the German steel industry. Some organisation will have to take the place of the pre-war Cartel—though not in the same restrictive spirit—in planning the future of the steel industry over Western Europe as a whole; and it is perfectly clear that, in the new world situation, this task will have to be performed directly by the European Governments and not through any private cartel of capitalist interests. Whatever may happen nationally, steel, on the international plane, is bound to continue under government regulation and to be planned by the co-operating Governments as an integral element in the general recovery plan. This is not a matter of political choice; it arises out of the sheer necessities of the case, whatever may be the political complexion of the Governments in power.

The State and the Federation

At the national level, any plan of public ownership covering the main branches of iron and steel manufacture will evidently need to include provisions for close interworking between the Board or Corporation that is put in charge of the nationalised sections and the firms which are left to carry on production for private profit. This will apply not only to the independent finishers but also to other important groups of steel consumers, from the already socialised railways and mines to the many branches of the engineering and shipbuilding and other metal-working trades and to civil engineering, building, and many other industries and services. The independent steel firms may decide, after nationalisation of the other branches of the steel industry, to retain some sort of Iron and Steel Federation to represent their common interests; and it may even be decided that the sections of the nationalised industry concerned with particular products covered by " product associations " shall maintain their connection with the Federation in its new form. Clearly, however, much of the work hitherto done by the Federation—as well as by the " Control " at the Ministry of Supply which has been the Federation's *alter ego* since 1939—will have to be transferred to the new body established to administer the socialised sections of the industry.

III

THE FEDERATION'S PLAN EXAMINED

In May 1946 the British Iron and Steel Federation, in response to a request from the Government, produced a plan for the development of the iron and steel industry, estimated to cost £168 millions at the prices then current and to be carried out by stages up to 1953—that is, in about eight years. This plan was mainly technical and dealt chiefly with proposals for the building of modern blast-furnaces and steelworks to replace obsolete plant and to provide for an increase in total output. It gave details of the new works to be constructed, of existing works to be modernised, and of the methods to be adopted in concentrating particular types of output at fewer points, in order to develop mass-production, and in re-arranging the units of the industry in the interests of fuel economy, lower transport charges, and other changes designed to reduce costs. In the ground covered, the Iron and Steel Federation's Report resembled the Reid Report on the requirements of coal-mining: the difference was that it was put forward not by a disinterested technician, but by the representatives of the industry, who were of course interested parties.

This factor of self-interest did not impair the technical soundness of many of the proposals included in the plan. Nobody supposes that the steel industry wishes to be inefficient or lacks good technical advisers. Indeed, if the steel industry is nationalised, the new public authority that takes charge of it will undoubtedly press on with most of the projects put forward by the Federation two years ago. The faults of the Federation's plan were not that it was technically bad—except where vested interests happened to run counter to technical considerations, as they sometimes did. The faults lay in the *scale* of the plan—that is, in its marked underestimate of the total capacity required, and in the methods proposed for financing it.

How Much Steel Do We Need?

Take first the question of capacity. The British steel industry has to meet the requirements both of home consumption and of the export trade, *minus* such imports as are allowed to be brought into the country and can be procured, in face of world shortages, if they are allowed. Before the war annual home consumption of steel was somewhere between $10\frac{1}{2}$ and $11\frac{1}{2}$ million tons. It was over $11\frac{1}{2}$ millions in 1937, the year of highest employment. Ten years earlier steel consumption had been running at an annual rate of 7 to 8 million tons, and before 1914 at about 5 millions. Between the middle twenties and 1937 it rose by about 50 per cent: if it had risen till now at the same rate it would have reached about 18 millions. Actually, war held up such modernisation and expansion plans as the industry had begun to carry out before 1939, and production, at the beginning of 1948, was not much above 14 million tons.* What did the Federation propose to do in order to meet expanding home demand in 1946? Despite the arrears of unsatisfied demand accumulated during the war, despite the crying need for steel for the re-building of Britain and the re-equipment of British industry, and despite the evident necessity of a really big expansion of exports, the Federation planned for a total output capacity of not more than 16 million tons, and for an actual output of about $15\frac{1}{2}$ millions. Moreover, these figures related not to 1947, but to the completion of the plan six years later, by which time there would surely have been a large further growth of demand.

This total of 16 million tons was divided by the Federation into 13 millions for the home market and 3 millions for export. Thus, the plan allowed for a home consumption of only $1\frac{1}{2}$ millions more than was actually consumed in 1937. This in face of the adoption of a policy of full employment as well as of the factors listed in the preceding paragraph! Nothing short of a tremendously monopolistic price policy could possibly keep demand down to such a level. If it were kept down, what would become of full employment, and how could other industries flourish in face of the shortage of their most vital material?

Nor was the export figure less surprising. The Federation based it on the fact that British steel exports had fallen in the years just before

---

* By April, 1945, the annual rate was over 15 million tons But see p. 27.

the war from 3½ to 2½ million tons a year. But why had they fallen? Because the Federation, as a partner in the European Steel Cartel, had given up export competition in many markets and was charging high prices and concentrating its efforts chiefly on the home market, in which it enjoyed a monopoly. Was it really supposed in 1946 that Great Britain, under an imperative necessity to raise total exports to at least 75 per cent above the pre-war level, and under a particular necessity to increase exports of capital goods based on iron and steel, could accept a target of a mere 15¼ million tons for both home consumption and exports—and that for as far ahead as 1953? The thing was ridiculous; but it was what the Iron and Steel Federation solemnly proposed.

Home and Export Targets

Clearly, the output target has to be of a totally different order from this. If total exports are to rise by 75 per cent at least, exports of iron and steel must rise by something nearer 150 per cent—to 6 or 7 million tons at the very least. Development plans in the less advanced countries could well absorb much more than that, if more could be supplied. As for potential home demand, by 1953, can it possibly be put at less than 20 million tons, including the increased quantities that will be used up in the larger volume of exports of engineering and other metal goods, including ships and vehicles, made largely of steel?

I know very well that 26 million tons is an impossible target for the iron and steel industry to reach, under any auspices, by 1953. There is not enough ore; steelworks and blast furnaces take a considerable time to build; and Great Britain is short of labour and of the industrial capacity needed for building them. But this was not the ground on which the Federation based its all too modest programme. The Report seriously argued that in all probability the total demand for British steel in the middle 'fifties would not be likely to exceed 15½, or at most 16, million tons. Persons who could put forward such an estimate are plainly not to be trusted to control the reorganisation of an industry on which, more than on any other save coal, the economic survival of Great Britain depends.

The Financial Aspect

The second outstanding fault in the Federation's Report was its casualness over finance. Wanting £168 million, at current prices, spread over 7 or 8 years, it estimated that the steel firms could find, say, from

£6 to £7 million a year—not more than a quarter of the total. It threw in another £10 million, as a lump sum to be received back from the Government to cover repairs deferred during the war; and it proceeded to demand higher depreciation allowances and allowances for obsolescence from the Government by way of tax remission, concluding that, given these, the industry might be able to find about half the total sum needed. As for the other half, it said only that " there should be no insuperable difficulty " in finding it by the raising of further capital. It urged that the steel industry would have a strong preferential claim on available funds, especially as two-thirds of its planned expenditure would take effect in the Development Areas. It did not say that it wanted a subsidy or a government guarantee; but the inference was fairly plain. Obviously it would be quite out of the question for the steel firms to raise anything like the amount required, even for their own inadequate plans, without government backing. Such capital as they could raise on their own would be got only at high interest rates, or on onerous terms of issue. In effect, they were asking the Government to stand behind them in carrying through a plan designed, not to give the nation the steel it needs, but to entrench their existing monopoly.

Obsolete Plant and the Federation Targets

I do not propose here to examine the detailed plans which the Federation put forward. As I have said, most of them were technically sound as far as they went: their fault lay in not going nearly far enough. One or two points that came out in connection with them, however, do call for some comment, as indicating the size of the job that has to be tackled in order to put the iron and steel industry into a satisfactory state. The parts of it that are in the worst state at present appear plainly from what is said in the Report. Thus, out of a blast-furnace capacity (for pig-iron making) of 7,320,000 tons, the Report states that only about 3 million tons can be obtained from plants that are reasonably efficient and up to date. Plant for producing from 4½ to 5 million tons (allowing for idle capacity, which is not wholly avoidable) needs to be built in order to replace obsolete units, quite apart from what is needed for increasing total output. The position is not quite so bad as this in most other branches; but in nearly all a very large proportion of the new plant proposed in the Federation's plan is for replacement of obsolete units, and not for expansion. This appears plainly in the following table, which is based on the figures given in the Report.

THE FEDERATION'S PLAN FOR BUILDING & SCRAPPING BY 1953
(Thousand Tons)

	Existing Capacity	New Building proposed	Future capacity	Increase in capacity	Plant to be scrapped	New Building as % of future capacity	Proposed percentage increase in total capacity
Blast-furnaces	7,320	4,750	9,100	1,780	2,970	52	24
Steel furnaces	14,100	5,835	15,950	1,850	3,985	37	13
Billet mills	3,700	2,200	4,500	800	1,400	49	22
Plate mills	1,750	500	1,750	—	500	29	0
Joist, Rail and Heavy Section mills	2,500	650	2,500	—	650	26	0
Sheet and Tinplate mills	2,400	1,100	2,700	300	800	41	12½
Wire Rod mills	675	150	750	75	75	20	11
Light Section, Bar and Strip mills	2,500	850	2,800	300	550	30	12

These figures make plain how very large, on the Federation's own showing, is the proportion of out of date plant that is only fit to be cleared away as speedily as it can be replaced. This bad plant, as long as the industry remains under private ownership, will hold up prices to a grossly inflated level; for even under government control private business has to be allowed a profit and, short of actual subsidies (which are given in some cases) all plant that is retained in use has to be made to pay. This involves fixing selling prices high enough to cover the costs of the inefficient producers, and prevents the economies of the better plants from being passed on to the consumers in lower prices. A public concern, of course, could average costs, and thus reduce prices at once, not to the full extent that would be possible when the old plant went out of use, but in proportion to the relative outputs produced at high and low cost.

How Much Can We Afford to Scrap?

This is a vitally important point, because it is all too plain that, faced by a very much bigger total demand for steel than the Federation has allowed for, we shall not be in a position to scrap even inefficient plant at anything like the rate it proposed. For want of better, much of the old plant will have kept in use for a good many years to come. If the industry stays in private hands, this will mean that high prices, based on the costs of the inefficient works, will stay too, hampering industry at home and putting disastrous obstacles in the way of increasing exports both of steel and of the countless products for which it is a material. Can anyone in his senses really contemplate such a prospect?

Costs and Prices

A further point is that the Federation, to say the least, is not at all optimistic about the reduction of costs that will be achieved even in the new plants which it proposes to build. For example, in the case of pig iron the fall in cost as between new plants and the *least* efficient 20 per cent of the plants now in use is put at no more than $21\frac{1}{2}$ per cent, and for steel billets 25 per cent; and, as an offset to these savings, there is charged up interest on the capital cost of the new plant, so as to reduce the total savings to $7\frac{1}{2}$ per cent for pig iron and to under 11 per cent for the steel. These estimates, of course, depend partly on the extent of the technical economies themselves and partly on the level of interest charged in respect of the new capital expenditure. The State, being able to borrow more cheaply, could cut down the latter figure: the estimate of the technical saving seems lower than it should be practicable to achieve by really thorough reorganisation.

IV

WHY NATIONALISATION?

We have now seen, broadly but sufficiently for the purpose, what will need to be nationalised, *if* the steel industry is to be nationalised at all. But of course the question is, whether it ought to be nationalised or not. To this we must now turn.

The case *against* nationalisation, we have seen already, is generally rested at present on the contention that the industry is doing very well as it is, under private ownership, and that it would be folly to start " monkeying " with it while the country is in the present state of crisis. Nationalisation, it is argued, would only upset the plans that are being carried out by the men who are at present in charge, and would mean less steel and not more. Is there any truth in these contentions?

Of course it is true that nationalisation would upset the present leaders of the industry. They have been making that clear enough ever since the Government first mooted the question. They refused to take any part in discussing with the Government any matter connected with nationalisation, and demanded that they should be let alone, to get on with the reconstruction of the industry in their own way. In short, they were out to fight against nationalisation, despite the Government's mandate for it, by every means in their power. I mention this, not by way of blaming them—for they no doubt believe that private enterprise is a good and public enterprise a thoroughly bad thing. I mention it simply as a matter of fact. That the capitalist owners of the steel industry are against nationalisation, and would be " upset " by it, goes without saying, and has no bearing on the merits of the question either way.

The Steel Industry's Record Considered

But what of the statement, so often made, that the industry is doing a fine job under private ownership and ought, on this score, to be let alone? Just where does this " fine job " come in? It is perfectly true that, from the technical standpoint, the steel industry is a great deal better organised than it was after the first world war—when, to speak bluntly, it had got itself into an appalling mess by its own fault. Instead of making their plants efficient, the leaders of the steel industry in those days went into an orgy of financial speculation, which left their businesses burdened with a great mass of watered capital and in much too unsound a state to be able to raise the new capital that was needed for technical reorganisation. Most of the big firms got into the hands of the banks and had to be put through a painful process of financial liquidation before they could even start on bringing themselves up to date. In 1924-5, despite heavy investment during the years of war, the output of the British steel industry was no higher than it had been in 1913; and though it rose in the later 'twenties, by 1930, even before the world slump had set in, it was down again below the output of 1913.

STEEL PRODUCTION (Great Britain), 1913 and 1924-1947

(Million Tons) 1913 7·7	1924 8·2	1930 7·3	1936 11·8	1940 13·0	1946 12·7
	1925 7·4	1931 5·2†	1937 13·0	1941 12·3	1947 13·1
	1926 3·6*	1932 5·3†	1938 10·4	1942 12·9	
	1927 9·1	1933 7·0	1939 13·2	1943 13·0	
	1928 8·5	1934 8·8		1944 12·1	
	1929 9·6	1935 9·9		1945 11·8	

* Coal stoppage. † World Depression.

IMPORTS OF STEEL INTO GREAT BRITAIN

(Thousand Tons)	1913	1929	1930	1931	1932	1933	1934	1935	1936	1937
Blooms, Billets and Slabs	514	573	566	531	360	230	331	262	453	437
Bars, Rods, Angles, Shapes and Sections	574	937	1,017	1,137	646	314	491	418	364	468
Plates and Sheets ..	169	197	162	150	76	37	46	48	43	51
Other Goods ..	747	962	854	719	358	269	335	296	311	362
TOTAL ...	2,004	2,669	2,599	2,537	1,440	850	1,203	1,024	1,171	1,318

No one can put upon it the main blame for the greatly reduced output of the next two years, during which it was meeting the impact of the world slump; but it has to be borne in mind that the slump served to get the steelmakers the tariff on imports for which they had been clamouring for a long while before. In 1928-9 Great Britain had been importing well over two and a half million tons of steel a year; in the 1930's total imports were less than half that amount. Indeed, from 1932 onwards no foreign steel at all was coming in except what the steel firms themselves wished to have imported. First the tariff and then, even more effectively, the cartel agreement shut out all other imports; and the Iron and Steel Federation itself took over control of the distribution of such foreign steel as it needed to supplement the British production. The British steelmakers, with every encouragement from the Governments of the 1930's, organised themselves into a close monopoly, and were able to regulate steel prices pretty much as they pleased, with the friendly assent of the official Import Duties Advisory Committee, which was supposed to watch over their proceedings in the public interest. Thus protected, they were able to maintain steel prices at a high level even during the worst period of the world depression and to keep them high when the depression was over. Profits recovered; share values picked up finely after the tribulations of the 'twenties; the tottering industry was put back firmly on its feet.

Steel Prices

A glance at the accompanying Table of prices will be enough to show what occured. The steel industry, except where it had to follow the American market, as in the case of tinplates, kept its price-levels unaltered through the years of slump, when most other prices were tumbling fast. After the slump, though wholesale prices in general remained a long way below the level of 1929, and even mineral prices as a group rose above that level only in the boom year, 1937, the steel industry—including the tinplate section—charged prices at first up to, and then well above, the 1929 prices. It was able to do this, at some sacrifice of exports, because of the high protection which it enjoyed in the home market and because its agreement with the continental producers, through the Cartel, gave it a practical monopoly in the Dominions and Colonies. Of course, these advantages did not extend to the users of steel, and the high prices were prejudicial to a wide range of British exports. The crude steel producers, however, and also most of the finishers were " sitting pretty," and felt under no obligation to pass on to the consumers the benefits of the considerable improvements made during the 'thirties in the technique of production. They were determined both to recoup themselves thoroughly for the losses of the previous decade, which had been largely their own fault (because of the speculative excesses of the post-war years,) and to build up a strong profit-making structure for the future; and it did not worry them if this were done at the expense of the wide range of steel-users or of other British export trades dependent on steel.

BRITISH STEEL PRICES AFTER 1929
Compared with general movement of Wholesale Prices
(Figures from " The Economist ")

	Steel Rails,* Middlesbro, per ton £	Index, 1929 =100	Tinplates,* S. Wales, per box s. d.	Index, 1929 =100	General Index† of Wholesale Prices 1929=100	Index† of Mineral Prices 1929=100
1929	8.5	100	18 9	100	100	100
1930	8 5	100	15 6	83	84	87
1931	8 5	100	14 6	77	70	77
1932	8.5	100	16 0	85	68	76
1933	8 5	100	16 7½	89	68	81
1934	8 5	100	18 2	97	71	81
1935	8 5	100	18 9	100	74	84
1936	8.5	100	19 9	105	79	89
1937	10 12	119	23 0	123	89	108
1938	10 12	119	21 6	115	78	97
1939	10 15	119	21 6	115	80	100

* End of Year. † Average of Year.

I am not suggesting that all this was simply a "ramp," connived at by the Government for the purpose of restoring the steelmakers' profits. The Government and the I.D.A.C. were no doubt sincerely convinced that it was necessary to put the industry back into a prosperous condition in order to enable it to raise capital for the technical modernisation which it badly needed and to ensure that the country would be well equipped, should need arise, to supply the requirements of war. As believers in private enterprise they naturally saw the restoration of a high level of profits as the only way of bringing about the desired results. And, up to a point, it was brought about. During the 1930's the steel industry, entrenched behind its monopoly and sure of good profits, did undertake quite considerable measures of technical reorganisation. Its output rose from the seven million tons of 1933 and the nine millions of 1934 to thirteen million tons in the boom year, 1937. It then fell back seriously, to only 10½ million tons in 1938; but war preparation and the actual war brought it up again to thirteen million tons in 1939—that is, rather more than it was producing in 1947[1].

The Fall in Exports

The pre-war expansion of output, however, was not accompanied by a corresponding growth of exports. In no major branch of the steel industry did exports in the 'thirties—even in 1937—nearly recover to the level of 1929, which was itself very near the level of 1913. In 1937 total steel exports were only 2,704,000 tons, as against 3,788,000 in 1929 and 3,772,000 in 1913. The steel industry in the 1930's concentrated on the home market, with its expanding output of motor-cars, electrical goods, minor metal ware, and structural steel, and, sheltered behind its tariff and its agreement with the German and other continental producers, made little attempt to push exports outside the empire market, which was reserved to it under the cartel agreement. Even in 1937, British exports of railway material, of girders and beams and joists were well under half those of 1929. Exports of bars and sections were only 72 per cent., of plates and sheets 60 per cent., and of tubes 83 per cent., of the exports of 1929. Total steel exports had fallen by more than one-third in quantity. Even in value, despite high prices, the total had fallen by 27 per cent.

BRITISH STEEL EXPORTS

Thousand Tons of	1913	1929	1930	1931	1932	1933	1934	1935	1936	1937
Bars, Rods, Angles, Shapes and Sections	251	330	231	123	106	130	195	234	206	237
Girders, Beams, Joists and Pillars	122	88	54	25	16	14	25	27	27	34
Plates and Sheets	1,533	1,808	1,281	894	1,019	972	923	996	918	1,076
Tubes, Pipes and Fittings	400	454	347	204	218	273	339	325	301	376
Railway Material	701	441	344	184	88	92	165	162	209	208
Wire and Wire Manufactures	116	130	86	57	60	67	74	87	91	106
Nails and Tacks	55	56	45	27	25	30	34	38	36	46
Other Goods	594	482	409	240	212	213	276	286	304	322
TOTAL	3,772	3,788	2,797	1,754	1,743	1,792	2,031	2,156	2,092	2,407

[1] In the early months of 1948 production rose to a much higher level—to an annual rate of 15 million tons in the first quarter of 1948, but this high output was achieved only by a considerable depletion of stocks of both scrap and pig iron, and it is not easy to believe that it can be sustained. Stocks of scrap fell by more than 50 per cent between February 1947 and February 1948, and stocks of pig iron were reduced over the same period from 534,000 to 352,000 tons.

This loss of exports was, and is, an exceedingly serious matter. The good health of the British economic system depends very greatly on the export of capital goods. The world output of steel, after being reduced by more than half in the world depression, rose from about 120 million tons in 1929 to about 135 millions in 1937, or, leaving out the United States, where the production of 1929 was not recovered until 1940, and also leaving out Great Britain, from under 54 million tons in 1929 to nearly 71 millions in 1937. The British steelmakers lost ground heavily in face of an expanding world demand. They were not, save in a few special lines, trying to expand exports : they were endeavouring to keep their productive capacity down to what they could hope to employ in production for a restricted market—restricted both by monopoly pricing and by agreement with their partners in the Cartel. It may well have been true that such a policy was best in the interests of profit-making and of secure yields. It assuredly was not best from the standpoint of British industrial prosperity as a whole, or of the British balance of payments, which was already unfavourable long before 1939.

Nor was the policy good even from the standpoint of national security. It was doubtless necessary, if the steel industry was to continue to be run for private profit, to get it out of the mess into which it had fallen, financially as well as technically, during the 1920s. In doing this, however, the Government, the Import Duties Advisory Committee, and the Iron and Steel Federation all adopted a policy which led, I agree, to some increase in average technical efficiency as well as to higher profits, but did so in such a way as to limit expansion and to provide a small total capacity in relation to the real needs of either war or peace.

Why the Steel Industry Tends to Restrictive Monopoly

Why was this so ? The industry, as we have seen, went in for a policy of high prices, which necessarily restricted demand. But there was more to it than that. The steel industry, it has always to be borne in mind, is one of the most highly capitalised branches of production. Its plants have to be large—larger and larger with every advance in technique—and their construction and maintenance costs, even apart from obsolescence, are exceedingly high. It takes a very big capital investment to set a single operative to work, and—what is the same thing put differently—the labour force is small in relation to the capital involved. Wages are thus a comparatively small part of the costs of production— a situation just the reverse of that which exists in the coal industry, where wages are the major part of costs. Overheads form a high proportion of total costs ; and as machines and buildings, unlike workers, cannot be discharged when times are bad, the steel industry has, from the standpoint of profit-making, a very strong inducement to keep its capital costs down by avoiding the construction of any plant which it cannot feel fairly sure of being able to put to full and continuous use. That is why there was so much talk between the wars of the need to eliminate " redundant capacity "; and that is why the steel firms, when they were given their head and assured of a protected home market, preferred a programme of limited output for that assured market to any launching out on risky ventures either abroad or at home. If they had tried to compete in world markets instead of entering into a restrictive international agreement through the Cartel, they would have had to take the risks of a fluctuating demand in a number of keenly competitive markets, and would have had to face the possibility of irregular employment for their plants. Even at home, if they had reduced their prices as their costs fell, in the hope of attracting a larger demand, they would very likely have made less profit than they were able to make by keeping prices high and sales relatively small.

These conditions are inherent in the technical economy of the steel industry; and they constitute the principal reasons why it ought to be nationalised. It is a key industry: its pricing policies affect the fortunes of many other industries, including those on which the long-run success of Britain as an exporter chiefly depends. It has a naturally strong tendency towards monopoly: the firms are large and few, and because of the high costs of plant construction the entry of new competitors is extremely difficult, or even, in many branches, impossible without the assent of the firms already in the field. It is an industry in which, because of the technical conditions, it pays the profit-seeking firms best to keep total productive capacity down as near as possible to the *minimum* level of expected demand, and to maintain high prices rather than pass on the benefit of technical economies to the consumers. Finally, because of its few firms and its tendency to monopolistic organisation it can easily enter into restrictive *international* agreements with the steel producers of other countries, and thus reproduce the conditions of scarcity and high prices over a wider field.

Steel and Armaments.

These inherent tendencies, taken together, make up an exceedingly strong case for public ownership. They constitute a case which is thoroughly cogent even apart from the fact that steel, with its related alloys, is the very foundation on which rests in every great country the making of armaments. Many people—and I am one of them—hold that there are overwhelmingly strong social reasons for removing the entire business of armament-making out of the hands of profit-making enterprise, and transferring it to public operation. It has often been pointed out that there is sheer indecency in making profit out of the instruments of death, and more than indecency in hawking them round the world and in maintaining "lobbies" to push their sales in Parliaments and Chancelleries, or in the courts of kings and chieftains, and sheer crime in making agreements with firms to render secret processes, patents, and scarce supplies available to potential enemies up to the very outbreak of war—as happened in British and American dealings with Nazi Germany. Even if there were no economic case for nationalising the steel industry, the moral case would be very strong; but it happens that in this instance morals and economics run together, and preach the same doctrine.

The Fears of Excess Capacity

Of course, the unwillingness of the steel firms to saddle themselves with potentially "redundant capacity," that would eat its head off in interest charges or in loss of profits if plans went wrong, was greatly accentuated in the 1930s by the fear that the great slump would recur, and that Great Britain would not escape its effects. This fear operated most of all to prevent any taking of risks in export markets, which were felt to be more precarious than the home market and as certain to be greatly contracted in a slump. But it acted also against taking risks even in the home market; for the policies of pre-war Governments were very far from offering the assurance that anything would be done to maintain full employment at home. The promises made first by the Churchill-Labour Coalition and later by the present Government to do all that can be done to keep employment high and steady may have done something to lessen these fears, as far as the home market is concerned; but they can, of course, do little to affect fears about export markets unless they can be expanded into worldwide undertakings, with the effective sanction of all the leading Governments behind them—and of this, despite the high-sounding clauses recently written into the World Trade Charter, there is all too little sign.

Steel and the Balance of Payments

Between the wars, the decline of iron and steel exports was sufficiently bad, but did not involve sheer calamity. The total deficit in the British balance of current payments was not big enough to lead

PRINCIPAL BRITISH EXPORTS OF IRON AND STEEL, 1938 & 1947

	Quantities (Thousand Tons)		Values (£ Thousand)	
	1938	1947	1938	1947
Pig Iron	93.9	42.5	565.0	635.7
Ferro-alloys	6.8	10.8	546.4	1,187.5
Ingots, Blooms and Billets	9.7	3.7	151.6	98.2
Iron Bars	3.2	5.7	62.1	181.4
Steel Bars and Rods	231.0	326.8	4,929.9	11,292.3
Angles Shapes and Sections	66.9	90.6	819.7	2,018.1
Castings and Forgings, Rough	1.6	5.2	68.9	376.3
Girders, Joists and Beams	33.5	25.5	407.0	594.7
Hoops and Strips	37.4	40.8	693.3	1,630.0
Plates and Sheets, Plain	209.0	216.1	3,374.8	6,637.3
Galvanised Sheets	146.9	66.3	2,742.8	2,116.9
Tinned Plates, Sheets, etc.	329.4	157.6	8,130.5	7,614.9
Tubes, Pipes and Fittings—Cast	91.9	95.8	1,076.8	2,393.6
,, ,, ,, —Wrought	220.0	253.9	5,277.7	11,954.0
Railway Material	158.2	161.1	2,126.3	4,055.2
Wire	55.2	45.8	1,402.8	2,334.4
Cables and Ropes	16.4	27.0	837.0	2,598.7
Wire Netting	13.1	24.3	472.6	1,614.0
Nails, Screws, Bolts and Rivets	32.4	43.0	1,162.4	3,448.6
Anchors, Grapnels and Chains	12.6	17.7	765.9	1,996.1
Fencing	5.1	6.7	123.2	172.2
Springs	3.9	5.9	211.9	463.3
Barrels, Drums and Churns	2.4	11.9	55.8	869.1
Trunks, Safes, etc.	1.4	2.9	136.5	515.3
Gas Containers	1.2	3.2	78.8	367.4
Bedsteads and Cabinets	4.8	11.8	347.7	1,835.8
Door and Window Frames	5.4	9.0	338.0	1,046.5
Stoves, Grates and Cisterns	9.8	7.9	442.5	1,056.6
Hollow-ware	10.6	64.7	737.9	4,503.5
Other Iron and Steel	204.0	233.1	5,695.9	12,495.6
TOTAL	1,915.9	1,877.1	41,692.0	84,298.1

OTHER BRITISH EXPORTS LARGELY DEPENDENT ON STEEL

	Values (£ Thousand)	
	1938	1947
Cutlery, Hardware and Implements	9,028	35,299
Electrical Goods and Apparatus	13,611	49,425
Machinery	57,868	180,545
Aircraft and Engines	5,408	24,818
Rail Vehicles	7,529	18,173
Motor Cars and Accessories	15,051	74,967
Motor Cycles and Accessories	1,087	5,037
Cycles and Accessories	3,087	13,480
Ships	8,491	18,976
Arms and Munitions	6,269	12,045

to crisis: it could be met by selling off a quite small proportion of British foreign investments, or, more usually, by not reinvesting abroad capital repayments from overseas. Nowadays, the situation is utterly different. Exports have to be increased greatly in order to provide the British people with the sheer means of living, as well as with the raw materials needed to keep them at work. Moreover, it is clear that a high proportion of British exports must consist of capital goods, produced either by the steel industry or by industries which depend directly upon it. Steel and its derivatives must be produced for large-scale export at competitive prices: and the competition is bound to become keen as the United States presses further into the world market, as German industry is allowed to be rebuilt, and as other steel-producing countries recover their efficiency. The steel is needed for world revival and development—there is no doubt about that—but it will have to be produced and sold at keenly competitive prices, and Great Britain's future standard of living depends on this being done. If, as has been officially estimated, total British exports of all kinds of goods will have to be increased to at least 75 per cent above the pre-war amount, exports of steel and of goods made with steel will have to be increased a great deal more.

A privately owned steel industry, working for maximum profit, can never be looked to to undertake this colossal task. The very attempt will necessarily run counter at many points to the quest for maximum profit, and will involve risks which will repel the private investor unless he is given a firm government guarantee of a good return on his capital. But to guarantee such a return would destroy the very incentives on which the case for private enterprise depends: it would be entirely inconsistent with the maintenance of efficient production. Nor would it be at all hopeful for the State to rely on control without ownership as an instrument for compelling the steel firms to follow an expansionist policy: they would, for thoroughly good reasons, be continually kicking against such coercion, which would run directly counter to their profit-making interests; and in such a situation control without ownership would be inevitably a blunt and ineffective weapon. It would show its defects even more plainly than it does to-day, when they are partly offset by the steel firms' desire to appear as " good boys," obediently attentive to national interests, because they hope, by behaving well for the next year or two, to stave off the threat of nationalisation and get back their freedom to do what suits them best from the standpoint of maximum profit. They are far wilier than the colliery owners, who did not even try to appear oncoming or efficient; and there is evidence that quite a few people are being taken in by their apparent zeal in the public interest.

Such a situation cannot last. It is against the very nature of private monopolists not to behave in such a way as to extract the highest returns in their own interests; and it is against the very nature of control without ownership to be effective when the divergences between public and private interest are very large and appear, not at one point, but at literally hundreds, in connection with almost every policy decision that has to be made. There is only one way of securing that the steel industry shall steadily serve the national interest both in its export policy and in its attitude to the home market. That way is to convert it into a public service, and to eliminate the profit motive altogether from its key sections, on which the rest depend.

The Problems of Centralisation

Of course, this solution is not without difficulties of its own. Steel is an immense, very complicated industry, with many branches and many problems; and there is manifest danger of top-heaviness and over-centralisation in placing it all, or even most of it, under a single operating authority. It is far more complex than coal or electricity, and fully as complicated as inland transport. Nationalisation will not work efficiently unless it can be combined with a generous measure of decentralisation. It has, however, to be borne in mind that in the steel industry policy control is already highly centralised, under private ownership, and was so before the war brought in the Ministry of Supply as a central controlling agency on behalf of the nation. The Iron and Steel Federation took over in the 'thirties all the separate " product associations " which existed among the firms which turned out the same type of product, as well as the formulation of policy in respect of the making and pricing of crude steel. The range and complexity of a nationalised steel service will be less than those of the Federation, because it will be possible to leave certain finishing sections of the industry wholly or mainly outside its scope. This point has been discussed in the preceding section and need not be gone over again. It is pertinent in reply to those who suggest that the steel industry is too complicated to be unified under a single authority, even for its main branches. The answer is that it has already been so unified, under private enterprise and in pursuit of private profit. The unification, up to a point, is unavoidable: it arises directly out of the conditions under which the industry works. What is necessary is to reconcile this monopolistic tendency with the public interest, by making it serve the public instead of a body of private shareholders and directors who are bound by the inherent conditions of production to put it to anti-social use.

V

THE METHOD AND THE PROBLEMS

If the arguments so far put forward are convincing, and the State ought to convert the steel industry, within the limits suggested, into a public service, *how* shall the job be tackled ? How can it be done with the least possible undesirable disturbance, and so on to avoid top-heaviness while ensuring that the national interest comes first ?

The Method of Acquisition

About the broad method of nationalisation there can be little doubt. The best course is to take over the existing *firms* just as they are, and to keep them running in every case as they are running now until they can be tackled, one by one or group by group, and the right adaptations and improvements introduced. When I say " as they are " I mean, of course, *minus* their shareholders and present boards of directors though many of the directors may reappear as public servants, where they possess the requisite competence. The existing firms should be acquired just as they stand, their working capital and reserves and their holdings in subsidiary or other business as well as their plant and stock-in-trade. The shareholders should be compensated, in securities of the new public Steel Board, or Corporation, or whatever it is to be called. They should receive fair market value—neither more nor less—based on stock market valuations of their holdings and on the current price-level of government bonds. All this technique of fair compensation has been fully worked out already and applied to mines and railways and electricity undertakings ; and there is every reason in equity for using the same method in dealing with steel.

All that is simple, and the application to steel presents no special problems[1]. Thus, on an " appointed day," the State will become the owner of all iron mines and iron and steel works that fall within the scope of the nationalisation plan and also of certain holdings, large or small, in concerns wholly or partly owned by the acquired firms. Where

[1] An alternative would be to take over the entire *equity* capital only, leaving the non-voting capital in private hands This would involve difficulties in amalgamating businesses subsequently, especially when it was a question of transferring only a part of a business to a new combined unit. I therefore prefer the complete requisition of the firms affected, but the difference is not really fundamental.

the steel firms have shareholdings right outside the steel industry it will be open to the State, or to the authority set up to act on its behalf, either to sell off such holdings in the open market (at once or gradually) or to keep them where it sees any good purpose to be served. It may well wish to keep them in some cases—for example, holdings in armament firms outside the steel industry, or in non-ferrous metal manufacture, or perhaps in key sections of engineering or shipbuilding in which the public has a special interest. But all such decisions will clearly have to be taken on the merits of each particular case, and cannot fruitfully be discussed here. A slightly different situation will arise in respect of shares held by the nationalised firms in steel-finishing firms which fall outside the general scope of the nationalisation plan; but here again each case will have to be considered on its merits, the difference being that in most the branches of production in question will also have been carried on to some extent directly by the nationalised firms, in conjunction with their main business : so that there will be a stronger presumption in favour of retaining their subsidiaries or firms with which they have a close interlocking interest.

Re-grouping and Planning

The main firms—that is, the firms mainly engaged in crude steel-making or in the processes which are commonly carried on in conjunction with it, and also the firms engaged in ore-mining or quarrying or in blast-furnace production of iron for steelmaking—will be taken over, then, as complete units, and will be told to continue production and to carry on with the plans of reorganisation already approved until further notice under instructions from the new authority set up by the State. As far as these firms are concerned, the new authority will take over the functions of the Iron and Steel Federation and its subordinate associations, and also presumably the powers now vested in the " Control " at the Ministry of Supply. There will be no interruption of production : only a change in the constitution of the body from which instructions about policy proceed. In the short run, the separate businesses which are taken over will retain their separate identities— not merely the individual plants, but the complexes of plants hitherto united under a common company ownership. Thereafter, it will of course be possible to undertake such re-grouping as may be necessary or convenient, especially between neighbouring works engaged in complementary processes; but this will have to be done gradually, in each case after careful enquiry into the economies of the proposal and after careful planning of the change-over. Some works will have to be re-built or expanded : some may have to be closed. In many cases the range of products and processes will need to be modified, in order to secure greater specialisation and further scope for mass-production. But, especially in view of the shortage of man-power and other resources for extensive immediate capital projects, even highly desirable changes of this sort are bound to be spread over a considerable time. There can be no very great speedy change in the steel industry's technical structure, though the aim will be to advance as fast as is deemed practicable along this line.

The need for increased over-all capacity is so pressing that, for some time to come, it will be necessary to keep relatively inefficient plants at work, subsidising their output out of the higher yield of those which are more efficient. The aim of course will be to end this situation as soon as possible; but it cannot be ended at once. What will no longer be necessary is the fixing of prices at a level high enough to yield a profit even to the most inefficient plant that it is necessary to maintain in use. Here is another point at which, from the consumers' standpoint, the advantages of public ownership can be plainly seen.

The Shortage of Capacity

The steel industry to-day has not nearly enough productive capacity, even including the less efficient plants, to meet the combined needs of the home and export markets. This is because the industry was conducted before the war on restrictive lines meant to keep capacity down to a low level, and also because this same policy was carried on into the war years. The leaders of the steel industry during the war steadily resisted proposals that they should increase their capacity, in order to meet war demands, beyond the level which they thought would give them the best assurance of maximum profitability after the war. They preferred, especially while the United States was still a neutral, to import American steel to fill up the gap in British supplies; and in formulating their reconstruction policies they stood out against any plans that they felt might threaten " redundancy " in relation to their monopolistic, high-price policies. There was much argument about the target that ought to be set for Great Britain's steel capacity after the war, between a lowest limit of about 15 million tons a year and a highest of about 17 millions. In the event, the industry was permitted to plan for the lowest limit, or for something very near it, after minimum allowance for the writing off of plant that was clearly obsolete. It is bound now to take a long time to rectify this gross mistake—which, of course, from the profit-making standpoint was not a mistake at all, but sound, if uncourageous, economic policy. The new public service will be run on the basis of an essentially different attitude; but the shortage of resources for huge capital projects will inevitably slow down the development of capacity in accordance with the changed objective.

The Steel Firms under Public Ownership

The new authority, then, will take over an inadequately equipped —though not, in some of its sections, a technically inefficient—industry, and will have, for some time, largely to make do with what already exists. This will make it the more desirable to maintain, for the time being, much of the existing business structure. I think, in the first instance, the best course will be to appoint new public boards of directors for all the major businesses that are acquired, and to include among them such of the present directors as are technically or administratively worth their salt, and prepared to play the game. In the case of the coal industry it was practicable to proceed fairly rapidly with new local and regional groupings of pits, because they were all engaged in the common business of getting coal. Steel manufacture is a much more heterogeneous affair, which cannot be simply sorted into areas or regions under common administrative control. Sorting out there will have to be, but it will be a complicated process, and in a good many cases the local basis of unification will not be the best. Regionalisation, over large regions such as South Wales or the North-East Coast, is another matter, and fits in, to a large extent, with the traditions of the steel industry. Local unification over small areas does not, because it cuts too much across the lines of product.

A National Steel Board

The likeliest course, then, seems to be that, at the outset, the nationalisation Act will set up some sort of National Board or Commission, more closely analogous to the Transport Commission, with its subordinate nation-wide executives, than to the National Coal Board. Under this national authority there will be, at first, the new boards of directors of the big firms that will have been taken over and also the new boards of a number of more specialised smaller firms. The new authority will presumably appoint these boards, to act under its instructions, and under the boards will be the separate managements of the individual plants belonging to the particular firms. From this beginning the national authority will proceed gradually to a sorting out, from which will emerge a mainly regional pattern of directing boards, endowed with a considerable, and increasing, amount of regional autonomy. But alongside this regional pattern, centred in the production of pig iron and of crude steel, there will have to be a distinct pattern of administration dealing with the more specialised products ; and it will be one of the chief tasks of the new national authority to devise the right system of relations between the regional and the specialised agencies. This will present difficult problems, because many of the works producing crude steel will be also making specialised products—semi-finished or finished. This, however is the same situation as exists in the Iron and Steel Federation and its interconnected " Product Associations " to-day : it is in no sense a problem peculiar to a nationalised industry.

Labour Relations

Other problems will arise in connection with labour relations. Labour, as in the coal mines, will demand its share in control and influence not only on the new national authority but also in the regions and in the affairs of the individual works ; and this will raise issues, apart from the relatively simple one of the form of collective bargaining, about the respective powers and spheres of regional or specialist administrative bodies and the " labour management " side of the nationalised industry. Such issues are giving much trouble and cause for thought in the coal industry just now ; and they cannot be settled except empirically. The labour function and the function of general administrative organisation are interdependent variables.

On the labour side, the problems are, however, less difficult than in the case of coal, both because the steel industry has a vastly better record of labour relations and because its methods of collective bargaining, within its general agreements, have usually been related closely to the partticular establishments. That its labour relations have been better is partly due to the fact that wages form a much smaller part of the total costs of production ; but it is due also to the smaller degree of isolation and to the greater diversity of crafts and skills and the closer interlocking with other forms of employment. The labour force of the steel industry is small in relation to the magnitude of its operations ; and there has been much less demand for " workers' control " than among the miners— who are, moreover, bound together by the close sense of community which the danger of their calling and the dependence of safety on good comradeship tend to create.

Consultation and Control

As a Guild Socialist, I believe that industry will not work really well until the responsibility for its efficient conduct is fairly shared with the workers by hand and brain, under conditions based on the recognition of every worker as a responsible partner in a democratically organised public service. I do not, however, regard it as practicable to leap straight from capitalism to such a system; nor do I undervalue the importance of trained technical and administrative ability, or the part played by leadership. What has to be worked out experimentally is the best way of reconciling the potentially conflicting claims of industrial democracy and of technical and managerial control, under conditions which will compel managers and technicians alike to pay much more regard than in the past to the human factor, because they will no longer be able to make the same use of the power of the sack. This power will be lessened both by conditions of labour shortage, which make men much less afraid of losing their jobs, and still more by increased solidarity, vested in stronger trade union organisations and in the greater accessibility of nationalised enterprises to public and Parliamentary criticism. It is already coming to be understood that these conditions necessitate much fuller joint consultation at the works and workshop level as well as on a regional or national scale: the question is how far and how quickly the advance can be made from mere consultation to an actual delegation of control, or to a sharing of it, and also how far the trade unions are themselves to become responsible partners in nationalised industry, or had better remain outside in order to serve as free agents for the formulation of the workers' collective grievances and demands. This is not the place for any attempt to do more than barely raise these issues, which are in no way peculiar to the steel industry, although they will arise in it as in any other industry which may be transferred from private to public operation.

The Board and the Minister

I am assuming that, as in the case of other nationalised industries, the administration of steel will be entrusted to a national Board or Commission, appointed by the appropriate Minister and instructed to work under general directions issued by him for the purpose of ensuring compliance with the Government's economic policy. This pattern seems now to be pretty generally accepted, though there are still many critics of its working. One vexed question is whether the Minister shall have complete discretion in making the appointments, subject only to a general provision that he must choose persons of experience in the industry or service or in related industries or services, or in such specialist matters as transport or finance, or in labour matters, or whether there should be some element of representation, at any rate to the extent of making the Minister choose some of the commissioners from lists of nominees submitted to him by the trade unions, or the consumers, or other legitimately interested groups. In France, nationalisation has followed the latter model, and has been based on a sharing of authority among nominees of workers and technicians and consumers and representatives of the general public interest. In this country the other line has been taken, with the advantage of freer choice for the Minister, but with the disadvantage of a diminished feeling of participation and responsibility on the workers' part. On the whole I prefer this method, but only on condition that it is accompanied and followed up by a real attempt to delegate responsibility not only upon regional and local bodies subject to the national authority of the industry but also, in each establishment, on the workers and technicians themselves.

Problems of Administration

There is, however, a related question which forces itself speedily to the front in any organisation as soon as it settles down to business. This concerns the relative powers of the technical experts—the professional "engineers" who are experts in plant construction and design—and the administrators, who are experts in business organisation and are also nearer to the human, as distinct from the mechanical, aspects of efficiency. There are, indeed, three claims to be reconciled —those of engineering, of administration, and of human relations; and any good set-up must rest on a balance between these three forces, subject in all cases to the overriding claims of the public interest as a whole and of the democratic ideal in its industrial application. The main task of the Minister in making his appointments to the national authority is that of achieving a right and harmonious balance in these respects; and the main task of the national authority is to reproduce this balance throughout the entire structure, at the regional, the local, and the works level. What is needed is, of course, not simply a right numerical admixture, but as far as possible a choice of men who have the imagination to understand and to sympathise with claims that belong mainly to fields other than their own—humane technical engineers and administrators, labour experts who appreciate administrative and technical points of view, technicians who are at any rate not allergic to administrative arrangements, administrators who know something of technique. Such men cannot be easy to find in sufficient numbers; and all too little has been done to train the various types of experts to appreciate one another's qualities. There will have to be much skilful shuffling to get the right men into the right places; and it will be vitally important for the nationalised industry to tackle the problem of training, at all levels, from this point of view.

Research and Development

A further problem to be faced—and one of particular importance in the case of steel—is that of research. Clearly a nationalised steel industry will need both to develop its own research organisation and to work in very closely with the metallurgical and allied departments of Universities and Technical Colleges and Institutes. It will need also to maintain very close relations with the research units connected with the steel-using industries and services, with the various bodies researching into fuels and their utilisation, and with the research sections of the branches of the steel industry itself that are left in private hands. It will have to collaborate closely with the National Physical Laboratory and with the Standards Institute; and it will need to work out the right arrangements for relating laboratory research to "development" research, as an intermediate stage between discovery and large-scale commercial application. In all these fields it will need to bear in mind both the danger of unduly commercialising scientific research and the point that research workers need a large amount of liberty if they are to give of their best. Not only "fundamental" scientific research, but also much applied research, needs independence if it is to be done well. A nationalised steel industry will be in an excellent position to allow such independence, and to afford to let its research agencies range freely, paying for work that leads to nothing in a commercial sense out of the rich yields of successful projects; but it will be necessary to plan deliberately for this independence, which will by no means always be pleasing to the technical and administrative personnel whose traditions and routines it will frequently upset. At the same time the opposite danger will have to be guarded against—I mean that of so isolating the researchers from the practitioners that research fails to make the required impact on everyday practice. The working technicians and managers must be kept in close touch with the research agencies; there must be continual coming and going between the laboratories and experimental stations and the works.

Costs and Prices under Public Ownership

These, I think, are the main practical problems which will arise immediately in connection with the transfer of the main sections of the steel industry from private to public operation. I am assuming that, broadly speaking, the nationalised industry will run on such a footing as to be required to cover its costs, including research costs, out of its earnings, except when the Government instructs it, in the national interest, to do something that is plainly uneconomic—in which case the cost should clearly be met by the Exchequer and not by the industry out of higher prices charged to the consumers of steel. I am assuming that the industry will be given power, subject to the sanction of the responsible Minister and of the Treasury, to raise fresh capital for development by the issue of bonds, either with or without a government guarantee of principal or interest, or of both. I assume that any international agreements or arrangements into which it may wish to enter will be subject to government approval, and that it will not be allowed to participate in any restrictive system designed to hold up prices at home or abroad. I assume that the regulation of imports competitive with home products will remain in the hands of the Government, even if the new authority is used for some purposes as the Government's agent for the distribution of imported supplies.

Export Policy

This brings me to the question of exports. At present there exists an Export Corporation under the control of the Iron and Steel Federation. This will presumably be taken over, as far as it handles the products of the firms which will pass under public operation. The next point is whether the State should take over the entire export business, including that of the sections of the industry which are to be left in private hands. On this issue I have to some extent an open mind. I am inclined to say "Yes, where the bulk of a product will in future be produced in publicly owned establishments," but "No, where the bulk will be produced privately and the share of the nationalised industry in it will be small or non-existent." It should not be difficult to find a reasonable solution of this problem: another possible way would be to leave the Export Corporation in existence as representing both the nationalised and the non-nationalised units.

VI

THE CASE CONCLUDED

When the steel industry passes under public ownership, an epoch will be at an end; for much more than an industry will be changing hands. It is not too much to say that the great age of Capitalism began with the discovery of cheap steel, or that the age of Economic Imperialism came swiftly in its wake. The earlier Capitalism of the ndustrial Revolution, built mainly on the production of cheap textile goods, was on the whole pacific in outlook. It wanted to sell its piece-goods and its clothing all over the world, and it felt no claim to interfere with the buyers or to disturb their social and political institutions further than was necessary to open the market to its wares. The Capitalism of the Age of Steel was a very different affair: it wanted not only markets but also sources of supply of scarce metals for its factories, and the very goods it set out to sell had to be marketed on essentially different terms. Trade was no longer just a matter of exchanging a length of cotton piece-goods for some native product: it involved selling very expensive things, such as railway plant and machinery, for which the inhabitants of the less wealthy countries could by no means afford to pay on the nail with their own products. In fact it involved *investment* by the capitalists of the wealthier countries in the less developed areas; and the investment could be made to pay only when it had been effective in opening up new regions to economic exploitation. New food producing areas were tapped, and sometimes occupied by white settlers, who either cultivated the land themselves or employed cheap native labour. New sources of minerals were developed, with native labour working in the mines at very low wages under white supervision. It was no accident that during the last quarter of the nineteenth century nearly all the African Continent was partitioned among the European Powers, while in Asia the British, Dutch and French Empires were continuously extended and Japan, imitating the Capitalism of the West, began to dream of an Empire spread over all Southern Asia up to India and to contend with Russia for the mastery of Northern Asia.

Steel and Economic Imperialism

All these developments rested largely upon steel, because steel underlay not only the building of railways and ships and factories equipped with steam and later with electrical power, but also the armed force on which rested the growing domination of the advanced countries over the less advanced. The world's steelmakers thus filled a double role: they played, in conjunction with the great heavy engineering concerns, the leading part in the worldwide process of capitalist exploitation, and in doing so they were themselves transformed from mere industrialists into merchants, financiers and politicians. They marketed their own products all over the world, directly or through subsidiaries; they became integrated into huge combines stretching back to their raw materials and forward to a vast variety of finished products; they linked up with bankers and company promoters and became much more financially than industrially minded; they set out to influence Governments to back and sometimes to guarantee their huge projects, and invoked the aid of their own Governments to protect, even by annexation, their investments in the less developed countries. They had also, inevitably, an interest in persuading Governments and peoples of the need for more and more armaments; and success in this field was much the easier because, the more arms one country bought, the more other countries felt they had to buy. The competitive race in armaments was wholly to the advantage of the steelmakers of the world, above all if the arms could be piled higher and higher without actually leading to worldwide war. Such war had its dangers for the steel-makers, as for everyone else—dangers of default, of revolution, or of causing the nations to bethink themselves of removing so dangerous an industry out of private hands. But this risk was not so great as to deter the steelmakers and their allies in the armament trade from doing all they could to push the sale of weapons in times of peace.

The "Steel International"

There was a paradox in the whole attitude of these people. On the one hand they worked in closely with their own Governments in each separate country, and became great powers behind the thrones. On the other, their economic interests and the conditions of their industries impelled them to link up internationally, both sharing and exchanging patents and secret processes across national frontiers and restricting competition in the world market by cartel arrangements and other agreements designed to keep prices and profits high. At the same time as they urged more and better weapons of war upon their own Governments they were selling the means of making similar weapons to the potential enemies against whom they were urging their Governments to re-arm.

All this happened not because of any particular wickedness among the steel- and armament-makers (though some pretty wicked individuals were attracted into the arms trade as the most congenial to their minds), but because it was of the very nature of the steel industry and of the industries grouped round it that these policies should be pursued, wherever the motive of private profit was allowed to prevail. Monopoly paid handsome dividends: arms-pushing was a highly remunerative business: risks could be reduced by bribing or cajoling Ministers or politicians or kings or tribal chiefs to favour the interests of the great firms and their investing associates.

Steel and the British People

An industry which possesses these inherent tendencies wherever it is allowed to remain in private hands is much too dangerous to the world's peace, as well as much too well able to entrench itself in a monopolistic position against the public, to be let alone. There is admittedly no guarantee that nationalisation will cure the evils, for in the hands of a predatory, imperialistic Government it might even accentuate the war danger, and such Governments, putting " guns " before " butter," can also exploit the people. Nothing, however, can be more certain than that the British people and the British Government are no war-mongers and are sincerely set on keeping the peace. This is true, henceforward, not only of a Labour Government, but of *any* British Government one can imagine being returned to power by the popular vote. It is so for the conclusive reason that everyone in Great Britain who is not a lunatic knows that another great war would mean final and irretrievable disaster for the British people. We can, then, from this point of view safely entrust the steel industry to the State, with the assurance that the State will not run it deliberately as an instrument of aggressive war. That leaves us free to consider the purely economic aspect of the matter. I think I have shown not only that, but also why, the steel industry has an inherent tendency to organise itself into a monopoly and to follow a policy of high prices and deliberate exploitation of the consumers for the enhancement of its profits. There is, however, an additional reason which I have not so far explicitly mentioned, though it has been implied. The extreme expensiveness of the industry's capital equipment involves that it has at any time a huge capital sum locked up in plant of widely varying age and efficiency. This plant represents a high proportion of its total capital, on which it is seeking to earn a profit. Accordingly, the steel industry has a strong interest in not scrapping more plant than it must until it is physically worn out, even if it has become obsolete, because of technical progress, long before. Under conditions of competition, each firm would be forced to scrap plant that was below the efficiency of its competitors, at home or abroad, and it would pay progressive firms to put in the best possible equipment in order to get a lead over the rest. It pays, however, still better to abandon, or rigidly to limit, competition ; for under monopoly the obsolescent plant can be kept in use, and prices can be maintained at a level high enough to make its use profitable. A monopolistic steel industry run for profit has inevitably an interest in slowing down the pace of technical improvement in order to conserve for as long as possible the value of its existing capital assets. This drives it to seek both protection against foreign competition in its home market and agreements with its foreign competitors to limit competition in the world market as a whole.

Steel Policy under Public Ownership

Of course, even if the steel industry were nationalised, the high cost of scrapping existing equipment would still be a factor to be taken into account. But under public ownership the choice between scrapping and keeping in use would be taken *in the national interest* and not in that of a limited group of shareholders and financiers. As matters stand in Great Britain to-day, it is indispensable to raise the steel industry to the highest possible level of efficiency and to get rid of all restrictive practices, even at the cost of lower profits, because Great Britain both needs extensive capital re-equipment, which depends on steel, and must raise exports to the highest possible level in order to procure the means of life. The raising of exports, as we have seen, also depends on steel; for the types of British goods for which there is the best long-run chance of an expanding market are finished steel products and the engineering and other goods made largely out of them. Therefore, in the interests both of the export trade and of speeding up the re-equipment of British industries, the nationalisation of steel is an immediate and urgent necessity.

The Problem of Quality and Location

Under nationalisation, as indeed under any system of operation, it will be indispensable to go out for high quality, as well as for high quantity, in production. A good many of the familiar comparisons between the efficiency of the British, American, German, and other steel industries in terms of production per man-hour are misleading because they do not take account of the factor of quality. It takes much less labour, and much less fuel, to produce a ton of " basic Bessemer " steel, from iron of a given quality, than it does to produce a ton of " open-hearth " steel, acid or basic, — to say nothing of the finer steel-alloys or of the " high-speed " steels, which cost still more to produce. It is meaningless to average costs, or labour used, over the total production of each of a number of countries and then to compare the results. Such comparisons are valid only when they are made for products of comparable quality. If, however, it is vitally important to maintain the high quality of British steel where it is to be put to uses for which high quality is required, it is also important not to inflate prices by using high-quality steel where cheaper steel will give a satisfactory result. Great Britain used up to 1932, to import much of its low-grade steel in a crude state and finish it here, the home-produced steel going mainly into the uses where relatively high quality was required. Then the cheap Belgian and German steels were cut out, and the British steel industry set to work to adapt itself to a higher degree of self-sufficiency. This involved establishing a new balance between different types of steel production for home use, and re-planning the location of the industry in order to take the fullest practicable advantage of continuous processes based on the use of relatively low-grade domestic supplies of iron ore. Those were the days in which the great new works at Corby and at Ebbw Vale were designed, to the accompaniment of heated controversy inside the industry. The new Corby works of Stewarts and Lloyds, built directly on the Northamptonshire ore-fields, were undoubtedly a great advance; but the new strip mill of Richard Thomas and Company at Ebbw Vale was from the first a much more doubtful economic venture, because it involved transport of the ore by land over a long distance from the Northamptonshire workings, and because the high cost of transport might more than offset the economy of continuous production. It is fortunately not necessary to go back upon the tangled story of the Ebbw Vale works and its difficulties, or upon the factors which led to the abandonment of the project for a large new steelworks at Jarrow. The information which alone could make it possible to tell these stories without distortion is not available; and I do not profess to be in a position to disentangle the truth from the confused accounts that have been made public. All I know is that the published record of the industry in the 1930's gives a clear impression of the jostling of rival interests and of the fears of those already in possession of new developments that might threaten their command of the market, rather than of any coherent attempt to replan the industry on a basis of high production at the lowest level of costs consistent with good working conditions for those whom it employs. The 1930's showed that the industry, left under private ownership, could not be trusted, even in conjunction with the Import Duties Advisory Committee, to work out adequate development plans or to prefer expansion to scarcity where expansion involved treading on the corns of vested interest. The monopolists were not in a position to prevent the introduction of new methods—indeed they had to do something to apply them themselves—but in general they were able to get control of the new processes and to make sure that competition did not so react on prices as to render the less up-to-date works unprofitable.

The Coming Battle

Steel, then, has to be nationalised. But we must expect a stiff fight before nationalisation becomes an accomplished fact. So far, the Government's socialising measures have had a remarkably easy passage. As we have seen, in the case of coal-mining the opposition was merely perfunctory, because everyone knew that public ownership was the only possible solution. Electricity nationalisation was no more than the completion of a process already well begun between the wars. The gas industry did not seem to mind at all : indeed, some of its leading units played an active part in the transfer. The railways put up a bit of a fight, but got no public support, and not even much from the Opposition in Parliament. Some of the road transport operators fought harder; but there was no real parliamentary battle even there. Steel, however, will be defended by the believers in private Capitalism, as well as by the steel interests themselves, to the bitter end; and every possible pressure will be put on the Government to delay action long enough to prevent nationalisation from going through before the next General Election. The Tories will fight hard in the Commons : the Lords will pretty certainly throw out the Bill, and will continue to do so till it can be passed over their heads.

So everyone who believes that the steel industry ought to be made a public service must stand ready to play his part in the struggle that lies ahead. We must expect the newspapers to be filled with praise of the industry's achievements, and *we must expect the industry itself to behave as well as it possibly can for the time being in the hope of convincing the public that there is no case for taking it over.* We must expect the output figures to be as good as they can be in face of coal shortage and the inadequacy of the industry's capacity to meet the full needs. In fact, we must *not* expect to be furnished with any fresh arguments for nationalisation arising out of the industry's *current* behaviour. The purpose of this booklet is to prevent the public from being misled by this evidence of death-bed repentance. If the industry can avert nationalisation now, it will not be long before it is back at its old games at the nation's expense.

EXPORTS DEPEND ON STEEL

The figures show the values of British Exports in 1947

DIRECT EXPORTS OF IRON AND STEEL

£84 million

Plates & Sheets including tinplates	16
Ingots & Semis	14½
Tubes & Pipes	14
Wire, Nails, Bolts & Rivets	8½
Hollow Ware	4½
Railway Materials	4
Pig Iron & Ferro Alloys	2
Other Iron & Steel	20½
	£84 m.

MACHINERY EXPORTS

£180 million

Textile Machinery	24½
Electrical Machinery	21
Machine Tools	15
Boiler Plant	11
Agricultural Machinery	9
Internal Combustion Engines	8½
Cranes	6
Pumps	5
Other Machinery	80
	£180 m.

OTHER EXPORTS DEPENDENT ON STEEL

£252 million

Motor Vehicles & Accessories	80
Electrical Goods	49½
Cutlery, Hardware & Implements	35
Aircraft & Engines	25
Ships	19
Rail Vehicles	18
Cycles & Accessories	13½
Arms & Munitions	12
	£252 m.

Fabian Society

BRITISH LABOUR MOVEMENT
—Retrospect and Prospect

G. D. H. COLE

Ralph Fox Memorial Lecture, April 1951
Fabian Special No. 8
Ninepence

Ralph Fox Memorial Committee

BRITISH LABOUR MOVEMENT
—Retrospect and Prospect

G. D. H. COLE

Ralph Fox Memorial Lecture, April 1951

Fabian Special No. 8

PREFATORY NOTE

THIS PAMPHLET is a reprint of a lecture which I gave at Halifax in April, 1951, at the request of the Ralph Fox Memorial Committee. It was the first of a series of annual lectures, to be given in memory of a citizen of Halifax, well known to the Socialist movement and as a writer, who died fighting for his faith in the Spanish Civil War.

Ralph Fox was born in Halifax on March 30, 1900. From his twentieth year he was actively associated with the Labour Movement and the Communist Party. He was best known as an historian for his biography of *Gengis Khan*, as a literary critic for his association with *Left Review*, the *Daily Review* and *New Writing*, to which papers he contributed articles, political journalism and short stories. On the outbreak of the Spanish Civil War he volunteered for the International Brigade and served as political officer to the British Battalion. He was killed in action before Cordoba on June 2, 1937. It seemed to me fitting to honour his memory by surveying, over the period covered by my own knowledge, the changing phases of Labour development, and trying to see what tendencies are at work in the movement to-day. After the lecture, it was suggested that a printed version might serve as a basis for discussion groups in some of the considerable number of Labour Party, Trade Union, and other organisations represented in the audience. I readily agreed, and the Fabian Society is publishing my lecture with this purpose, as well as its own members, in view. Those interested or needing copies of this pamphlet can apply either to the Fabian Society or to the Ralph Fox Memorial Committee's Secretary, Mrs F Edwards, 20, West View Drive, Halifax, Yorkshire.

G D H C

May, 1951

G D H Cole is a member of the Fabian Society Executive Committee and was until recently its Chairman He is Chichele Professor of Social and Political Theory at Oxford

NOTE —This pamphlet, like all publications of the Fabian Society, represents not the collective view of the Society but only the view of the individual who prepared it The responsibility of the Society is limited to approving the publications which it issues as worthy of consideration within the Labour Movement.

June, 1951.

THE BRITISH LABOUR MOVEMENT —RETROSPECT AND PROSPECT

Ralph Fox Memorial Lecture. Halifax, April 1951

By Professor G. D. H. COLE

MY OWN recollections of the British Labour movement go back over forty-five years I became a Socialist as a schoolboy a year or so before the General Election of 1906, which first put the Labour Party firmly on the parliamentary map Till then it was only the Labour Representation Committee, with no more M P s than could be counted on the fingers of one hand In 1906 it rose suddenly to a party of thirty members—still a mere handful besides the 400 Liberals and not much more than a third as many as the Irish Nationalists Nevertheless, Labour became a party, and from 1906 there was no longer any doubt that it was destined to become a major force in British parliamentary affairs—though it was then impossible to foresee the speedy break-up of the Liberal Party, which seemed at the very height of its powers, or the great accession to the strength of the Labour movement during the First World War

Why I became a Socialist

My conversion to Socialism had very little to do with parliamentary politics, which were at the time of it mainly occupied with the struggle over Free Trade and Tariff Reform, with the issues of Irish Home Rule and Women's Suffrage ranking next in current estimation, and that of Trade Union rights, challenged by the Taff Vale Judgment, a poor fourth, outside a few industrial areas I was converted, quite simply, by reading William Morris's *News from Nowhere,* which made me feel, suddenly and irrevocably, that there was nothing except a Socialist that it was possible for me to be. I did not at once join any Socialist body I was only sixteen, and had the best part of three years more school in front of me before going up to Oxford, which was already my planned destination I do not remember even taking a great deal of interest in the General Election of 1906 until it was over—when I shared in the common excitement and wonder about what would happen next. My Socialism, at that stage, had very little to do with parliamentary politics, my instinctive aversion from which has never left me—and never will. Converted by reading Morris's utopia, I became an Utopian Socialist, and I suppose that is what I have been all my life since. I became a Socialist, as many others did in those days, on grounds of morals and decency and æsthetic sensibility. I wanted to do the decent thing by my fellow-men: I could not see why every human being should not have as good a chance in life as I, and I hated the ugliness both of poverty and of the money-grubbing way of life that I saw around me as its complement. I still think these are three excellent grounds for being a Socialist: indeed, I know no others as good. They have nothing to do with any particular economic theory, or theory of history: they are not based on any worship of efficiency, or of the superior virtue or the historic mission of the working class. They have nothing to do with Marxism, or Fabianism, or even Labourism—though all these have no doubt a good deal to do with them. They are simple affirmations about the root principles of comely and decent human relations, leading irresistibly to a Socialist conclusion. If I were talking to-day to persons who had grown up in the same mental climate as I did, I should hardly need to add that before long my favourite weekly reading was the *New Age*. I was, of course, an 'intellectual' of the middle class: had I been a worker it would probably have been the *Clarion*, to which I took a little later, after overcoming an initial distaste for its jollity and its liking for getting people to go about in droves. Judged by any standard, the *Clarion* was well past its prime when I first met with it, but it was still a considerable force in the industrial centres.

I did not join up with any Socialist body until 1908. Then, shortly before leaving school, I discovered a small branch of the Independent Labour Party in my home town, and joined it, but found it rather depressing. A few months later, I celebrated my first week in Oxford by joining the University Fabian Society and its parent body in London, and my second week by starting, with one friend I had made a few days before, a new paper, called *The Oxford Socialist*. I remember waylaying R. H. Tawney in the quadrangle at Balliol and getting him to write me an article. That was our first meeting: he was then the leading figure in the small band of University Tutorial Class Tutors connected with the Workers' Educational Association.

Socialist Prospects Forty Years Ago

As I look back and try to discover what were my expectations in those days about the future of Socialism and of the Labour movement, I find it difficult to be sure what I felt or expected. I think I felt sure that Socialism was the cause of the future, and that some day there would be a Socialist society from which poverty would have been banished—and therewith the unpleasant necessity of worrying one's head about economic or social problems, as against the many more attractive things one wanted to do instead I was then reading and writing poetry at a great rate, and much more interested in literature than in economics, of which I knew nothing I did not want to be a politician, or to concern myself with such matters as economics except in the hope of pushing them away by getting their problems solved on Socialist lines Socialism presented itself to me, not as an economic or political doctrine, but as a complete alternative way of living—as I still regard it In this guise, it offered itself as something which seemed at one moment very near, and at another a long way off When it seemed very near, I was feeling revolutionary, and dreaming of a day when, how I hardly knew, the masses would rise up and overthrow capitalism and create on the morrow a complete Socialist society But at other moments capitalism looked to me very well entrenched, and I envisaged a long process of Socialist education and propaganda culminating in its destruction at some distant date in the future I do not think I ever, though I became a Fabian, contemplated a gradual evolution into Socialism by a cumulative process of social reforms My notion of the advent of Socialism was always catastrophic, whether it should come late or soon I was never in the very least a 'Lib-Lab', and the last thought that could have entered my head would have been to look hopefully on the Labour Party as the heir to the Liberal tradition

Indeed, in those days I had no love for the Labour Party, though as a member of the I L P as well as of the Fabian Society I belonged to it The Labour Party of the years between 1906 and 1914 was much too 'Lib-Lab' for me I was well aware that nearly all the Labour victors of 1906 owed their seats in Parliament to Liberal support, and that not a few of them were ex-Liberals who at the behest of their trade unions had changed their party but not their opinions Year by year after 1906, and even more after the elections of 1910, which left the Liberal Government more dependent on Labour support, I could not help seeing more and more plainly the ties in which the Labour Party was held by its support of the Government, the bargaining with the Liberals over seats and electoral alliances, and the wide gap between the Labour right wing and the left A left, may I remind you, that was becoming stronger and more vocal as the cost of living rose, and as the claims of the workers were postponed to the exigencies of party politics or side-tracked—as I saw it—by Lloyd George's Bismarckian social insurance measures—denounced by Hilaire Belloc as leading to the 'Servile State.'

British Socialism before 1914

Two things impress me above all others as I look back on the feelings of those years One is the insularity not only of my own outlook, but of that of most of my contemporaries—if 'insularity' is the right word The other is the sense of squeezability of the capitalist orange By our 'insularity' I mean, not that we were unaware of foreign countries or of a community between our problems and theirs, or that we ignored ideas from abroad, but that, despite our awareness and our openness to other peoples' ideas, we thought of ourselves as fighting the battle for Socialism as a national battle, side by side with similar battles that were being fought elsewhere, and had no notion of our particular struggle being altered in its nature or seriously deflected by the course of international affairs We were simply not considering world war as a factor, or social revolution as a world event We were, in effect, most of the time assuming that capitalism would continue, developing but not essentially changing, until we were ready to supersede it, and that it could afford, out of its surplus earnings, to make large concessions to working-class claims without losing its potency to 'deliver the goods' We were very far from the mood in which Marx and Engels had confidently expected a rapid intensification of the 'contradictions' of capitalism, to be manifested in recurrent and increasingly severe crises, each of which might prove to be the last—the death-throe of capitalist exploitation, the birth-pang of Socialism We expected capitalism to last our time, unless we roused the workers to overthrow it, and this, I feel sure as I look back, gave us confidence to preach left-wing doctrines, because we were not afraid that labour revolt might paralyse or slow down capitalist production without putting any alternative system in its place

Syndicalism and the Labour Unrest

I am of course speaking now, not of the Labour leaders of my youth, but of my contemporaries of the Socialist left and of their analogues in the trade unions The political conditions which confined the Labour Party of the years before 1914 to playing a secondary rôle as the ally of Liberalism helped to breed in the young a spirit of antagonism to the compromises of politics and to prepare a welcome for the industrialist theories of working-class action which were influencing many workers in France and in the United States The great 'Labour Unrest' of the years immediately before the First World War was not in any sense a product of French Syndicalist or of American Industrial Unionist theory These became influential in Great Britain as a *result* of the unrest and as attempts to give it a clear meaning they were rationalisations rather than causes The causes were rather the freeing of trade unionism from the chains of the Taff Vale Judgment by the Trade

Disputes Act of 1906 and the rising prices which parliamentary action seemed able to do nothing about, *plus* a sense of power which the advent of the Labour Party had first stimulated and then flouted. The rise of the militant suffrage movement also had a little to do with it, and it is undeniable that there was in the air a feeling of impatience of old restraints which affected not only Bergsonian philosophers but also the man in the street. The victory of 1906 had seemed at the time to promise so much: within a very few years it seemed to contemporaries to have achieved so little—infinitely less than, looking back on it now, we can see that it had actually brought to birth.

The wave of 'Labour Unrest,' with militant Syndicalist and Industrial Unionist ideas carried on its crest, struck Great Britain in the middle of my university career. It struck me, and my student contemporaries. We watched the strikes of 1910, 1911, and 1912 with fascinated attention, attracted above all in them by anything that involved an assertion of the worker's claim to equality of human rights with his 'betters'. Strikes against tyrannical employers or foremen, strikes for the right to a share in determining industrial policy, strikes for the right of workmen to do as they pleased in their hours of freedom from labour, strikes for trade union 'recognition,' sympathetic strikes in which workers asserted their right to refuse to handle 'tainted goods'—all these possessed a human appeal which seemed to us, in comparison with the familiar processes of collective bargaining about wages and hours, to involve an assertion of higher status—a revolt against the 'undemocracy' of capitalist enterprise and of the bureaucratic State.

Guild Socialism

Yet most of us were very moderate revolutionaries after all—trade unionists and young intellectuals alike. Most of us did not swallow whole the Syndicalist gospel of 'Direct Action,' or throw overboard the parliamentary method of advance towards social equality, or even accept in full the Marxist doctrine that the State was to be regarded as simply an instrument of the capitalist class, and would have to be overthrown and replaced by a new proletarian State made in the imagine of the governing class of the coming revolutionary era. We tried to construct a theory of Socialism that would embody and reconcile what was good in the conflicting theories of Fabians and Syndicalists, of the Labour Party—as far as it then had a theory—and of the Industrial Workers of the World. For the group with which I was associated, this attempt was embodied in Guild Socialism, which for a time, though sponsored mainly by a small body of Socialist intellectuals, exerted a widespread influence on the trade union leaders—especially on those younger leaders who were in search of a halfway house between old-style trade unionism, with its limited objectives, and the full-blooded revolutionism of Tom Mann and the Industrial Unionists

I am not suggesting that Guild Socialism ever bit deeply into the consciousness of the Labour movement I think it was too intellectual a creed ever to do that, and too little capable of being simplified down to such emotive slogans as gave Marxism, despite its intellectual complexity, its mass-appeal But an idea closely associated with Guild Socialism, with Syndicalism, and with Industrial Unionism did get across to large numbers of the younger workers This was the idea of the 'control of industry'—of 'workers' control' This idea, however, in its Syndicalist and Industrial Unionist forms, came sharply up against the traditional Socialist advocacy of nationalisation, as it had been preached by the stalwarts of both the Independent Labour Party and the Social Democratic Federation It was therefore unacceptable to most Socialists, whereas Guild Socialism, which retained the demand for national ownership of the means of production, while advocating that the administration should be entrusted to 'Guilds' representing all the workers 'by hand and brain' organised on an industrial basis, enabled Socialists to take over the libertarian drive behind the Syndicalist movement without breaking with Socialism as they had understood it in the past Even the Webbs, in their *Constitution for the Socialist Commonwealth of Great Britain*, went some way towards compromise with the Guild idea, and most of the younger working-class Socialists of the I L P went a good deal further, though most of the older leaders did not Philip Snowden, in particular, fought Guild Socialism and 'workers' control' as forms of anarchy quite as implacably as he had fought Lloyd George's Insurance Act as an attempt to introduce the 'slave State' The old collectivist Socialism, he kept saying, was good enough for him Ramsay MacDonald, too, disliked the new ideas, but characteristically temporised, and tried to capture the slogans of the Guild Socialists without changing his meaning

The battle of ideas continued to be fought out during the First World War. The many and quick changes in the factories called for by war needs—the dilution of labour, the suspension of cherished craft union practices, the questions about who should be called up for the armed forces and who left in the workshops—gave a strong impetus to the demand for 'workers' control' But, as the war dragged on, the emphasis shifted more and more from matters of workshop organisation to matters of the 'call-up', and anti-war feeling grew stronger when all who were willing to go to the forces had gone and it came to be a question of prising more and more reluctant workers out of their jobs Moreover, the workers became more and more uncertain what the war was about, and more inclined to call for a negotiated peace as against the entire victory required by Lloyd George and his government colleagues, who by that time included the leaders of the parliamentary Labour Party

The Russian Revolution

Into this cauldron of conflict was thrown the Russian Revolution of 1917 I think nearly all of us recognised this as the earth-shattering event it was, but we held differing views about its nature, and these differences grew steadily wider after the Bolshevik seizure of power As long as the war lasted, the growing numbers who wanted peace rather than absolute victory were held together, support for the Stockholm Conference which the Russians tried to convene acting for some time as a bond of union But even during the war the Russian Revolution caused the shop stewards' movement to take a more militant turn, which foreshadowed the coming of the Communist Party There was a growing cleavage between those who regarded 'workers' control' as a form of industrial self-government, to serve as the complement to parliamentary democracy, and those for whom 'workers' control' meant the social revolution and the dictatorship of the proletariat The one group insisted on the internal democratisation of each industry, through the strengthening of the trade unions and the development of 'encroaching control' by means of an extension of collective workshop bargaining: the other insisted that the workers could win no real control until they had made themselves masters of the State, and that the true democratic control was control by the whole working class, organised as the masters of a new revolutionary State I am of course here over-simplifying, for there were many intermediate attitudes, and most active Socialists did not formulate the issues clearly in their own minds But the shop stewards' movement did break up into revolutionary and 'constitutional' factions, and then went to pieces as soon as the wartime scarcity of man-power disappeared, and the Guild Socialists were riven into three fractions, one of which was speedily in full cry against the authoritarian tendencies of Bolshevism, while a second was in process of going over to the Communist side, leaving a centre, to which I belonged, supporting the Russian Revolution but standing out strongly against any attempt to apply its 'democratic centralism' or its method of dictatorship to the half-democracies of the West

The New Labour Party of 1918

This struggle was only beginning when Arthur Henderson, driven out of the War Cabinet because of his support of the Stockholm Conference, set about reorganising the Labour Party on a wider basis as a claimant to political power It needs to be remembered that up to 1918 the Labour Party had never had any pretensions to be so regarded. It had contested only a small number of seats, mostly in alliance with the Liberals, and it owed a high proportion of its election successes to the existence of two-member constituencies in which the Liberals could be persuaded to concede it one of the seats in return for a common front against the Conservatives But after 1916 the Liberal Party was rent into two, and Henderson saw the chance of making the Labour Party the heir to its historic position Where there had been only a few constituency Labour Parties and a scatter of small I L P branches, he set about the huge task of organising a party machine capable of fighting nearly every seat at the first post-war election, and in order to achieve this he converted what had been a loose federation of trade unions and small Socialist societies into a nation-wide party aiming at mass individual membership The I L P leaders, who had been from 1914 an anti-war opposition within the Labour Party—an opposition which Henderson resisted all attempts to drive outside its ranks—did not at all like the new plan, because it threatened to deprive the I L P of its key position of influence as the chief propagandist agency and policy-maker for the party as a whole But, weakened by their differences with the trade union leaders over the war, they were in no position to resist, and MacDonald, their foremost leader, was already preparing to shift his main allegiance from the I L P to the Labour Party as soon as the war was over Henderson, aided by Sidney Webb, was able to carry his plans through the Party Conference with only a scattered opposition from a few I L P ers on the left and a few trade union leaders, who wanted a purely working-class party without the intellectuals, on the right The reorganised Labour Party was heavily defeated by the Lloyd George Coalition in the election of 1918, but the new machine had been made, and its chance was soon to come

The Acceptance of Gradualism

Looking back, it is easy to see—much easier than it was at the time—the immense significance of the Labour Party reorganisation of 1918 In terms of declared policy, there was a sharp move to the left Up to 1918, the Labour Party had never formally adopted a Socialist creed it had been an exponent of immediate working-class demands and of a vague social idealism which trade union divisions forbade it to formulate into a Socialist definition of its aims Webb and Henderson and MacDonald, in drafting and getting accepted the new declaration of policy embodied in *Labour and the New Social Order*, committed it to Socialism, but also committed it equally to seek Socialism exclusively by constitutional and gradualist means At the same time, by enlarging the basis of membership and making a general appeal to men and women of goodwill to join, they replaced the I L P as the principal local organising and propagandist agency of the movement by a network of local Labour Parties concerned much more with electioneering than with preaching Socialism, and therefore disposed to keep off militant tactics that were liable to estrange the marginal electors

The effect was not that the Labour Party became less Socialist than it had previously been: that could hardly have happened It was that it became more completely committed to a middle way This indeed was involved in the whole conception of making it the heir of Liberalism and aiming at the speedy attainment of office An outright Socialist Party could not, in 1918 or for long afterwards—could not, indeed, to-day—hope to be more than a minority group in Parliament There were neither enough Socialists nor good enough prospects of making them to wrest the position of His Majesty's Opposition from the Liberals without making Socialism appear to be a moderate creed, which could win the support of citizens who were by no means ready to welcome a revolutionary transformation of their way of life The main body of the British people did not want revolution the most it could be hopefully asked to vote for was social reform, with a dash of Socialism by way of seasoning But the seasoning had to be just hot enough to keep the main body of believing Socialists willing to remain in the Party, and to campaign for it, rather than desert it and join up with the small revolutionary wing, which was beginning to take on a Communist shape

The Non-Communist Left

Between the constitutional Social Democracy of the new Labour Party and the militant Communism of the new extreme left, the middle groups, to which the Guild Socialists mostly belonged, could find no place to stand, when once the post-war slump had set in, and the militant movement in the workshops had been destroyed by the advent of large-scale unemployment They became a permanent minority, invoking vainly the spirits of the pioneers—of Keir Hardie, of Blatchford, and of William Morris—while the leaders of the party, with the support of most of the rank and file, got on with the 'real business' of winning parliamentary power It was obviously impracticable—as the I L P discovered after 1931—to establish a new party of the left in opposition to both the Labour Party and the Communists, and attempts to work inside the Labour Party could be effective only on condition that they did not endanger its electoral success There was always in the local Labour Parties a considerable amount of left-wing sentiment, which was able to find expression at particular moments, but never to establish any lasting ascendency After the depression of the early 1920's this sentiment at first expressed itself chiefly in industrial action Disappointment with the minority Labour Government of 1924 combined with anger at the policies of its Conservative successor to provoke the movement which culminated in the General Strike of 1926 During this period *Lansbury's*

Labour Weekly became the principal organ of non-Communist left-wing sentiment, but the collapse of the General Strike and the defeat of the miners brought the phase of industrial militancy to an abrupt end and shifted trade union policy sharply to the right

Mond-Turnerism and MacDonaldism

Then followed the Mond-Turner negotiations for industrial peace and the second minority Labour Government under MacDonald, which lasted from 1929 to 1931 There is no need for me to re-tell the calamitous story of those years The second Labour Government doubtless had bad luck in being faced by the earlier phases of the great world slump, but this cannot excuse either its sheer failure to cope with the growing problem of unemployment or its evident lack of understanding of the forces with which it had to contend It was made all too clear that MacDonald had abandoned his Socialist beliefs, that Philip Snowden was an orthodox capitalist financier and Free Trader much more than a Socialist, and that most of the Cabinet were merely bewildered by the crisis and had no notion of the right ways of meeting it The one excuse that can be made for MacDonald is that he became exasperated at the futility of his Cabinet, but it is a poor excuse, for he was quite as futile as the rest

The Labour Party after 1931

The defection of MacDonald, Snowden and J H Thomas, and the crushing defeat which the Labour Party sustained in 1931, had a momentary effect of strengthening the Labour left and causing the Party Conference to adopt a stronger Socialist programme But even in 1932 it was apparent that the leadership was nervous about the new line The test issue that year was the proposal to include in the party programme nationalisation not only of the Bank of England but also of the joint stock banks This was carried, against the platform and against Ernest Bevin's strong opposition, but it soon became plain that the party leadership did not intend to act on the decision They were willing to include in the short-term programme considerable measures of nationalisation of industry and the taking over of the Bank of England, but taking over the joint stock banks they regarded as bad electioneering, because it would offend the middle classes, and they managed to persuade themselves that the conditions necessary for Socialist planning could be secured without it Moreover, in the nationalisation plans that were worked out by a series of committees after 1931 the model adopted was that of the Public Corporation, taken over from the Conservatives who had used it for the Central Electricity Board as well as for the BBC, and on the question of 'workers' control,' which was advocated by some of the trade unions but opposed by others, the Labour Party leaders showed themselves strongly hostile. Their plans of nationalisation were substantial and challenging to some great capitalist interests, especially in the cases of coal and steel, but they were plans which could be carried out without interfering seriously with the main structure of capitalist ownership and control.

As against this, the Labour Party of the 1930's stood for a great development of the social services and of redistributive taxation of incomes—but not of property. Except for a prolonged hesitation over family allowances, about which the trade unions were sharply divided, the Party came to stand for a far-reaching programme of social welfare, as well as for a substantial amount of public ownership (with full compensation) and a not very clearly defined measure of national economic planning. In its proposals for dealing with unemployment it was deeply influenced by Keynes: indeed, it came to put almost entire faith in the Keynesian mechanisms for maintaining full employment under capitalism. Apart from its advocacy of nationalisation, it was coming to be more and more plainly the inheritor of the traditions of progressive Liberalism, and less and less tolerant of the more aggressive Socialists who remained within its ranks.

Foreign Policy in the 1930's

While these policies were being worked out in relation to home affairs, the international situation was becoming continually more menacing as the belligerent intentions of the Nazis grew more and more evident. But the Labour Party found great difficulty in adapting its foreign policy to the new conditions. It had been in the 1920's the party of peace and disarmament and of fair treatment of Germany, and it was not easy for it to change its line in face of Nazi aggression. George Lansbury, its best-loved leader, was a pacifist, and, even when the danger from Germany had become plain, many Socialists hesitated to support rearmament under Conservative rule, fearing that the strength thus acquired would be used in the wrong way. Even after the Party had declared for rearmament and Lansbury had resigned from the leadership, fear of world war kept the Party from advocating effective help to the Spanish Government in the Civil War and induced it to take its stand by the policy of 'non-intervention.'

This hesitancy was responsible for the revival of left-wing activity in the years before Munich. There were movements, in which some Liberals and even a few Tories joined, for a 'Popular Front' or an 'United Front' against Fascism, in the hope of rallying sufficient support to turn out the Government. But the Labour Party leadership set its face firmly against all such movements, partly because it was suspicious of Liberal help, but mainly because it would have nothing to do with the Communists, who threw their entire energy into the anti-Fascist campaign and contrived to get a great deal of its organisation into their hands

By this time, the feelings of the Labour Party leaders towards the Communists had become much too embittered for any sort of collaboration to be accepted This is hardly to be wondered at, in view of the continual vilification to which they had been subjected and of the struggle that had been going on in the trade unions ever since the turn towards industrial pacifism that had followed the defeat of the General Strike The trade union leaders regarded the Communists as intolerable trouble-makers at home, and much of the friendly feeling towards the Soviet Union had evaporated in face of the increasing totalitarianism of the Stalinist régime. In Great Britain the Communist Party was small but active, and it saw in the condition of international affairs in the middle 1930's its chance to establish a leadership of the left against the existing leaderships of the Labour Party and the trade unions The non-Communist left thus found itself in a very difficult position If it joined hands with the Communists in the anti-Fascist crusade, it ran the risk of being driven out of the Labour Party and of becoming their captive But if it refused to act with the Communists against Fascism, it was powerless to bring any effective pressure to bear on the official Labour leadership This was the dilemma that led Sir Stafford Cripps and Aneurin Bevan into courses which resulted in their expulsion from the Labour Party and the dissolution of the left-wing, non-Communist movement they had set up

The Second World War

The Second World War, and the Nazi-Soviet Pact which heralded it, reunited the Party, and for the time threw the Communists into deep discredit and unpopularity But the Nazi invasion of the Soviet Union presently rehabilitated them, and enabled them to play a leading part in the workshop movements for high production Their influence in the trade unions increased, and remains considerable in some unions even now, but there was no parallel movement in the political sphere The Labour Party remained as determinedly hostile to the Communists as ever, and a good deal of the non-Communist left returned to it, while others found a temporary outlet during the suspension of parliamentary contests under the Churchill Coalition in Sir Richard Acland's Common Wealth movement As soon as the Coalition broke up, most of these latter joined the Labour Party, and the election of 1945 was fought by a reunited movement which had temporarily buried its dissensions The programme on which the Labour Party fought the election, though vague about international affairs, was in other respects strong enough to satisfy the left the victory sent a wave of enthusiasm through the movement During the five years that followed, the programme was carried into effect with remarkable completeness and fidelity. Yet, even by 1950, a great deal of the enthusiasm had died away. We must ask why.

1945 and After

Part of the answer is obvious enough. The enthusiasts of 1945 had not taken account of Great Britain's changed economic position in the post-war world, so as to expect a continuance of shortages and a stop on wage-movements in face of mounting profits and conditions of full employment. Nor had the workers in the industries due for nationalisation realised how little difference the establishment of Public Corporations would make to their actual status and conditions of work. Nationalisation had been a dream: the reality brought disillusion. Nor, again, had the main body of active Labour workers visualised in advance a state of affairs under a majority Labour Government at all like that which they found to exist. There had been vague anticipations of a changed way of life and of a putting down of the mighty from their seats. But, after five years, the upper and middle classes remained, grumbling but unsubdued, and the class structure still seemed to be much as before. Perhaps good Socialists ought not to have been disappointed at this, but they were. Perhaps they ought not to have felt uneasy when so many of the key positions in the new Corporations and in other branches of public life were given to anti-Socialists, and when Labour Honours Lists—except for a sprinkling of trade union and co-operative ennoblements—looked very like those of previous Governments. Perhaps they ought to have been satisfied with the great advance made in the social services, with the practical disappearance of destitution and really grinding poverty, and with the undoubted improvement in social security and in the standards of living of a large part of the people, and ought not to have expected a long-established and well-entrenched class system to be greatly altered overnight. The fact remains that the limitations of what had been achieved were evident, whereas the improvements were no sooner made than they came to be taken almost for granted. It is always easy to absorb an addition to real income, and gratitude for past favours is seldom a powerful political sentiment.

World Affairs since 1945

A second factor making for disillusionment among Socialists has been the steady worsening of the international situation, both from a specifically Socialist and from a more general point of view. In 1945 I think most British Socialists expected democratic Socialism to emerge as the dominant force over most of Europe— in France and Italy, in Belgium and Holland, in Czechoslovakia, and in Germany, as well as in Scandinavia. They felt that the

British Labour Government, especially in Germany, could have done much more than it actually did to forward the Socialist cause and to strengthen the Socialists' hold on society: it seemed that, in the name of democracy, the Government was following a neutral policy which in practice played into its opponents' hands. They felt that little attempt was being made to establish a common front of European Socialism against the capitalist parties, or even to prevent a revival of Fascist tendencies. They were encouraged by the statesmanlike handling of the problems of India and Burma and by a forward policy in most of the Colonies, but they could not make out what Mr Bevin was playing at in Palestine and the Middle East, and they were acutely disturbed by what was going on in Greece. I think most of them also disliked the increasing subserviance of Great Britain to America, but did not see how to avoid it. They were not prepared as a body to face the serious deprivations that would have resulted from a withdrawal of American help, even before that help had got tangled up with the cold war between the Soviet Union and the West.

Disquietude about international affairs became much deeper and more pervasive as, step by step, Great Britain became more deeply committed to an alliance under American leadership against the Soviet Union, and as, on the American side, the alliance turned more and more into an anti-Communist crusade in which Western values came to be identified with those of capitalist (called 'free') enterprise and Socialism came to be confused with Communism in an indiscriminate warfare against the left all over the world. I cannot by any means exempt the Soviet leaders from a share in the blame for this unhappy state of affairs. Their fears of American 'imperialism' and ideological belief in the inevitability of a world conflict between capitalism and Communism, with the non-Communist Socialists counted as part of the capitalist *bloc* and denounced as the betrayers of the revolution, destroyed the possibilities of pan-European economic co-operation, and their liquidation of the non-Communist democratic régimes in Czechoslovakia and Poland, together with their destruction of Social Democracy in Eastern Germany, helped to force West European Socialists to the acceptance of the American alliance as the only course left open. But I think most of us felt that a more Socialist foreign policy in 1945 could have prevented the disastrous series of developments which began in 1947 and reached their height in the Korean crisis and the threat of war against China in 1950-51.

Gradualism at Home and Abroad

Indeed, it was all too evident throughout the period after 1945 that British Socialism had no international policy of its own and was in no way minded to put itself at the head of an international

Socialist movement distinct both from Communism and from American conceptions of the 'free world' order I am sure this disastrous lack of an international policy was not due merely to Mr Bevin's presence at the Foreign Office or to Mr Attlee's dislike of the left to which he once belonged Its roots went much deeper: it was an outcome of the tendency to model foreign policy on the conditions prevalent at home In home affairs, the Labour Party stood entirely committed to gradualist constitutionalism it was the declared enemy of all revolutionary notions What its leaders could not see was that, even if this was the correct policy under British or Scandinavian conditions, its transference to other parts of the world might rest on a fundamental misunderstanding of the facts What was the use of telling peoples who had no experience of parliamentary democracy and had come through the searing experience of social war between the classes that they must do everything by strictly constitutional and parliamentary methods? Where the first necessity was to overthrow a still feudal aristocracy and to build up swiftly a new political régime to replace a ruling class tainted by collaboration with the Nazis, what was the sense in urging that the first need was to have free elections and that the displacement of the landlords and capitalists should be deferred until it could be done in due order under the auspices of a democratically chosen Parliament? Such precepts made nonsense, and were an invitation to the defeats which they have helped to bring about But Labour leaders who knew little about international affairs and had been accustomed to thinking politically in terms of purely national problems could not see an inch beyond their British noses, and it is not altogether surprising that the acutely suspicious leaders of the Soviet Union mistook their parochialism for subservience to capitalist and imperialist designs

Whether there is now any way back from the mistakes made in international policy since 1945 I do not profess to know Certainly there is no present possibility of establishing that democratic Socialist 'Third Force' which could, I feel sure, have become predominant in Western Europe if the task had been rightly tackled in the first instance Had that been done, such a Third Force, joining hands with India and Indonesia and Burma, could have prevented the division of the world into two hostile *bloes,* the one under Russian Communist and the other under American capitalist domination The danger of world war, which now overshadows everything, would have been much less, and democratic Socialism would have been, not third man out, but a great world influence in its own right This chance has been cast away, I repeat, not because Ernest Bevin was a bad Foreign Secretary, but because almost the entire leadership of British Labour has shown itself incapable of putting itself in the place of peoples who have not grown up in the British parliamentary tradition.

The Future: at Home and Abroad

What then of the future? It is none too promising, even if we concentrate our attention for the moment wholly on home affairs For the time being, the Labour Party has done most of what it can afford to do towards the establishment of the 'Welfare State'—fully as much as it can afford if we are to be burdened for years to come with an immense expenditure on armaments out of resources which are scanty enough without such claims upon them As for nationalisation, the gilt is off the gingerbread, and, apart from that, the election programme of 1950 made it clear that the Labour Party did not know what it wanted to nationalise next and was quite unprepared with any further ambitious plans for the supersession of capitalist enterprise What is left with which to appeal to the electorate, or even to its own stalwarts, if neither social services nor nationalisation can play the major part? Very little, except 'Down with the Tories,' and that will serve only when the Tories have had a spell of power, and have given the poor something fresh to hate them for

On the international plane, the prospects are even worse—yet they could be more hopeful if the Government would take a firmer stand against American and Communist hysteria and would, even now, constitute itself, with India and the majority of the peoples of Western Europe, the champion of peace There is no doubt at all that most of its supporters want peace, and would like to see their Government mediating between intransigent Americans and intransigent Russians, rather than lined up on one side of a divided world in company with Syngman Rhee and Chiang Kai-shek and General Franco and all the reactionaries from pole to pole I say this, not out of any love for Communism, or any will to see Great Britain lined up on the other side I say it as a democratic Socialist, wishing to save the world from domination by either capitalism or Communism, and, above all, from war But I almost despair of our Government, at the eleventh hour, giving such a lead

The Pioneers and Ourselves

These are not comfortable words I have, alas, no comfortable words to give you I cannot even offer you the usual consolation prize of a peroration about the spirit of Keir Hardie and Robert Blatchford and William Morris For these pioneers of the modern Labour movement were products of a situation which it is impossible to recall They were moved to strong indignation by the sight, everywhere they looked around them, of unmerited and unnecessary human suffering, among men and women and children whom they recognised as like unto themselves and as members of the same social family They were men who had grown up in a social atmosphere that was at one and the same time moral and hard, and they inherited its moral tendency while they revolted against its hardness Growing up in the great days of British capitalist expansion, they saw lying ready the wealth that could be used to relieve distress, and they hated the system which in the name of individual self-reliance denied this use of it They became Socialists because they regarded capitalism and human suffering as inseparable partners, and saw no way save Socialism of making an end of both

But to-day, though poverty is still widespread, the sheer misery the pioneers saw around them has been either done away with or tidied away out of sight There is very much less in the sights and contacts of everyday life to stir the sentiments of compassion and moral indignation, and misery afar off, which we do not see with our own eyes, has a great deal less power to move us than misery that directly affronts our senses Nor are most of us as sure about our morals as the Socialists were sixty or seventy years ago Two World Wars and the threat of more have dulled our sensibilities to other people's troubles, and have made the road to Utopia look much rougher and stonier than it used to look We trust our feelings less, and have much less confidence that everything will be brought to rights if we only do our duty by our fellow-men. The political realist and the logical positivist are abroad, to reinforce Communist jibes at Socialist sentimentalism After all, we can say, most people are not so badly off nowadays: the great threat to human happiness is no longer capitalism, but war and the totalitarian spirit which it encourages Can we not afford to relax our efforts for Socialism, having already achieved so many reforms? Is it even worth while to try really hard, when at any time a few atom bombs may sweep away all the fruits of our labours—not to mention ourselves?

What We Need Now

I find this attitude fully understandable among those for whom politics and social affairs have never been more than a minor interest I find it partly understandable even among the more convinced Socialists, in face of the deep disappointments of the past few years It is not, however, my attitude, or I hope yours What I do recognise is that the British Labour movement has, over the past six years, exhausted the impetus that has driven it on since the 1880's and stands in need of a new interpretation of the Socialist gospel There is a great deal still to be done in developing the social services—education above all—as means of advance towards the classless society, but, even were the economic circumstances less restrictive, the gospel of human compassion could no longer have the same compelling power as it did There is an immense task still ahead in devising new forms of social ownership and control to replace capitalist enterprise, but few hearts will be lifted up by the prospect of more nationalisation on the model of the existing schemes There is a keen desire for a world organised on a basis of friendly co-operation among the peoples to lift the poorer countries out of their primitive poverty, but how can we enlist that desire on the side of Socialism while we are showing ourselves the friends of reaction and the foes of revolution in countries which need revolution, even if we do not?

I do not know how far Ralph Fox would have agreed with what I have said in this lecture, had he been alive to-day I do know that he was a fighter for the ideals and values which I have been trying to put before you, and that he died faithful to them. I pay tribute to his memory

WEAKNESS
THE ECONOMICS
THROUGH
OF RE-ARMAMENT
STRENGTH
BY G·D·H·COLE

ONE SHILLING

A UNION OF DEMOCRATIC CONTROL PUBLICATION

What is the UDC?

THE Union of Democratic Control is a non-party organisation, backed by voluntary subscriptions, which seeks to provide the facts upon which enlightened foreign policy may be formed Founded in 1914 by E D Morel and other outstanding champions of the democratic control of foreign policy, the U.D.C has campaigned without fear or favour on many great issues which have stirred this country and the world During the 'twenties the U.D C stood for full support of the League of Nations and for international disarmament Early in the 'thirties, in a series of remarkable pamphlets which achieved great influence at the time, the U D.C. exposed the international arms racket Later it opposed the betrayal of Abyssinia to Mussolini, supported the cause of the Spanish Republic, and warned of the dangers of Munich and appeasement. During the war it used its unique contacts in Europe to publish almost the first information that became available about the growth of resistance to Hitler in the occupied countries There is perhaps no other organisation in this country which has better or more numerous contacts with the new men and movements of Asia Further information about the work of the U.D C may be obtained from the General Secretary, the Union of Democratic Control, 32 Victoria Street, London, S W.1 (ABBey 3770).

EXECUTIVE COMMITTEE
Chairman F ELWYN JONES, M P.

LEONARD BARNES	LESLIE HALE, M P
PRESTON BENSON	MAURICE LICHTIG
FENNER BROCKWAY, M P	CATHERINE MARSHALL
RITCHIE CALDER	GUY ROUTH
HAROLD DAVIES, M P	REGINALD SORENSEN, M P
BARBARA DRAKE	DOROTHY WOODMAN
TOM DRIBERG, M P	EDGAR YOUNG (CDR R N RETD)

Hon Treasurer BEN PARKIN
General Secretary BASIL DAVIDSON
Organising Secretary AUDREY JUPP

THE ECONOMICS OF RE-ARMAMENT
by G. D. H. COLE

One thing the plain man and his wife would like to know about re-armament is how it is likely to re-act on their standard of living. They have been warned that it will involve sacrifices; but they have been given little idea how big the sacrifices are likely to be, or on whom they will mainly fall These questions are admittedly very difficult to answer in any exact way, for the answers depend on so many factors—some of them entirely outside British control. Indeed, the heaviest part of the burden of re-armament for the British people may well be, not the amount that the British Government spends on it, but the effect of other countries', and especially of America's, spending on the prices of the things we import, not only for making armaments but for meeting our ordinary civilian needs.

How much Priority for Arms-Making?

THUS, EVEN IF Mr Aneurin Bevan is right in maintaining that it is a sheer physical impossibility for Great Britain to carry out the Government's proposed re-armament programme for 1951–2, it does not follow that failure to spend the projected sums on armaments, on account of shortage of the required raw materials, will do much to ease the burden on the common man It may indeed make matters worse if it leads to unemployment at home, while the prices of British imports continue to soar because of the general inflation of world demand Of course, if the supply of raw materials that can be made available for our industries, even at very high prices, falls badly short of our needs and if, in such a situation, a very high priority is given to armament-making, the effect will be to reduce supplies of goods to the consumers still further, and to lower standards of living for the employed as well as for the unemployed and the under-employed.

It is not clear how nearly absolute a priority has in fact been accorded to armaments over civilian requirements Mr George Strauss, in a speech explaining his own attitude after the resignations of Mr Bevan and Mr Harold Wilson, asserted that the arms programme remained conditional on the obtaining of enough materials to meet civilian claims, whereas speeches by Mr Herbert Morrison and others have suggested that the priority allowed to re-armament is to be, if not absolute, at any rate very high Whatever the precise intention may be in this matter, the fact remains that the actual and prospective forcing up of prices in Great Britain is a consequence mainly, not of British, but of world re-armament

The Effects of American Stock-piling

AS A GREAT importing country, heavily dependent on imported materials as well as on imported food, Great Britain is already suffering severely from the shortages and from the tremendous rise in world prices that have resulted mainly from American re-armament and stock-piling of essential materials The prices of our imports have risen much faster than the prices of the goods we export, and this tendency is likely to continue unless measures are taken on a world scale not only to allocate supplies of scarce materials, but also to control their prices and to stimulate additional production

Such measures cannot be taken without the consent and full participation of the United States, which would need, in order to make them effective, not only to slow down its own buying from abroad but also to release for foreign use American materials for which there is an unsatisfied domestic demand It will take a great deal to persuade the Americans to act in this way, which will be represented as undermining their own re-armament programme, already proceeding at a furious pace, and it would be most unwise for us to reckon on enough being done to prevent world prices from continuing to rise sharply, and shortages from getting very much worse, as long as world re-armament goes on *

Exports and the "Terms of Trade"

EVEN IF BRITISH export prices, stimulated by the upward movement of material prices, were to rise sharply enough to narrow the gap, or, in more technical language, to bring about some improvement in the "terms of trade", this would not solve our problem, because our re-armament measures will mean holding back from export, and using for our own military purposes, precisely those goods for which we are in the best position to raise our prices in the world market Even if the prices of such goods were to go up, we should have many fewer of them to sell

In practice, the prices of our exports are most unlikely to rise as fast as the prices of our imports, because we shall be trying to fill the gap caused by the withdrawal of the goods other countries want most by selling more of

---

In a few cases, where speculation has driven prices up even beyond the levels corresponding to increased American demand, there may be price recessions, even while the prices of most materials continue to rise This has occurred already (May, 1951) in the case of wool

things they want less urgently, *e g*, textiles. Moreover, in the world market for textiles and other exports which we shall be trying to push instead of goods now needed at home we are faced with rapidly growing competition from Japan and from Germany—countries whose absence from the world market helped us greatly in building up our export trade after 1945 Japan is already selling abroad more cotton goods than we are, and is in a position to supply even more, and at prices with which we shall find it hard to compete

The Adverse Balance

WE MUST THEN expect the "terms of trade"—that is, import prices as compared with export prices—to continue to move against us, unless the Americans show much more readiness than seems at all probable both to join with us and other countries in regulating supplies and prices, and to slow down their own re-armament in order to ease the burdens of other countries Already, on the figures for the first quarter of 1951, our adverse balance of trade had risen again to nearly £235 millions as against an average of £87 millions in 1950, and much less than that in the latter part of 1950

But for re-armament we should now be more than paying our way in terms of visible trade† As things are, we are already dissipating the balances we had begun to accumulate last year out of the earnings of our "invisible exports"—shipping and financial services and returns on overseas investments A small part of this deterioration in our overseas position may be due to our own buying of stocks of goods of which prices are rising and supply difficulties growing greater. But this can hardly account for much, because there have not been large supplies available for us to buy, and we are already faced with a sharp fall in our supplies of a number of vital materials—above all, of sulphur.

The Consequences of the Cold War

I AM STRESSING the adverse effects of *world* re-armament on our national economy because I want above all else to make it clear that this is capable of being a much bigger factor in depressing our standard of living than any re-armament we undertake ourselves Even if we did not propose to spend an additional penny on our own defence services we should still feel severely the adverse effects of re-armament by other countries, and above all by the United States, which, with their immense purchasing power and command of gold, are in a position to control the world market and to force up prices against other buyers to a practically unlimited extent.

(†) *I am speaking now of Great Britain's own balance of payments, and not of that of the whole sterling area A very large proportion of the increase in gold and dollar holdings in Great Britain during the past year has been due to the large sales of highly priced materials made to the dollar area by Commonwealth countries and colonial areas, which have in consequence increased their holdings of sterling These sums, though lodged in Great Britain, belong to the countries which have earned them, and not to us The improvement in gold and dollar assets gives an entirely misleading picture of Great Britain's international economic position*

If we want to avoid having our standards of living forced down we must somehow *stop the cold war as a whole* and not merely contract out of the part we are at present committed to taking in it. We must work for an improvement in world relations, for an agreement to restrict armaments all over the world, and for a *modus vivendi* between the Communist and the non-Communist sectors of the world: without this we shall be bound to suffer a fall in our standards of living, even if we were to give up re-arming ourselves.

Mr. Gaitskell's Assumptions and Trade Union Reactions

EVEN IF THAT is likely to be the most disastrous factor, the burden imposed by our own re-armament is of course a very serious addition to it. Mr Gaitskell's comparatively mild Budget has led some people to believe that the economic consequences of re-armament will be less onerous than was feared. This is, for several reasons, a thorough misunderstanding of the facts. The Budget was "mild", in appearance, (*a*) because the Chancellor refused to increase subsidies to offset part of the rising cost of living, (*b*) because he limited to the barest minimum his concessions to old age pensioners and other groups most adversely affected, and (*c*) not least, because he assumed that the workers would allow their wages to lag behind rising prices, and would thus accept a fall in their living standards without using their economic power to resist it. If he had not made this assumption he would have needed to budget for a much bigger surplus—that is, to raise a considerably larger amount by taxation—in order to reduce inflationary pressure.

Personally, I do not think the Trade Unions are likely to allow real wages to fall seriously without putting up a good deal of a struggle ; and I expect the inflationary pressure to become considerably greater than the Chancellor has allowed for. This, however, does not mean that the workers will be able to avert a fall in their living standards: it means that the more they succeed in raising money wages, the less their money will buy. They might be able to transfer a small part of the burden from their own shoulders to pensioners and others, rich or poor, who live on fixed incomes. But the fall in consumption will have to be felt *somewhere*, for the simple reason that, in face of the demands of re-armament on some industries and of the need to export more consumers' goods to replace the goods we need to keep at home for use in re-armament, there will be fewer consumers' goods and services to be shared out among all sections of the population. Even if the richer people reduce their consumption to a certain extent—and it is very doubtful if most of them will—the main impact is bound to fall on the largest body of consumers, the working classes.

Re-armament Costs in Future Years

SECONDLY, THE BUDGET was "mild" because only a small part of the total cost of our national re-armament programme is expected to fall into the current financial year. We have promised the Americans that we will spend £4,700 millions on defence services over a period of three years. We cannot, however, spend anything like a third of this amount in the first year, because it takes a considerable time to shift factories over from making goods for the home civilian market or for export to armament-making The Budget estimate for this year is £1,300 millions—and that is unlikely to be reached except as a consequence of a further sharp rise in costs If costs do rise sharply, we may spend as much this year as Mr Gaitskell has budgeted for, *but the higher cost will leave us with much less than one-third of our estimated programme actually carried out*

Moreover, in view of rising costs, the total sum we shall need to spend in order to carry out our three years' programme *in real terms* is certain to be much more than £4,700 millions—even apart from the fact that the original estimate made no provision for the higher running costs involved in the maintenance of the increased force under arms The bill for defence services is bound, unless the not-so-cold war ceases, to be a great deal higher in 1952–3 and in 1953–4 than it can be in 1951–2, and to involve a much bigger disturbance of industrial production and a much greater re-distribution of man-power at the expense of civilian supplies

We are now spending about 10 per cent of our gross national product on armaments, as against less than 7 per cent a year ago Two years hence we may easily be spending 15 or even 20 per cent, but no one is in a position to make an exact estimate, since both the cost of armaments and the total volume of production are uncertain factors

The Shortage of Materials and its Effects

How HEAVY THE burden will actually be, and how it will affect our standards of living, obviously depends on what happens to productivity in Great Britain as well as on the relative movements of import and export prices We have been quite remarkably successful during the past few years in increasing both our total production and the productivity of each worker's effort, in spite of the fact that we have been short of capital for investment and have had to keep a large quantity of obsolescent plant and buildings in use This success has been partly due to full employment, which has eliminated a great deal of waste of time that used to occur during working hours in waiting for work when orders were slack It has been partly due to greater effort, as in the case of the steelworkers, whose acceptance of a continuous working week alone made possible the big increase in the output of steel *

One effect of re-armament will be to make it much harder to maintain the increasing rate of productivity that has so greatly eased our economic difficulties The shortage of key materials is already resulting in short-time working, and in waste of working time, in a number of important industries, and this adverse factor will become very much more widely operative unless we are able to secure some better allocation of materials that are in short world supply—sulphur, non-ferrous metals, cotton, and a number more The rayon industry is already threatened with a disastrous fall in output because of the sulphur shortage, which also affects many other industries, as well as agriculture Motor-car firms are already working short-time because

---

* *An achievement now likely to be brought to an end by the world shortage of scrap*

there is not enough steel the steel industry is menaced by shortage not only of scrap steel but also of high-grade iron ore The cotton industry needs more raw cotton than the Americans are ready to spare—and so on, through a wide range of materials and of industries affected by the inadequacy of available supplies

The estimates given in the official *Economic Survey* for 1951 assumed an increase of production in that year of only 4 per cent, as compared with 9 per cent in 1950—a figure which required only that the actual level of output achieved during the final quarter of 1950 should be maintained But even this estimate may be very difficult to make into reality if there is a serious shortage of essential materials nor should it be overlooked that there is bound to be a loss of output while factories are re-tooling for the change-over from civilian work to arms manufacture. At the very best, it is clear that increased productivity cannot be expected to provide for the increased output of munitions of war, and of machinery for making them, without a substantial fall in other supplies Moreover, a considerable proportion of these other supplies will have to be diverted to export in order to buy materials at inflated world prices

Wages and Profits

It is sometimes argued that the workers' standard of living can be maintained, despite higher expenditure on armaments, by raising money wages at the expense of profits But this is not really possible under existing conditions to more than a very limited extent Profits have been running at an exceedingly high level, and it is true enough that many industries—though by no means all—could easily afford to pay higher money wages But, if they did, the increase in money wages would of itself do nothing to add to supplies of consumers' goods—that is, unless the increase were given as a return for a correspondingly greater output—which would mean that more materials would be required It would result mainly in higher prices Or, if prices were held down by government control, there would be a chase after scarce goods and a diversion into buying more of whatever could be supplied at least real cost in productive resources—that is to say, highly taxed goods and services of which the major part of the price goes straight back to the Government Even of such goods, for example beer and tobacco, it would not be easy to increase the supply.

Alternatively, if prices were kept down, the workers would have money to spare which they could save, but not spend, because there would be nothing to buy with it Such saving would have to be made compulsory, or it would be impossible to prevent the growth of black markets in defiance of the price controls But in practice, in face of rapidly rising costs for materials, transport, and other services which enter into the costs of production of most finished goods, the Government cannot keep prices down except by higher subsidies, which would require still higher taxes and would thus raise the whole problem over again

Even apart from the administrative difficulty of controlling the prices of an immense variety of finished goods, the notion that prices can be held down by cutting into capitalist profit margins is not so feasible as it sounds Profits are high and getting higher, not only because of full employment, but also largely because in most industries there is a very wide gap between the costs of the most efficient firms and those of the least efficient which it is necessary to keep in business if we are to maintain a high aggregate output of essential goods These less efficient firms cannot at present be either driven out of business and replaced, or compelled to improve their efficiency, because it is not possible to spare resources for building better factories and installing improved plant on more than a small scale indeed, this will be possible now only on a reduced scale in most branches of production because of the diversion of capital to the re-equipment of the arms industries As long as high-cost firms have to be kept in production and allowed to cover their costs, as they must be under capitalist conditions, prices have to be allowed to stand at a level which yields very big profits to the more efficient firms, for otherwise the inefficient firms would not be able to carry on Higher wages in these circumstances could not be taken out of profits without reducing total output by forcing the inefficient factories to close down.

What Happens to Profits

THERE IS, APART from this, a further reason why profits cannot be used on any considerable scale to supplement working-class purchasing power The major part of the high profits now being made is not passed over as spendable income to the owners of business concerns The State takes a large share of it in taxation, both directly on business profits and on the incomes of the owners, and a large part of the rest is not distributed as dividends but is retained in the businesses as reserves, and is used for investment in new plant and buildings If either of these elements in the profits total were transferred to the workers *for spending on consumers' goods and services* there would be a fall in the sums available for investment in new capital equipment, and production would soon suffer, unless the State took back an equivalent sum in taxes, and used it for investment—in which case it would *not* be available for spending on consumers' goods

It is necessary to maintain a high level of investment in order to improve industrial efficiency, and even to prevent it from falling off, and it would do the workers no good to increase their current spending if the effect were to reduce productivity and thus lead to a fall in the total supplies of goods and services in the near future

Who Gets the Distributed Profits?

THERE REMAINS THE part of profits that is paid out in dividends and interest to the owners of capital, and, after the State has taken toll of it through income tax and surtax, is available for consumption or investment No doubt some part of this income could be diverted from richer to poorer spenders if direct taxes on incomes were increased still further, but it has to be remembered that by no means all recipients of incomes derived from profits are wealthy people They include retired persons living on their savings, or on small inherited incomes, private traders and proprietors of small-scale productive enterprises, and other "independent workers" whose gains are in many cases no larger than many workmen's wages, and a part of profits also goes to educational and other trusts and agencies which exist to maintain services it is highly undesirable to cut down The total sum left in the hands of really rich people, though considerable in itself and provocative when it is used for luxurious living, would go only a little way if it were shared out among the poorer sections of the population

That is no good reason against cutting down still further the spending-power of the rich, but do not let us deceive ourselves into the belief that re-distribution of this kind could make any substantial difference in reducing the effects of re-armament on the standard of living of the main body of the working class The men who spend large sums to-day do so for the most part, not out of incomes derived from business profits, but out of capital gains or by allowing their capital to run down while it is still theirs to make hay with

How Much Re-distribution of Incomes is possible?

INDEED, IT IS obvious on the face of it that further re-distribution of incomes cannot under present conditions do much to avert a fall in the standards of living of the main body of the people If investment has to be kept up in the national interest—that is, if a high proportion of total output has to be used not for consumption but for maintaining and improving productive power—and if, further, there has to be a large diversion of what remains to the production of munitions of war, the brunt of this diversion has to be borne by those who would have been the consumers of the goods and services which either cannot be produced at all, because there is no more productive power available, or which have to be sent abroad in payment for imports of materials The only alternative is that total output should be increased to bridge the gap, but such an increase involves more imports and the finding of more exports to pay for them By far the greater part of total consumption is done already by the workers, and by other persons whose standards of living are no higher than those of many wage-earners

How are Incomes Distributed Now?

LET US CONSIDER the actual figures for the year 1949–50, as shown in the current White Paper on the National Income The total of personal incomes before tax in that year was £10,507 millions Of this, £1,460 millions cannot be assigned to incomes of any particular size It is made up of such items as Co-operative dividends, interest on Savings Certificates, income paid in kind and not in money, the income from investments of charities, educational bodies, and insurance companies, the part of employees' incomes that is deducted before assessment for income tax (*e g*, national insurance contributions), and a few other items

If we leave aside this £1,460 millions there remains a total of £9,047 millions of personal incomes before tax. Out of this, £5,755 millions went to persons with less than £500 a year, and a further £1,614 millions to persons with from £500 to £1,000. Thus, the total received by persons with more than £1,000 *gross* was £1,678 millions, which was shared between 775,000 recipients. If these persons each kept £1,000 *gross*, and no more, there would be a total sum of £903 millions *gross* which could apparently be re-distributed to the less wealthy. But out of the £1,678 millions the State was already taking £659 millions in income tax and surtax, leaving £1,019 millions in the hands of the original recipients. If they were allowed to keep *an average* of no more than £750 a year *net*, the total sum remaining for re-distribution would amount to no more than £438 millions, or roughly 7½ per cent of the total of *net* incomes under £500.

May I repeat that the inadequacy of this sum to make a really considerable contribution towards raising the smaller incomes, if it were spread evenly over them all, is no good reason against taxing large incomes generally, or large incomes derived from ownership of property, at a very high rate. I have given the figures, not by way of objection to such taxation, but simply in order to show how little what the most drastic measures of income redistribution could do towards preventing re-armament from involving a fall in the general standard of living.

Who Should Own Reserved Profits?

SAVE TO THE extent necessary for making this plain, I have no intention in this short pamphlet of embarking on any discussion about what can or should be done, either by further taxation of profits or incomes, or by other means, to bring about a nearer approach to economic equality. Nor do I propose to discuss the wider question of what can or should be done to prevent excess spending out of capital, or to reduce inequalities of ownership. That is another subject, on which my friend, Roy Jenkins, has recently written an excellent *Tribune* pamphlet.

It would, I think, be quite practicable to devise ways and means of transferring a part of the reserved profits which are piling up in capitalist hands to working-class ownership, provided that the workers saved and did not spend on current consumption the amounts thus placed to their credit. But it would not be possible to give them more than a little out of current profits *to spend on consumption*, because any such increased spending would come immediately up against the absolute shortage of consumers' goods. Apart from increased total production, the supply of consumers' goods could not be increased without taking away man-power and other resources that are either needed for making capital goods or destined for use in re-armament.

Housing and Education

IT WOULD, OF course, be possible to increase somewhat the supplies of some kinds of consumers' goods at the expense of others of a more durable kind. It would be possible to stop building houses, schools and hospitals, and to transfer the man-power and resources employed in these branches of production to re-armament activities, and thus to lessen the need to draw man-power and other resources out of other industries supplying civilian needs But to do this would be only to accept a fall in living standards in an alternative form The consumers need more houses, schools and hospitals as much as they need the consumers' goods they could get instead or rather, it is a question of striking a right balance in deciding of what kinds of goods and services we are to go short if re-armament is to be carried through on the projected scale Rightly, I think, the Government has decided not to cut the housing programme , but for how long it will be able to maintain it in face of the increasing demands of re-armament I do not profess to know

The Long-run Outlook

INDEED, THE WORST thing that confronts us in relation to the armaments programme is not its immediate size, though that is bad enough, but the prospect of its continuance on an ever-increasing scale Assuming increased armaments to be desirable, we could bear a demand to tighten our belts for a short period if we could count on the emergency ending fairly soon and the resources locked up in armament-making being speedily released for other uses But that is very far from being the nature of the demand that is now being made upon us

If American policy remains as it appears to be, and if we continue to follow it, we are faced with a continuance for an indefinite period to come of a division of the world into two vast armed camps, each wildly spending against the other in the supposed interest of its own security

It is in the very nature of such armament races to involve continually rising costs, as deadlier and more expensive weapons are introduced and as the rate of obsolescence of weapons of destruction grows continually more rapid *The burden we are committed to bearing over the next three years is heavy enough , but it is nothing to what we are likely soon to be called on to bear unless we can stop the cold war*

Obsolescence and the Arms Race

THIS POINT ABOUT obsolescence is of fundamental importance The pace of technical advance in the production of munitions of war has now become fantastically swift Armaments now not only cost immensely more to make than they ever did, but also become out-of-date very much faster so that the total burden is increased by much more than the rise in the cost of each unit This is a much less deterrent consideration to the United States than to Great Britain, both because American industry is used to a high rate of obsolescence and because American national resources are so much greater than ours

The Americans can afford to expand their armaments at a great rate, not, of course, without adverse effects on their consuming power, but mainly by slowing down the increase of supplies for consumers rather than by actually reducing their standards of living We, on the other hand, not only need all our productive power if we are to make even modest improvements in general living standards, but are also badly in arrears with the maintenance and modernisation of our industrial structure We can very ill afford to cut down either supplies of consumers' goods or the amount of resources devoted to capital development.

The Position of the Soviet Union

IN THIS RESPECT the Soviet Union's position is much more like ours than it is like that of the United States , for despite all the advances of recent years the Soviet Union is still a very poor country and requires to make provision for the needs of a rapidly increasing population It is disastrous for the people of the Soviet Union to be spending a large part of their productive resources on armaments, and to be facing an indefinite continuance of the arms race

I do not wish, in this pamphlet, to embark on any discussion of foreign policy I am trying to keep strictly to the economic facts But it is surely evident that the peace propaganda of the Soviet Union and the support given to it are not wholly a sham, and that the Soviet peoples have an interest fully as strong as ours in halting the arms race in the interests of their standards of life Mutual suspicions, and the conflict of Communist and capitalist philosophies, make it exceedingly difficult to persuade the ruling groups in either the Soviet Union or the United States that in arming madly against each other they are doing anything other than each is forced to do by the attitude and policy of its antagonist.

But we in Great Britain, and with us the peoples of Western Europe, have nothing to gain by war and have the strongest reasons for knowing both that if it comes it is likely to be utterly disastrous for us, whichever side wins, and that a prolonged condition of near-war will wear us out long before it has exhausted either the Americans with their vast productive power or the Russians with their immense capacity for enduring hardship I am quite unable to believe that either the American people or the people of the Soviet Union want war, or would willingly resort to it unless they had been induced to believe that there was no other way open to them of defending their several ways of life

Will Re-armament make us Stronger ?

We in Great Britain and our neighbours in Western Europe have even stronger motives for the preservation of peace , for it is clear to most of us that war, far from enabling us to defend our ways of life, would be fatal to them. If intensive re-armament were in very truth the best means open to us of avoiding war, we should be right to meet the cost of it, whatever the economic effects. But we need to be very sure of this to be justified in throwing away the gains in real income and in social security which by an intense effort we have made in recent years for the main body of our peoples

Are we so sure? May it not be that the social discontents which will be created by the economic upsets of re-armament will leave us not stronger but weaker in facing the perils of a divided world, from whatever quarter they come? If armies march on their bellies, so do whole peoples. A weakened economy, rent by internal dissensions, can be in no good case either for preventing a war or for fighting one

APPENDIX

ESTIMATED NATIONAL EXPENDITURE, 1950 AND 1951-2 (£ MILLIONS)

DEFENCE SERVICES	1950–1*	1951–2†
Army	309	419
Navy	190	278
Air	225	329
Supply	49	82
Ministry of Defence	4	6
Civil Defence	7	13
Strategic Reserves	—	143
Margin for Supplementary Estimates	—	160
	784	1,430

OTHER SERVICES	1950–1†	1951–2†
National Services (Health, Insurance, Pensions)	756	776
National Assistance to Local Services	459	474
Food Services	400	403
Agriculture, Forestry and Fisheries	67	57
Development Services	513	581
Other Services and Expenses	501	522
	2,696	2,813

*Exchequer Issues   †Budget Estimates

CURRENT TOTAL £4,243,000,000, of which Defence expenditure accounts for more than a third.

DISTRIBUTION OF PERSONAL INCOMES, 1949‡

	Before Direct Tax £ Millions	After Direct Tax £ Millions	Number of Recipients Thousands
Under £250	2,209	2,185	?
£250—£499	3,546	3,360	10,310
£500—£999	1,614	1,375	2,443
£1,000—£1,999	728	539	545
£2,000—£9,999	760	436	219
Over £10,000	190	44	11
	9,047	7,939	—

‡*Excluding £1,460 millions unallocated. See page 10.*

THE COURSE OF PRICES (1938=100)

A.—British Wholesale Prices *(Board of Trade)*

	March 1949	Sept. 1949	March 1950	Sept. 1950	March 1951
(a) Mainly Home produced					
Coal	245	248	248	246	270
Iron and Steel	171	185	185	188	199
Chemicals	203	199	208	227	246
(b) Mainly Imported					
Non-ferrous Metals	285	254	291	403	478
Cotton	373	385	441	491	641
Wool	293	290	390	639	1,070

B.—World Prices *(The Economist)*

	June 1950	End of March 1951
Rubber (d. per lb.)	24	$62\frac{3}{4}$
Wool 56's (d. per lb.)	81	277
Lead (soft pig) (£ per ton)	88	136
Copper, electrolytic (£ per ton)	186	202
Tin, London (£ per ton)	$607\frac{5}{8}$	1,255
Aluminium scrap sheets (£ per ton)	$8\frac{3}{4}$	16
Antimony 99% (£ per ton)	160	360
Tungsten (sh. per unit)	127	550

DISTRIBUTION OF PERSONAL INCOMES, 1949¹

	Before Direct Tax £ Millions	After Direct Tax £ Millions	Number of Recipients Thousands
Under £250	2,209	2,105	
£250—£499	3,540	3,460	10,310
£500—£999	1,614	1,357	2,443
£1,000—£1,999	738	530	848
£2,000—£9,999	760	436	217
Over £10,000	190	44	11
	9,047	7,939	

¹ Excluding £1,750 millions unallocated. See page 10.

THE COURSE OF PRICES (1938=100)

A.—British Wholesale Prices (Board of Trade)

	March 1947	March 1948	March 1950	Sept. 1950	March 1951
(a) Mainly Home produced					
Coal	245	248	248	266	270
Iron and Steel	171	185	185	189	199
Clothing	202	199	212	227	276
(b) Mainly Imported					
Non-ferrous Metals	285	254	291	403	478
Cotton	277	365	441	401	641
Wool	283	290	390	635	1,070

B.—World Prices (The Economist)

	June 1950	End March 1951
Rubber (d. per lb.)	24	161
Wool 50s (d. per lb.)	81	217
Lead (£cif. pig) (£ per ton)	118	150
Copper, electrolytic (£ per ton)	181	202
Tin, London (£ per ton)	602	1,155
Aluminium ingot, shapes (£ per ton)	81	15
Antimony 99% (£ per ton)	160	360
Tungsten (ore per unit)	122	550

THE FABIAN SOCIETY

PAST and PRESENT

(REVISED EDITION)

BY

G. D. H. COLE

TRACT SERIES No. 258

Fabian Publications Ltd.
11, Dartmouth Street, London, S.W.1

CONTENTS

		Page
1	**FABIAN FUNCTIONS**	
	Practical Proposals	3
	"Permeation"	3
2	**WHO THE FABIANS ARE**	
	Fabian Standards	5
	Are the Fabians Middle Class?	6
3	**WHAT THE FABIANS ARE DOING**	
	Publications	9
	Research	10
4	**FABIANISM AND POLITICS**	
	Fabians and the Labour Party	12
	Policy Making	13
	Local Societies and Socialist Propaganda Committee	14
5	**FABIAN HISTORY AND FABIAN FUTURE**	
	A Word to Fabians	17

NOTE *This pamphlet, like all publications of the Fabian Society, represents not the collective view of the Society, but only the view of the individual who prepared it. The responsibility of the Fabian Society is limited to approving the publications which it issues as embodying facts and opinions worthy of consideration within the Labour Movement. It is the aim of the Society to encourage among socialists a high standard of free and independent research.*

(*Revised Edition, June, 1946*)

THE FABIAN SOCIETY
Past and Present

by G. D. H. COLE

The Fabian Society, in the words of its Constitution, "consists of Socialists". The same fundamental rule, to which all its members must subscribe, goes on to define this phrase by saying that the Fabian Society "therefore aims at the establishment of a society in which equality of opportunity will be assured and the economic power and privileges of individuals and classes abolished through the collective ownership and democratic control of the economic resources of the community". The rule adds that "it seeks to secure these ends by the methods of political democracy".

That, together with a profession of faith in equal citizenship open to persons "irrespective of sex, race or creed", is the whole basis of belief to which those who wish to join the Fabian Society are asked to subscribe. The words have been changed from time to time during the long life of the Society, but for some time past they appear to have given so much satisfaction that no one has even tried to alter or to enlarge upon them.

The Fabian Society was founded in 1884. Throughout more than sixty years it has done its best to keep the conditions of membership wide enough to admit a large diversity of views. It insists on Socialism, and does its best to define Socialism in the broadest possible terms. In all other matters of faith and doctrine, it prefers to leave its members free. There is no Fabian 'orthodoxy' on matters of controversy within the Socialist movement, save to the extent to which the brief statements quoted above are regarded as controversial. Up to a point, no doubt, they can be so regarded. They would exclude an anarchist, or anyone who does not believe in political democracy. But of genuine Socialists they are meant to exclude as few as possible. The Fabian Society is not a sect: within the limits set by its affiliation to the Labour Party, which it helped to found, it is open to all democratic Socialists.

The Fabian Society was named, more than half a century ago, after a certain Roman general, Quintus Fabius Maximus Cunctator—which means 'the Delayer'. This may appear an odd way of naming a Society which has stood throughout its existence for Socialism, and has become famous throughout the world as a planner of Socialist policies and an inspirer of Socialist ideas. For, by and large, most people tend to think of Socialists rather as rushing in where more timorous angels fear to tread than as biding their time, as Fabius did against Hannibal, from whom he saved Rome. I doubt if anyone, founding a Socialist Society nowadays, would think of calling it 'Fabian'. The name is a bit of history it derives from the state of the British Socialist movement nearly sixty years ago.

Let me remind you. In 1884, when the Fabian Society was born, there was no Labour Party in Great Britain. The beginning of the Labour Party was sixteen years ahead, and nine years were to pass before Keir Hardie founded its forerunner, the I L P. The only pebbles on the British Socialist beach in the Society's early days were Hyndman's Social Democratic Federation and William Morris's Socialist League, which shortly after the birth of Fabianism split off from the S D F; and both these bodies, though they did good work for Socialism in their day and generation, were adepts at 'rushing in'. In the same year the S D F rushed into the General Election to such purpose that two of its three candidates scored respectively 27 votes against 4,695 and 32 votes against 6,342. Such miserable polls, to say nothing of other circumstances, discredited the Socialist cause, and it was one object of the Fabians to call a halt to such tactics and to set on foot a campaign of Socialist education that would prevent similar fiascos for the future. The Fabian Society set out to spread a knowledge of Socialism; and its propaganda played no small part in preparing the way for the wider successes of the I L P and for the coming of the Labour Party and its adoption of a broadly Socialist creed.

1 Fabian Functions

The early Fabians, though they favoured 'delay' in Parliamentary action until Socialism had acquired a substantial following, were under no illusion that delay by itself could win the day. They invented for themselves quite soon a motto. It was "*For the right moment you must wait, as Fabius did, but when the right moment comes you must strike hard, or your waiting will have been vain and fruitless.*"

That is the attitude to which the Fabian Society has remained constant throughout its history. Between times, it has gone ahead steadily and quietly with its work of Socialist education, sending out speakers, issuing tracts, pamphlets, books and manifestos, patiently devising policies for anyone who would listen to it—and for many who would not listen. But whenever there has come a crisis in the affairs of men, the Fabian Society has been ready to throw aside its delaying tactics and to take its stand boldly for what it has believed to be the right course of action.

Sometimes this attitude has involved the Society in a great deal of self-denial. In its early years it built up a network of local Fabian Societies over Great Britain. But in 1893, when the I L P was founded, it seemed best in the interests of Socialism to consolidate the available forces in the constituencies under its banner; and the parent Fabian Society readily acquiesced in the absorption of most of the local Fabian Societies into the I L P. During the years after 1906, when there was a great ferment of labour unrest and Socialist thought in Great Britain, a second crop of local Fabian Societies grew up, but again the parent Society readily let most of them merge themselves into the re-organised Labour Party of 1918, when local Labour Parties with individual members were first set up throughout the country. During the last few years there has been a third crop, larger than either of the others, of local Fabian Societies and Socialist Propaganda Committees under Fabian auspices, to fill the void left by the secession and practical disappearance of the I L P. There is always need, side by side with the Labour Party, and in close connection with it, for a body which can devote itself primarily to thinking about the long-run problems of Socialist policy, rather than about immediate election issues and electoral problems; and this need exists, not only centrally, but also up and down the country, wherever there are groups of Socialists who can help both themselves and the Labour Movement by keeping their ideas and knowledge continually up to date, and by fitting themselves to play the part of Socialist educators and propagandists in the places where they live and work. At one time these functions were performed largely by the I L P. to-day, the Fabian Society is the only body which is setting out to perform them. Its success is attested by the rapid growth of local

Fabian Societies in recent years, and by the close contacts which these Societies have established with the wider Labour Movement in their areas. This third crop of local Fabian activity is developing splendidly just now; and I hope and believe it will continue to grow. Yet if, at any time, it appeared to be in the interests of the Labour Movement as a whole for any particular local Society to merge itself in some other body, the parent Fabian Society would be no more disposed to stand in the way than it has shown itself in the past It has no desire to create local Societies for its own aggrandisement · it values them for what they do, not for the Fabian Society, but for the Socialist cause.

PRACTICAL PROPOSALS

The truth is that the Fabian Society has always believed its mission to lie more in ideas than in organisation. Throughout its long life it has always, in greater or less degree, combined three functions. It has tried to think out practical proposals for the reformation of particular political, social and economic evils along broadly Socialist lines, and to enlist, in support of its particular schemes, those who have been in key positions for helping to carry them out and have not had their ears stopped by vested interest to the appeal of reason, and it has tried to make plain to ordinary people who are intelligent enough to care about the possibilities of a better social system the necessity of Socialism, and the best means of achieving it. All these things it has done to such extent as its resources have allowed, at various stages in its history. For example—before there was a Labour Party in existence Fabians, largely under the inspiration of Sidney Webb, had a good deal to do with persuading the Liberal Party to adopt a more advanced programme of social reform—the Newcastle Programme of 1898. It was again Sidney Webb who drafted, in 1918, the first comprehensive programme ever put forward by the Labour Party—*Labour and the New Social Order* Persons who had been converted by Fabian propaganda were largely responsible for the social legislation passed by the Liberal Government after 1906—until Lloyd George, instead of acting on the Fabian-inspired proposals of the Minority Report of the Poor Law Commission, again the work of the Webbs, sent the Liberals haring off after social insurance on the German model. At all times, Fabian lecturers and writers have been busy, as they were busy in the midst of war, telling people about Socialism in terms which bring it down from generalities to concrete practicable proposals. It is the Fabian view that the " good news' of Socialism needs putting squarely and realistically before everyone, in every class and group, who can be persuaded to listen to it.

" PERMEATION "

The second Fabian method, that of trying to convert those who hold the key positions, was called in the Society's early days by the name of ' Permeation ', and a good deal of mud was slung at the Society for trying to talk commonsense to anyone who had ears to hear instead of spending all its time speaking comfortable words to those who had been converted already. Naturally, the Fabian Society expected its ideas to get the warmest welcome from those who were already Socialists, and especially from the livelier elements in the working-class movement. But it saw no reason for confining its efforts to those who were easiest to persuade. Not that Fabian ' permeation ' ever really meant simply the conversion of a few leading officials or ' high-ups '. Far from it. The person whom the Fabian Society, on this side of its work, most wishes to convert is the man or woman who is in the best position for influencing others, either over a wide area or in his or her comparatively narrow group. Such persons may be Civil Servants or professional men and women or Trade Union or Co-operative leaders, local as well as national, or parsons with a loyal following in their own churches, or speakers with a gift for moving men, or regimental officers or common soldiers, or shop stewards. They may be business men who have realised the futility of capitalism, or scientists, or teachers in school or university—or students. They may, in effect, be anybody who is a real living person, trying to think for himself and not content to be merely a passive recipient of mass-propaganda or a feebly acquiescent victim of things as they are. The Fabian Society regards each individual in its relatively tiny membership of a few thousands as a stone thrown into a pool, spreading rings of influence all round him.

2 Who The Fabians Are

The Fabian membership has always been small, not because the Society wants it to be small, but because reasoning has, and probably always will have, a limited appeal. The Fabian Society's essential appeal is to certain particular kinds of people, and not to all and sundry. It wants, of course, to influence as many people as it possibly can, and it has been, throughout its long history, an agent in converting to Socialism, directly or indirectly, very many times as many persons as have joined it. But it does not expect more than a small fraction of those to whom it appeals actually to join its ranks, or at any rate the ranks of the parent Society. Of course, the more who do join it the better it is pleased, and it seeks to enrol in its local Societies and groups many more than are likely to become national members of the parent body. This is partly because the effectiveness of its work depends on supplying its members with a great deal of literature, itself the product of a great deal of careful research. Such a service cannot be financed, even with the aid of some large ponations, without a rate of subscription that is bound to seem high to those who are used to small weekly payments The parent Fabian Society cannot afford weekly collections from a membership scattered all over the country. It has to collect an annual sum from each member, and this in practice limits its membership. In fact, a guinea a year is not much more than fourpence a week; but it is apt to seem much more, when it is asked for as a lump sum.[1] Moreover, our smaller subscribers contribute little or nothing to the general expenses of the Society· they get back from it most of what they pay in the actual expenses of supplying them with literature and keeping them in touch with the Society's work. So the parent Society has to get larger subscriptions from all who can afford to pay them—and of course a good deal more from some of its members, or it could not go on at all. The local Fabian Societies do not suffer under this particular handicap, and can therefore aim at a wider membership.

But, even in their case, there are reasons why the Fabian membership is likely not to become large, in comparison with that of other political bodies seeking to exert a widespread influence. Although of late the Fabian Society has been growing fast, and though it looks like growing faster still, it will never, in the nature of things, become a mass-movement.

---

[1] The Fabian Society's *minimum* national subscription is only 10/6 , but all members who can possibly afford it are asked to pay at least one guinea a year, and there is a large class of two-guinea subscribers, besides those who contribute larger sums.

It does not aim at mass-conversions or at mass emotional appeals. While recognising their political necessity and value, it leaves them to others, within whose province they lie. Mass-appeal is a different art from research and education; and the Fabian Society prefers to get on with its own different job, which is to put the right equipment of ideas and information into the possession of that not inconsiderable body of persons (some hundreds of thousands at the least, if they could all be reached) who believe in the value of getting at the real facts and thinking hard about them, and are aware that, even if politics depend fundamentally on men's emotions, emotional appeals by themselves will not get far in practice, unless clear thinking comes to their aid when it is a question of translating desires and ideals into positive achievements.

This type of clear thinking is not a monopoly of any class of specialists, or of those who have received the benefit of any particular kind of education. Men and women who are prepared to use their brains for thinking lucidly about politics are found in all classes; and in all classes they are at present the exceptions. It is much easier for the educated as well as for the uneducated man, in the ordinary sense of the words, to live by the rule of prejudice and tradition than to think things out in an objective way. Indeed, in this respect the highly educated are often among the worst offenders, both because they are blinded by social prejudice and because, even when they are not, they are very apt to think unrealistically, and with much too little understanding of the wants and sentiments of ordinary people. Those who have missed the chance of higher education often offend also against the rule of reason, and with much better excuse. The educated obscurantist turns his back on the truth, because it offends his prejudices or seems to involve knowing things too mean for his mind. The uneducated man, on the other hand, is apt to be unable to get his aspirations into a shape in which they are realisable, and consequently tends to flounder about in generalities.

The Fabian Society consists, to a quite remarkable extent, of reasonable people—by which I mean people who believe in using their reason and in not allowing themselves to be the victims either of prejudice or of intellectual dilettantism or of muddled good-will. It is bound to make fairly high demands of its members in these respects in order to be true to its essential function. Not, of course, that it requires that all its members shall be original thinkers, or exceptionally able persons. What it demands of them is not exceptional ability, but a kind of intellectual courage which will not let them run away from the facts of contemporary society, whether it likes them or not. It calls, not for high educational attainments, but for a positive state of mind which refuses to be satisfied with phrases or to take things for granted, and insists on having everything carefully examined again and again, in order to find out whether what once held good holds good still, and to seek new ways of dealing with changing situations instead of trying to meet them by the application of ancient formulæ that no longer fit the facts.

FABIAN STANDARDS

This means that the Fabian Society has, within the limits imposed by its resources, to set itself a high standard in both research and the propaganda which it bases on its research. It is appealing to people who *know*, whether about the hewing of coal or the drafting of forms; it cannot afford to be ignorant or silly. Nor, as it believes in reason and the use of reason in argument, is it prepared to tell lies or compound slogans which it knows to be false for the sake of producing some immediate emotional result. It can be said with confidence that during the whole of its history the Fabian Society has steadfastly endeavoured, subject to human frailty,

(1) To check and counter-check the *facts* contained in its publications;
(2) To *argue*, fairly and fully, the case for any proposal which it puts forward, and not to put forward any case which it does not believe to be substantially true, merely because it would like to believe it true, or because it forms part of the recognised Socialist ' orthodoxy ' of the moment;
(3) To check, by consultation with those who know, the practicability, under existing conditions, of any proposals which it makes—i e., not to be visionary or foolish.

These three ambitions may sound modest. But they are not particularly easy to work out in practice. They involve a fairly high standard of accuracy and competence in work, and sometimes a measure of self-abnegation, which the Society has often in fact employed, in withholding from the public work which has seemed to it to fall short of the standard it tries to keep.

ARE THE FABIANS MIDDLE-CLASS?

A society which takes this line inevitably, as matters stand to-day, has to face two sorts of misrepresentation. It will be attacked by some working-class people as being 'middle-class' and by some people, including members of all classes, as being a home of the 'long-haired intelligentsia'. Let me deal first with the second line of attack So far from attracting what are called the 'Bloomsburyites', the Fabian Society definitely repels them by its practicality. It is always nosing about in the drains, and attending to all sorts of sanitary affairs that have no romance about them in the eyes of the intellectual revolutionary remote from the realities of working-class life. The 'Bloomsburyites' do not join the Fabian Society: they prefer as a rule something much more exciting and a good deal less solid. I ought perhaps to apologise at this point for seeming to insult the inhabitants of Bloomsbury who do happen to belong to the Fabian Society; but they will readily understand that there are two Bloomsburys, one a district of London including the British Museum and the other a Cloudcuckooland which has somehow usurped its name. The 'Bloomsburyites' belong to this second Bloomsbury; and it is of them I say that they do not belong to the Fabian Society.

The second charge—that of being middle-class—involves a more subtle misconception. It is a most curious habit of the English people to regard as belonging to the 'middle class' almost everybody who has received a higher education, even if his father is a miner or an agricultural labourer, or if he himself has hewed coal or served at the plough. The Labour movement unwaveringly demands a broad highway leading to the summit of the educational system: yet many Labour adherents regard as having dropped out of their class anyone who advances at all far along this highway. But one purpose of higher education—it should be the main purpose, though often at present it is not—is to teach people to think clearly and to be able to express their thoughts. The Fabian Society therefore is bound to have a more obvious and immediate appeal to those educated persons who are not blinded by their prejudices than to most of those who have missed the chance of higher education. Exceptional men and women—especially those who find their opportunity later, in the adult education movement, but not only they—can rise above the defects of the educational system and think clearly for themselves even though they have never been taught to think. But they are bound to be the exceptions, wherever the demands of thought are exacting and the things that need to be thought about inherently difficult or technical.

It is therefore unavoidable that a society such as the Fabian Society should consist largely of members who have in one way or another become highly educated. Such members may be workmen, or salary-earners, or anything else you please. But there will be, until things change a lot, a strong propensity in certain working-class quarters to dub them 'middle-class', merely because they are educated, whatever their jobs, or their family connections, or their opinions, or their level of income may be. In this sense only is the Fabian Society a 'middle-class' body, and not in the least ashamed of being so, but ashamed only of a social system so unfair and lop-sided as to regard education as the prerogative of a single social class.

A society of educated men and women (including, of course, 'self-educated' men and women) the Fabian Society must remain, if it is to do its work well. It must set a high standard for those who work for it, either in devising plans and policies or in spreading the results. It must remain in that sense, a society of specialists—specialists in the art of clear, courageous, Socialist thinking and planning for the future. That it is this should be its strongest recommendation in the eyes of the Labour Movement, which stands in need of just this sort of help. Whoever you are, if you want legal advice you go to a lawyer. Trade Unionists do so every day, and would be failing in their task if they did not. If you want bricks laid you go to a bricklayer. Persons who dislike and despise bricklayers do this as much as others, and would not get their houses well-built if they did not. Similarly, if the Socialist movement wants research done into social and economic problems, it has to go to the people who have trained themselves to understand these problems, or it will not get good results. This is why the Fabian Society is the organisation to which educated Socialists naturally gravitate. If it gave up this character, if it tried to turn into another sort of organisation, it would lose the capacity to do its own special Socialist job well, and it is very doubtful whether it would develop a capacity to do any other.

3 What The Fabians Are Doing

At any rate that is the Fabian 'line'. Let us try to see what it means in practice—in terms of what the Fabian Society is actually doing, or attempting to do. There are now, in June, 1946, over 4,500 of us—members and Associates of the parent Fabian Society, apart from the members of our 67 local Fabian Societies scattered over the country. That, by the way, represents a remarkable rate of increase; for four years ago the main Society had only 2,070 members, and the local Societies numbered no more than 14. Moreover, our pace of growth has been limited of late, not by the numbers who are ready to join us, but by our ability to undertake the necessary work of local organisation. It would not serve our purpose to let anyone who feels like forming a local Fabian Society go ahead and form it without making as sure as we can that the Society, when it has been formed, will act in accordance with Fabian methods and the Fabian spirit. We have to keep our standards high, in local as well as in national work; and that involves care in picking our people, and seeing to it that local Societies are not started by enthusiasts who, however well-intentioned, may do the Fabian movement more harm than good.

Lest this sound unduly deterrent, let us see what it means in terms of the kinds of people we wish to attract. A great deal of our research work needs the reinforcement of local information, and the criticism of those who are in close touch with local conditions. Suppose we are setting out to make a study of some contemporary social problems—Housing, for example, on which we have a special Committee at work—we depend absolutely on the help of our members who know the actual conditions in different parts of the country. The same thing applies to town and country planning, or health services, or education, or to any of a hundred other problems that we attempt to survey in an objective way. In such cases, we want as members the Socialists who have been active in connection with these services in their own areas, whether as Councillors or as social workers or as active participants in the local working-class movement. Nor is this help needed only for the Society's central work. We expect our local membership to be prepared to do local research and survey work that will be of help to the Labour Group on the local Council, or to the local Labour Party or Trades Council or Cooperative Society. We want to get into our ranks in each area the men and women who know things because they do things; and we believe we can help them as much as they can help us.

This, I hope, makes it clear what we want our local Societies to be and to do. We want them, of course, to be propagandists for Socialism as well as research workers; but in our view the best kind of propaganda they can engage in is very often that which emerges directly from their own study of their local conditions and their success in relating it to the national policies which the Society as a whole is working out.

All this, if it is to go well in the localities, puts a very big burden of work on the parent Society. If you were to visit our offices at 11 Dartmouth Street, Westminster, you would appreciate what the rapid increase in membership has involved. We have no money to spare for expensive accommodation, for we need it all for financing our research and spreading its results. Consequently, in relation to what the Society is doing, it is ridiculously under-housed. It is also, for lack of money, seriously under-staffed. Crowded into a small and inconvenient building are the general offices of the Fabian Society, the Research Department, the Library, the Publications Department, the Bookshop and Despatch Department. The very active Colonial and International Bureaux, the Indian Affairs Group, and the offices of the Local Societies Committee are across the way, crowded out of the main building. The Women's Group, and a large number of other special activities, fit themselves in where they can; and during the war we tried to provide a centre for meetings for a number of our comrades from overseas who were in exile as a result of the Nazi occupation of Europe. It is ten to one that, when you call, you will find every room fully occupied, and even have some difficulty in getting a chair.

The reader may well ask how this congestion squares with what I said about the Society being understaffed. I can assure him that it does square. Although our staff is too large for our premises, it is much too small for the work we are trying to do. Moreover, as we cannot pay enough people to do even the regular office work for us, we have to supplement the services of the paid staff by using volunteers, not only for research (practically all our research work is unpaid) but also for office jobs. We can always do with more volunteers for what is called ' the donkey work ', as well as for speaking and research, though we cannot promise them either that we will have just the job ready for them that they will prefer to do or that we can give them all comfortable quarters to work in if the work needs to be done on the spot.

PUBLICATIONS

What does all this activity lead to? In the first place, it leads to publication—of books, pamphlets, periodicals, cyclostyled memoranda, covering a wide field. *Fabian News*, our official organ, is essentially a newssheet of our activities, meant for members and indispensable to them, but with no room, in these days of paper shortage, to do more than announce and chronicle the crowded hours of the Society's life. Through it, we tell our members about our publications, our summer schools and week-end schools and conferences (which are always crowded out), the lunch meetings organised by the Society and its groups and bureaux, and as far as space allows the activities of our local societies. *Fabian News* does duty in place of many notices; and any member who fails to study it carefully is not doing his job.

Fabian Quarterly is a journal of a different sort. In it, we publish special research articles and reports which are either too short or too specialised to be issued in pamphlet or booklet form, but are of real, though sometimes only of temporary, importance to our members as material for their Socialist work. There, too, we record our research activities, and give room for controversies about questions on which opinion needs to be formed. But most of the product of our research appears in books or pamphlets. Our series of *Fabian Tracts* has now reached number 261, *Dumbarton Oaks A Fabian Commentary*, in which a Committee of the Society examines the proposals made for the creation of an international authority after the war. *Fabian Tracts* go right back to the beginning of the Society, and include the invaluable *Facts for Socialists* which, first issued in 1887, has, for upwards of half a century, supplied generations of propagandists with good ammunition for shooting at the enemies of our cause. Side by side with the *Tracts* we have our younger *Research Series*, each dealing with a special problem from a practical Socialist angle. Recent examples of these are No. 109, *European Transport The Way to Unity* and No. 110, *The Rate for the Job*. This *Research Series* is meant to be solidly constructive, and needs more than cursory reading, though it is simply and straightforwardly written. It is intended for readers who want the hard facts as well as the conclusions, in order that they may be well equipped for arguing the Socialist case. Where we can, we produce the results of our research in the form of pamphlets, so as to keep them cheap. But some things that need saying cannot be said in a pamphlet, and need full-length presentation in book-form. We believe that the books in which we embody many of the major results of our research are among our most important products and that we have succeeded in keeping their quality high. Among our latest books are *Towards a Socialist Agriculture*, a study of *Cooperation in the Colonies*, and *The Condition of the British People, 1911–1945*, by Mark Abrams—all mines of information for anyone who wants to study the particular subjects with which they deal.

Yet another of our ventures is a series of booklets and pamphlets called 'Fabian Specials'. This series is definitely meant to be more popularly written than the others It includes purely occasional pamphlets arising out of some contemporary event or controversy, on which it seems desirable to express a Fabian point of view, or, to put concise, clearly written information into the hands of the public. In this series we also publish special propagandist appeals, such as our series of *Letters* to a Soldier, A Teacher, an Industrial Manager, and so on. Among the most popular 'Fabian Specials' have been *How the Russians Live* and *Beveridge Quiz*, and we are specially anxious to find better methods of distributing these pamphlets through the Labour Movement, which is in these days seriously short of well-written popular publications.

Then we have another journal—*Empire*, the organ of our exceedingly successful Colonial Bureau, which exists to focus Socialist opinion on problems of empire and of colonial development and exploitation; and right through the war we issued *France and Britain*, which was founded to help in building up a community of sentiment and idea between two neighbouring countries whose close mutual understanding is indispensable for the future settlement of Europe. It was issued by our International Bureau, which is seeking to establish co-operation over a much wider field and has committees for joint action between British Socialists and those of a number of countries.

RESEARCH

Parallel to this activity in international matters is the work we are doing on home affairs through our Home Research Department, which is the pivot on which the whole of our work in home affairs is meant to turn. Until a few years ago the New Fabian Research Bureau was an independent body, working in friendship with the Fabian Society, but apart from it. The New Fabian Research Bureau was founded in 1931, during the period of office of the second Labour Government, and as the result of a good deal of preparatory work during the preceding years. Its founders, who included, besides many of those now in leading positions in the Society, such men as Attlee, Cripps, Dalton, Arthur Henderson, Bevin and Pritt—a good mixed bag—felt the urgent need in the Socialist movement for a new organ of collective thinking and planning for a better social order. So they set to work, and ever since 1931 the results of their efforts have been flowing forth in a steady stream of constructive research. Originally, there was associated with the New Fabian Research Bureau a parallel body designed to conduct propaganda based upon its research. But this body—the Society for Socialist Inquiry and Propaganda—did not survive; and for some time the effectiveness of the N F R B was limited by its lack of adequate local contacts. Then, in 1939, the N F R B and the Fabian Society were fused into a single body, and the gain to both has been immense. The research work thereafter reached directly a wider membership, and was thus passed on more effectively to others, and the Fabian Summer School, the lecturing work, and the other activities of the older Society got a freshness and a more solid content which greatly increased their influence. Moreover, whereas the Fabian Society had lost most of its local Societies, and N F R B had founded only a very few local Research Groups, the combined body has been able to go forward with a new drive for local contacts; and the place which S S I P was meant to fill is being taken by the new Societies and Groups which are being formed under the auspices of the Local Societies and Socialist Propaganda Committee.

The Research work now undertaken by the Society covers a wide range. As our financial resources are scanty—terribly scanty in relation to the tasks we are called upon to undertake—it has nearly all to be done by our members in their spare time, and on a voluntary basis. We have no rule about its organisation. A matter needing research goes sometimes to a committee of the Society, and sometimes to a single member; but in either case, when it is done, it undergoes a fire of criticism from readers appointed by the Executive. Our instructions to our readers are simple. They are asked so say, not whether they agree with what has been written, but only whether the job has been competently done from a definitely Socialist point of view. I have said earlier that, within our general profession of Socialist faith, we as a Fabian Society have no rigid orthodoxy. We believe in free Socialist inquiry, and in publishing the results of such inquiry whether we agree with them or not. None of our publications represent the views of the Fabian Society as such; for, beyond the general declaration of Socialist faith embodied in the rules, which I quoted at the beginning, the Fabian Society has no collective views on particular questions. There is no Fabian 'party line'—no more than a common determination to work for Socialism and democracy on a broad basis of agreement which is rather implicit in the entire record of the Society than set down anywhere in so many words.

The Society wants this to be clearly understood—for it is very easy to misunderstand. Most Socialist bodies have Annual Conferences at which they decide upon their policies, which are thereafter supposed to be binding on their members. The Fabian Society's annual gathering is a business meeting, which does not, save quite exceptionally, deal at all with questions of policy in the ordinary sense. It is not precluded from dealing with them; for it is always open to the members, at the annual meeting, to criticise the Society's publications or its conduct of the Society's policy during the year. But in practice this hardly ever happens. The Executive may be criticised for not having done more than it has done, or for having tackled some problem of Socialist research in the wrong way; but it is hardly ever confronted with any proposal to pin down its activities to a definite line. This is because our principle of fostering free Socialist research and publishing the results without attempting to reach detailed agreement is understood and valued by our members.

4 Fabianism And Politics

There are two reasons why the Fabian Society attaches particular importance to preserving this undogmatic attitude. We believe there is need, somewhere in the Socialist movement, for a body which is entirely free to think out and to give publicity to new ideas, even where they run counter to Socialist orthodoxies inherited from the past. Socialism is not a set of fixed dogmas, always ready to be applied irrespective of time and place. It is a set of principles, which need continual re-interpretation in the light of changing needs and conditions. There is always a danger of mistaking dogmas for principles, and of allowing policies and programmes to become ossified; and this danger can be held off only by continual fresh thinking of an essentially objective sort. A political party can never be quite free to do this, because it has to act solidly in support of a united policy in order to achieve its ends. But the Fabian Society is not a political party, and its object is to influence others rather than to carry out its ideas in practice. It is organised for thought and discussion, and not for electoral action, which it leaves to other bodies, though it encourages its members, in their individual capacities, to play an active part in the work of these other bodies. It counts among its members a great many leading members of Local Labour Parties, Trade Unions, Co-operative Societies, and other working-class agencies; a large number of Labour Members of Parliament and of Labour representatives on municipal and other local authorities, and it expects all its members to take an active part in the political work of the Socialist movement, in their several spheres. But as a Society it keeps itself apart from electoral affairs, and values its freedom from the day-to-day exigencies of party politics. Thought must be free if it is to remain alive; and thinking about politics and economics is the Fabian Society's special job.

The second reason is closely connected with the first. The chief body of opinion which the Fabian Society seeks to influence is the Labour movement. But it would be entirely fatal to our prospects if we, as a body of people who specialise in plans and ideas, were to produce a programme of our own, separate from and in rivalry with the accepted programmes of the Labour Party and the Trade Unions, and were we to attempt to force our programme down the throats of the millions whose lives it would vitally effect. It is legitimate and necessary for the Fabian Society continually to throw out ideas and suggestions for notice by those who have the task of formulating the official programmes, and to hope that these ideas and suggestions will influence official policy. But our chance of exerting this constructive influence would be gone if we appeared to be pushing our own programme against the official programmes.

That is precisely what has happened to other Socialist bodies which have tried to act in this way. The I L P and the Socialist League in turn got the reputation of trying to force their own particular medicines down the throats of the Labour Party and the Trade Unions. Many of the leaders of these bodies thereupon refused to have anything to do with them, and denounced them as bodies of irresponsible persons who were trying to teach their grandmothers to suck eggs. It does not matter, for the present purpose, whether the policies advocated by the I L P and the Socialist League were right or wrong. Personally, I hold that they were largely right. The point is that they were put forward in such a way that there was no chance of their being listened to, and that any fool who got up and denounced them as the work of a bunch of superior intellectual idiots was certain of rapturous applause. The Fabian Society does not mean to fall into that error. It is not trying to push anything down anybody's throat. It simply researches and thinks, publishes the results of its thinking in speech and writing—and hopes for the best. It trusts to the wisdom of the common people to ensure that what it does well will in course of time pass into the general stock of Socialist ideas and policy, and that what it does badly will be set aside.

FABIANS AND THE LABOUR PARTY

That has been the Fabian way ever since it helped to found the Labour Party more than forty-six years ago. All that time the Fabian Society has been affiliated to the Labour Party, and has never quarrelled with it, even if again and again many Fabians have disapproved of something the party has done. We have watched other Socialist bodies break their heads against a brick wall, and knock their brains out in the process. We, as a Society, have sat tight, leaving our individual members to make the running in support of this or that idea through the local Labour Parties or other bodies to which they belong, but refusing to commit the Society collectively on any internal quarrel—jealously guarding our independence of thought and seeing to it that our identity as a Socialist body is maintained. For though we are affiliated to the Labour Party and working in loyalty to it, let it be clearly understood that the Fabian Society is not simply a part of the Labour Party, but an independent body of persons organised for furthering the Socialist cause.

It is of vital importance that both our numbers and others who have dealings with us shall understand this difference. We cannot as a Society be simply a part of the Labour Party, because Socialism is not simply a political question. Socialism is a theory and a way of life: it is what some-people call a religion and others an ethical creed. It involves political action for achieving many of its ends; and for this purpose there is need of a political party committed to a Socialist programme. But Socialism involves much besides this—much that is not 'politics' in any ordinary sense. The Fabian Society, when it wishes to act politically, acts as a part of the Labour Party. But this is not all it does, and in view of its special character, its non-political work is fully as important as that part of its work which falls within the field of politics.

For example, the Fabian Society has among its members a good sprinkling of men and women from many different professions—doctors, teachers, industrial managers and technicians, and so on. It wants all these persons to face as Socialists the special problems of their own professions, and to work out, not merely how these professions ought to be organised in a Socialist Society, but what can be done in them now both to improve the immediate quality of their service to the community, and to lead on towards their reorganisation on sounder lines. What Fabians are trying to do in these spheres of action is hardly politics at all—certainly not 'party politics', but it is of immense importance for creating in the key positions of Society the states of mind and preparation that will make Socialism work, if and when the politicians succeed in establishing it. Nor is it of less importance in the immediate cause of human happiness and decency under the existing order; for every doctor, or industrial manager or teacher who becomes a convert to Fabian Socialism is one more man or woman holding a key position who appreciates that his job is to work in terms of fellowship and social equality with others, irrespective of class or status, for improving the quality of human life.

POLICY-MAKING

A few examples of what the Society is doing in these fields of action will serve to illustrate what I mean. We try from time to time to get together those of our members who hold positions as managers or technicians in industrial concerns for the discussion of the forms of management and control of industry that need to be established in a democratic society. We try to get them to understand the claims of the Trade Unions and our Trade Union members to realise the importance of the problems of technical management and administration. In this way we do what we can to build a bridge between the workers 'by hand and brain' for the essential tasks of Socialist construction. Again, on the economic side, we have a group of members busy studying the forms of State control in industry and commerce, in order to find out how the systems of control need to be changed and developed in order to fit in with the requirements of Socialist planning. On the social side, we had a group which did excellent work on the problems of Social Security in preparation for the Social Insurance Act of 1946. This group gave important evidence to the Beveridge Committee, and subsequently brought out a comprehensive book on the reconstruction of the social services as a whole. We have had a similar group working on population problems, which has produced an admirable report, presented in the first instance to the official Commission that was studying the subject; and our Economic Committee covers a wide range of important contemporary issues, such as the problems involved in the acceptance of a policy of Full Employment. Our Women's Group has made a special study of the problems of women's employment, also in connection with an official inquiry; and another group has been at work on the question of the future organisation of the B B C. These are only a few instances of what the Society is doing to enlist the help of the many specialists who are among its members, and to ensure that Socialists who have expert knowledge are given every opportunity of putting their wisdom and experience at the disposal of the whole Labour movement.

We of the Fabian Society wish most heartily that we could do more than we are doing in these fields—especially in these days when Labour is in power, and there is so much needing to be done. Both in wartime and since the war ended it has been exceptionally hard to get people together; and we, like other societies, have been badly hampered, first by blackout, evacuation and difficulties of travel, and latterly by the much harder work that most of our members have been doing since the General Election of 1945. For we have now a large Fabian contingent in the House of Commons; and many other Fabians have been engulfed in one form of public service or another, so as to have all too little time left for the Society's calls upon them. If, in spite of all these difficulties, the Society's activities are to-day greater and more varied than they have ever been, that is no reason for our feeling satisfied, for the times have aroused in many more men and women a readiness to respond to the Socialist appeal and to perform prodigies of energy beyond what they would have deemed possible in normal times. We have to recognise that we have touched only a tiny fraction of those who would be ready to help us if we could get near to them and explain to them where we stand and what we want them to do. Our resources are so pitifully limited in relation to our opportunities that we are continually conscious of a dozen opportunities missed for every one that we are able to take. We can avoid this only to the extent to which our present members not only work for us, but also bring in others, and thus widen the range of what we can put in hand. The experiences of the past year or two have sufficiently shown us that the members are waiting to be made, as fast as any of us can get round to the job of making them.

LOCAL SOCIETIES AND SOCIALIST PROPAGANDA COMMITTEE

Especially is this the lesson of what has happened since we launched our Local Societies and Socialist Propaganda Committee. It is worth while to explain how this Committee came into being. Every year the Fabian Society runs a Summer School, which is at once a holiday in pleasant country surroundings, and an opportunity for many of our keener members from all over the country to get together and discuss their common problems. In 1941 our Summer School met soon after the Nazi onslaught on the Soviet Union, just when the Russians were being forced back dangerously towards Moscow by the terrific weight of the German offensive. Those of us who were present were all keyed up by the sense of the war having become something new and different, and much more vital for the future of our civilisation, as a result of the German attack on Russia. We felt an intense sympathy with our Russian comrades, an immense desire to do all we could to help them, and a sense of obligation to join hands with them not only in winning the war in a military sense, but in winning it for Socialism.

In this mood, we felt ashamed at the little we were doing and at the little that anybody was doing in Great Britain to bring Socialism home to the people. We compared what was being done with the work of Keir Hardie, Robert Blatchford, and other early propagandists for Socialism, and we found ourselves wanting. There arose among us, without any premeditation, the demand for a new Socialist drive; and we, as Fabians, could see no body other than our own Society through which that drive could be organised. Tiny as our numbers and resources were in relation to the need, we determined to do what we could, and the Socialist Propaganda Committee came into being.

Our original idea, in creating the new Committee, was not to push the Fabian Society, but to reanimate the propagandist activities of the Local Labour Parties and other bodies, larger than ourselves, upon which the work would most naturally have devolved. We did this where we could; but very soon, almost against our will, we found ourselves creating new Fabian Societies up and down the country. This was not because we aimed at becoming ourselves a really big body: far from it. But we found there was need, and a demand, nearly everywhere, for a nucleus of convinced Socialists who could meet together for Socialist education, and for improving their usefulness as apostles of Socialism, and who would be ready to turn their hands to any job that needed doing for the wider Labour movement in each particular place—from working up facts and policies for the Labour group on the local Council to training bands of speakers or writing letters to the local press and focusing local attention on pressing grievances and problems. The figures of the growth of local Fabian Societies during the past few years speak for themselves, and it is a plain fact that we could already have founded twice as many if we had had enough speakers and organisers to help them start.

5 Fabian History And Fabian Future

This is not bad going for a Society which I have heard more than once described as being already in its second childhood. There were many who, when Sidney and Beatrice Webb and Bernard Shaw retired from active work for the Fabian Society—though not, I am glad to say, from a keen interest in its doings—prophesied that our end was near. We owe a tremendous debt to the Webbs and to Shaw for the great work they did in building the Society and keeping it lively and original for so many years; but we are not handing in our checks now that they are no longer available to give us active help. Their names will be for ever associated with what we do, and we shall be able to do it better for having their record behind us. But we do not propose to live on the legacy they have left us. We are doing our own job in our own way, honouring our fathers and our mothers, but trying to advance beyond them, as good children ought to do. Which does not mean that we are the less grateful to them for not having embarrassed us by turning into 'old fogeys' in their latter days, as so many of the pioneers have done. It has been of immense help to us that the Webbs, more than anyone else, have helped British people to understand the Soviet Union and to build the needed bridge between the older Socialism and the new. The Webbs' *Soviet Communism* is not our Bible; for we do not deal in Bibles. But it has helped not a little in the new renaissance of the Fabian Society during these latter years.

This brings me back to saying a little more about the Fabian Society's history, of which I think we have some right to be reasonably proud. I have space to say but little about it here; but those who are interested in it will find the story told in full in Edward R. Pease's *History of the Fabian Society*, which can be got from the Fabian Bookshop; and a part of it is also fascinatingly presented in one of our tracts, Bernard Shaw's *Early History of the Fabian Society*, obtainable from the same source. We hope before long to issue a pamphlet history of the Society, which will bring the record up to date and include the important phase which began with the foundation of the New Fabian Research Bureau in 1931 and culminated in the amalgamation of 1939 Our Society began, in 1884, as a quite tiny group, and ' Fabianism ' became a word known all the world over when there were only a few hundred Fabians. That worldwide reputation came to us chiefly after the publication of *Fabian Essays*, in which Sidney Webb, Bernard Shaw and the other leaders of the movement in its early days stated their essential philosophy of Socialism. *Fabian Essays* appeared in 1889—the year in which the present writer was born, and after so many years the book still sells. It sells because nowhere else is there written down so clear an exposition of what has been called ' English Socialism '—a conception of Socialism which fits it in with the English tradition, and shows the Socialist doctrine as the logical outcome of the Benthamite utilitarian philosophy which provided the main driving force of nineteenth-century social reform. *Fabian Essays* showed that it was no longer possible, in face of modern capitalist development, to pursue ' the greatest happiness of the greatest number ' under the ægis of individualist liberalism. It showed that reform was bound to become sterile unless it based itself solidly on the public possession of the basic instruments of production, which were fated to become the tools of antisocial monopoly unless they were transferred from private exploitation to common ownership and control. The conception of Socialism outlined in *Fabian Essays* was, like Marx's, an evolutionary concept; unlike Marx's, it was conceived in times of the British tradition and admitted of ' gradualism ' in that it envisaged Socialism as coming into existence by steps and stages, rather than all at once.

Fabian Essays was by no means the only noteworthy product of the Society in those early days. The early Fabians, few as they were, poured forth a spate of tracts which served as valuable ammunition for the active propagandists of Keir Hardie's I L P. It was largely by the sales of these tracts and booklets that the message of Socialism was put into the hands of those who were best in a position to pass it on to the general body of the people—active local Trade Unionists and Co-operators, progressives who were becoming more and more dissatisfied with the Liberal Party, Christians who had come to the conclusion that Christ's Kingdom needed to be realised in this world as well as the next, idealists and workers for human welfare in every field of social life. The Fabians, of course, were not the inventors of this kind of propaganda, but they raised it to a higher level and saw to it that their tracts were always good solid value for the price they cost The most successful of all these smaller Fabian publications was H G. Wells's famous tract *This Misery of Boots*, still one of the most effective pieces of popular Socialist exposition.

It has been one of the main difficulties of the Fabian Society in these latter days that there is no longer the same zeal as there once was for selling Socialist literature. The Fabians were never in a position to spread their own publications far and wide. Their membership was much too small for that. But others did the work for them—I L P branches, local Trades Councils or Trade Union groups, and later local Labour Parties, after the Labour Party had brought into being a local political organisation of its own. But latterly there has been, mainly since the eclipse of the I L P, a sad falling off in the Labour movement's equipment for the sale of literature, and the machinery that is needed for this purpose is only now being slowly and painfully re-built. Yet how, without it, can the Labour movement hope to gain, not merely voting supporters, but well-armed and intelligent exponents of the Socialist case ? Very much of the movement's shortcoming to-day is the outcome of its failure to keep this essential link in the work of propaganda in good condition; and, until this fault is remedied, even the best written advocacy of Socialism is fated to fail of its full effect.

A WORD TO FABIANS

The purpose of this brief pamphlet has been twofold—to tell Socialists something about the Fabian Society, and to tell those who are attracted to it how they can serve it best. They can serve it best by working hard for it along its own special lines and not by trying to turn it into anything other than what it is. Above all, they must avoid setting it up as a body apart from the main stream of the Labour movement, or as in any sense a rival to the mass organisations which it exists to serve. They must preserve its character as a Society carried on mainly for research and for propaganda based on research, and they must remember always that research cannot be effective unless it is free always to seek and to confront the truth. They must not seek to set up any Fabian ' orthodoxy ', or to put fetters upon one another in this quest. Always, to the best of their power, they must try to serve the wider Labour movement, and not to ' come the clever ' over it; and always they must be ready to sacrifice the immediate interests of the Fabian Society when that is necessary in the greater cause of Socialism. If they do that, they will be understood and liked; whereas if there is any hint about them of playing the superior person they will do nothing but harm, however excellent their intentions may happen to be.

The Fabian Society is, I feel sure, in these days a good society to belong to. It has, what so many people lack, and feel that they lack, a feeling of hope about it, and a sense of working together for a cause that is worth while. It is, you will agree if you know it from the inside, a singularly friendly and unquarrelsome society. Its members are no more agreed about everything than you can expect several thousand people who are in the habit of using their brains to be; but they are agreed in thinking the Fabian Society well worth while and in supporting its attitude of wide tolerance and frank and open discussion. They may differ; but that does not cause them to quarrel, because they have a democratic belief that out of the frank statement of their several points of view, and the discussions to which these statements give rise, the right course of action stands a good chance of emerging more clearly than it could by any other means. That is why, in a world that gives so much ground for unhappiness, we Fabians give on the whole the impression of being a happy family of plotters and planners for a better future which we feel we are really helping to bring to pass. A sense of thwartedness besets so many people nowadays that it is a real relief to get into an atmosphere of busy hopefulness and friendly working together. The Fabian Society does not feel thwarted: it is much too busy getting on with its job to suffer from cynicism or disillusionment, or to waste its time in unproductive grumbling.

NEW STATESMAN PAMPHLET

Is This Socialism?

by G. D. H. COLE

★

1954
NEW STATESMAN AND NATION
in association with
THE FABIAN SOCIETY

First published July 1954
by the New Statesman & Nation
*Great Turnstile, London, W.C.*1

PRINTED IN GREAT BRITAIN BY
THE STELLAR PRESS LTD
UNION STREET, BARNET
HERTFORDSHIRE

FOREWORD

I HAD better begin by explaining as clearly as I can what this pamphlet is, and is not, about. It *is* about Socialism, by which I mean nothing less than a society without classes, and not one in which a new class-structure has replaced the old. It is *not* about the policy to be followed by a Labour Government which is not seeking to establish a classless society, but only to nationalise a few more industries and add a few more pieces to the equipment of the Welfare State. I have not tried in it to argue the case for Socialism I have taken that case for granted, and have asked only how the given Socialist objective can be achieved in a non-revolutionary way. It is not addressed to Labourites who are satisfied with the way things have been going, and, if they call themselves Socialists at all, regard Socialism only as an objective too remote to be taken account of in formulating policies for the near future. It is an attempt to indicate a way of action to those Socialists who feel a sense of frustration because Socialism means to them something radically different from the managerial Welfare State. It may well be that such persons are too few at present either to bring the Labour Party over to their point of view or, should they do so, to carry it to electoral victory. About that I do not pretend to know. I am not electioneering· I am only saying that, *if* we do wish to advance towards Socialism, these are the kind of measures we must try to persuade the electorate to accept.

G.D.H.C.

21st May, 1954

IS THIS SOCIALISM?

A SOCIALIST, we used to be told, is 'one who has yearnings for the equal division of unequal earnings'. This description neatly slurred over the fact that the inequalities the Socialists were most intent on getting rid of did not arise out of earnings at all, but out of the possession of claims to income based on ownership and, above all, on inherited wealth. Socialists saw the gross inequalities of income as proceeding much more from the 'rights of property' than from differential rewards in return for unequal services. Most of them did, no doubt, hold that the large disparities of *earned* incomes were due to a considerable extent to the existence of large *unearned* incomes, and that, if the latter were eliminated, it would become much easier to narrow differences in earned incomes. They denied the contention of many orthodox economists that differences in earned incomes corresponded to real differences in the value of services rendered, and were dictated by inexorable economic laws. They held, as against this view, that the high salaries and fees paid to professional and managerial workers were in part a reflection of the social inequality inherent in a social system which accepted unearned incomes based on property as legitimate and as carrying high prestige, and were in part due to the near-monopoly of higher education by the children of the well-to-do. They wished to diminish the inequalities of earned as well as of unearned income; but their main attack was concentrated on the inequality due to ownership. On that ground, in the main, they demanded the socialisation of the means of production, distribution and exchange, and the elimination of the toll levied by individuals on the social product on the score of ownership.

Incomes and Property

In practice, however, Socialists – as exemplified by the Labour Government of 1945 – have attacked inequalities of *income* much more than inequalities of *property*, and earned incomes almost, though not quite, as much as unearned. True, they have nationalised a number of industries and services; but they have compensated the owners, if not with generosity, at any rate so as to leave them with their claims to income broadly intact. As against this, they have taken over a structure of taxes on incomes erected to meet the emergency of war and have used it to help finance an expansion of social services in time of peace with very little discrimination between incomes derived from property and incomes received as a return for personal services. Admittedly, it is often difficult, or even impossible, to draw a clear line between earned and unearned incomes where a person gives his services to a business in in which his property, or some of it, is also invested; for in such cases there is no valid way of deciding how much of his 'profit' comes from his invested capital and how much from his work. But, in practice, lines are drawn, however arbitrarily, for tax purposes; and it would have been possible to discriminate further against unearned incomes if the Labour Government had really wished to do so. It did not, because it did not really want to in the main, it concerned itself rather with finding the money to pay for the social services and for other public outgoings in the easiest way, rather than with attacking unearned incomes as such.

Why was this? And why was it that the Labour Government made no attempt, or almost none, to attack inequalities of ownership, and contented itself with lopping off by taxation a large fraction of the really big incomes, while leaving the property that gave rise to most of them practically intact? It would certainly have surprised the Socialist pioneers very much to find a Socialist Government proceeding in this way, for they took it for granted that the advances towards Socialism would involve the abolition of the toll levied by private owners of the means of production on the current product of social labour.

Is the answer that the Labour Government of 1945 had no mandate to introduce a Socialist system, but only to carry through certain social reforms representing an advance towards the Welfare State, and to nationalise certain industries and services only on condition of *not* socialising the property rights of their previous owners? This is part of the answer, and it is reasonable to plead that the Labour Government could not have gone beyond what it did without seeking a fresh mandate. That, however, only involves re-casting the question. Why, we are impelled to ask, did the Labour Party, when it put forward a programme for further advances, beyond what it had received a mandate to do in 1945, produce in succession three further programmes in which there was still virtually no attempt to attack inequality at its roots or to advance beyond mere piecemeal nationalisations to the socialisation without which it was clearly impossible to set about the establishment of a classless society?

Why has Labour not Attacked Inequality at its Roots?

It did not, because it did not want to – at any rate for the time being. Why then, did it not want to do what its professed Socialist faith surely required of it? Largely, no doubt, because it did not believe that a majority of the electors would be prepared to give it a mandate to do anything of the kind The electors who returned the Labour Government of 1945 voted, for the most part, not for Socialism but for a change – and not too great a change As far as they envisaged anything clearly, they thought of the change they wanted mainly in terms of better social services, including more equal educational opportunities, and of 'full employment' as against a return to the depressed conditions of the 1930s They did not for the most part think of it at all largely in terms of nationalisation of industries – much less of socialisation of property –

though they were quite prepared to see some industries that had got into a mess taken into public ownership. They certainly did not see it as a sudden uprooting of established ways of life, either for themselves or for others.

That, indeed, was how most of the electors were bound to envisage the situation. Most people are neither Socialists nor anti-Socialists in the sense of having a thought-out view of the social and economic system they want. They have certain wants, for particular things, and certain broad preferences for one sort of society over another. But for most of them the particular wants are much more clearly present, and much more of a driving force, than the vaguer ideals they entertain, and, in a society such as ours, with its long traditions of gradual adaptation as against revolution, most voters vote on the assumption that the Government they vote for will do less than it says it intends to do, even if its declared intentions are not very extensive. Under conditions of universal suffrage, electorates do not vote for revolutions – unless the revolutions have already happened. If, in 1950 or in 1954, the Labour Party had put forward a really challenging election programme, involving a large advance in the direction of Socialism, one thing certain would have been, and would be, the loss of the ensuing General Election by the defection of the 'marginal' voters.

In part, then, the absence of a more Socialist programme is to be attributed to the Labour Party's wish to get back to power – or at least to office. This is a very natural desire, not only because politicians naturally prefer winning to losing, but also because they honestly believe that they have a better case than their opponents. This latter belief is shared by their active supporters, and makes them also eager to win. Accordingly, if a moderate programme offers the best prospect of electoral victory, the odds are very heavily in favour of the party, as well as the politicians, preferring it to anything more drastic. If any of the latter feel qualms about it not being socialistic enough, they can always tell themselves that they must not run too far ahead of popular opinion, and that it will at any rate help to prepare the way for something further-reaching later on.

Does the Labour Party Want Socialism?

But is this the whole explanation? I feel sure that it is not. I feel sure that many politicians who are professed Socialists, and not a few of their active supporters, have lost the simple faith in Socialism with which most of them began – and which, up to a point, they still hold to with part of their minds – and have come to entertain doubts whether the attempt to establish Socialism does not involve too great risks for the game to be worth the candle. Quite serious and even cogent reasons can be advanced in support of this doubt. They are very often not openly admitted, but haunt the backs of people's minds and are half-repressed. Let us try to drag some of them into daylight.

More Nationalisation?

First – to take one which lies quite near the surface – nationalisation, in the form of public management of industries and services, does not look quite so enticing as it did now that we have had some of it and can see how it works out in our society as it is. It is not so easy as it was to contemplate with extasy, or even with equanimity, the prospect of all or most of the means of production, etc. being nationalised, if that is to mean their administration by a series of Public Boards on the model of the Coal Board, the Transport Commission, and the B.E.A. We may, or may not, approve of these bodies, whether or no, it is not very easy to look forward to their extension to cover most branches of production, nor is it easy to see what alternative Socialists have to offer. So we fall to disputing about how much of industry we still need to nationalise after all, in order to infuse *enough* Socialism – if it is Socialism – into the economic system, and, in doing that, we soon find ourselves a long way off the old formula of socialisation – or even nationalisation – of 'the means of production, distribution and exchange.'

Social Equality?

Secondly – to go a good deal deeper – equality, or even near-equality, does not look quite so simply desirable an objective as it used to do. The Labour Government thought it saw good reasons for paying the administrators and managers it needed for the nationalised enterprises as good salaries as they would have got under private ownership, or as those holding analogous positions in capitalist industry were continuing to get. It also thought there were good reasons for not paying those of its own supporters whom it appointed to such positions less than it paid to persons taken over from capitalist industry. It therefore, on what appeared to be valid grounds, created a new Labour aristocracy of officials in the public service, and in doing so had at any rate some influence in causing such bodies as Trade Unions to increase the salaries of officials who were *not* so transferred. In effect, it sanctioned degrees of inequality of earned incomes which would have horrified the Socialist pioneers. It did this the more easily and with fewer doubts because there was proceeding at the same time so considerable an uplifting of standards at the bottom of the social scale and because so many workers in positions of superior vantage had actually become able to earn good middle-class incomes that it seemed natural for those who were higher in the scale of incomes earned by honest work to move up too. So, no doubt, it was, but that cannot alter the fact that the consequence was to undermine the old belief in a much nearer approach to economic equality, and to make it very much more difficult to launch any attack on middle-class, or even upper middle-class, incomes in general

More State Power?

Thirdly – and here we come nearest of all to the bone – the experience of one kind of totalitarian rule under Hitler and of another kind of totalitarianism under Stalin unavoidably put into the minds of reasonable persons a fear of placing too much power into the State's hands, even if the State professed to be Socialist. The workings of universal suffrage under totalitarian conditions did not encourage the continuance of the faith that, where the 'people' had the right to vote – all nominally on equal terms and with the secrecy of the ballot guaranteed – democratic government would necessarily follow as a result. Democracy came to be thought of less exclusively in terms of electoral rights and more in terms of personal freedom – of speech and writing and association – and with this went a greater preparedness to take account of the claims of minorities and of groups within the larger society. This reacted on, and interacted with, the new look of nationalised enterprise. It began to be seen that the government of an industry by a National Board could not be simply identified with its government by 'the people', and that there was a real problem of finding out how to control the controllers.

In Great Britain, this fear of putting too much power into the State's hands has hardly come, as yet, to be more than an uneasiness. We are in no present danger of losing our rights of free speech or association, or of passing under the control of a 'one-party' State machine. But we cannot quite avoid asking ourselves whether our present immunity in this respect may not have something to do with the fact that what we have been engaged in setting up has been, not Socialism, but only a partial embodiment, within our limited opportunities, of the Welfare State.

Socialism and the Welfare State

Of course Socialism involves the Welfare State that is implied in the old slogan 'From each according to his capacities, to each according to his needs.' It has always been one of the essential Socialist objectives to put an end to poverty and to ensure that in the distribution of incomes the children, the aged and the incapacitated are not pushed aside by the predatory or the strong. To the extent of our success in advancing towards this we have been doing what every Socialist must wish to do. But the Welfare State is, all the same, not Socialism in the form in which we have been attempting to move towards it in recent years it is at most only socialistic – if even that. For what we have been doing is not to put people on an equal footing, but only to lessen the extremes of inequality by re-distributing grossly unequal incomes through taxation; and even this re-distribution has quite largely taken the form of making the poor pay for one another's basic needs. No doubt, the taxation levied on large incomes has been severe no doubt, it would have been quite impossible to develop even such social services as we have developed without putting the major part of the cost on the workers and the middle classes, for the simple reason that the total income of the rich, even had it been possible to take it all, would not have been nearly enough. Nevertheless, we need only use the evidence of our senses to assure ourselves that the rich are still among us and that the class structure of our society remains, if not intact, very much in being.

What is Happening to the Class-Structure?

What has happened, stated in the broadest terms, appears to be something like this

1. *The Bottom Dogs*

At the bottom of the scale, sheer hunger and malnutrition have been greatly diminished. Nobody need starve nobody, in the last resort, need go without the absolute minimum needs of life. I know that many old age pensioners are having a raw deal, and that the conditions are still heavily weighted against large families, but it will hardly be denied that, in comparison with 1939 or any earlier date, there has been a great improvement in the position of both these groups, especially when the supplementary payments from the Assistance Board are taken into account Those who suffer sheer want to-day for absolute lack of means are fewer by far than they used to be In spite of this, the 'bottom dogs' remain there is still a stratum that lives under conditions of want and mal-adjustment. But this stratum owes its inferior position to-day less to the lack of social legislation designed to meet general needs than to a failure to devise special means of dealing with special cases. The 'submerged tenth', which is to-day much less than a 'tenth', presents a long-run problem which is not so much one of further re-distribution through taxation as of devising, by education and training, improved ways of equipping for useful activity those who have something mentally or physically 'wrong with them,' but are not incapable of earning their livings and looking after themselves if we help them to discover how.

2. *The Unskilled Workers*

At the next level, that of ordinary unskilled labour, the improvement in economic conditions has been immense. This stratum has benefited most by full employment, both in its ability to command a better wage and in the increased regularity of employment. These factors have been much more important for it than the development of the social services, though that of course has counted too – especially sickness benefit and the supplementary help given through the Assistance Board, and also children's allowances, despite their inadequacy. Many of the families belonging to this stratum are, no doubt, still rather bad at spending their money, and many of them are hampered by very bad housing. But there can be no doubt that this is the part of society that is benefiting most from what has been accomplished, and will continue to benefit – if full employment holds. We must not, however, forget that it is also the group that would be flung back most disastrously were full employment to disappear – though even so its lot would be better than in the past because of the better social services on which it would be able to fall back, if it can be assumed that these services could and would be maintained intact in face of a slump.

3. *The Semi-Skilled Workers and the White-Collar Brigade*

At the next higher level, we come to the main body, not of highly skilled workers, but of the semi-skilled in manual jobs and to the corresponding groups of non-manual workers, such as shop assistants and the lower grades in clerical employment. These groups include a rather high proportion of women workers who are not heads of households and are in many cases living in households in which there is also a male earner – a father or a husband. Such earners – men as well as women – have also benefited greatly from full employment, as well as from the growth of the social services On the other hand, there are in this stratum a good many heads of households, especially those with young families, who have benefited much less because they are in time-working jobs for which wages have risen less than the average. This applies particularly to some of the non-manual groups, and also particularly to those who are engaged in employments that do not produce profits – such as the public services But side by side with these relatively unfortunate groups there are others, especially piece-workers on repetitive work in flourishing industries, whose earnings have risen by much more than the average, and for such workers the gain has been large. Economically, they have risen to parity, if not beyond parity, with large bodies of skilled manual and non-manual workers who used to have both higher incomes and higher social prestige

4. *The Highly Skilled and the Lesser Professions*

Fourthly, we come to the definitely skilled manual workers and, on a broad level with them, to the higher grades of clerical and distributive workers and to such large bodies of professional workers as draughtsmen, teachers, nurses, and professional 'auxiliaries' of many other kinds. In comparison with most of those in the groups lower down the scale, this stratum has fared rather badly. The manual workers included in it have benefited much more than most of the non-maual workers from full employment, and also more, I think, from the extension of the social services. But wage-differentials between skilled and less skilled manual workers have been reduced except for a smallish minority which has been enabled by special bonuses and allowances, or by high piecework payments, to earn very good money indeed – mainly because certain kinds of highly skilled labour have been seriously scarce, so that employers have gone out of their way to retain its services These small privileged groups have risen notably in the economic scale, whereas the highly skilled non-manual workers, except those who have been promoted to managerial positions, have lost ground – especially those in non-profit-making salaried employment that allows no scope for extra earnings. On the whole, skilled manual workers have gained more than salaried employees, and among skilled manual workers there has appeared an increasing differentiation between those who have been able to secure special treatment and those who have found the margin of difference between their wages and those of the less skilled considerably reduced. But even the manual groups to which this last condition applies have in many cases reaped great gains through full employment.

5. *The Lesser Bourgeois Classes*

Partly on a parity with the fourth stratum, partly rising above it, and partly below it comes the large mass of shopkeepers and independent jobbing small masters in such trades as building repairs and decoration. About these it is difficult to generalise. Many small traders complain of cut margins, but I think it is undoubted that in general their position has been improved by quicker and more assured turnover resulting from full employment and from scarcities of goods, which have reduced dead and idle stocks. Some traders have undoubtedly done remarkably well – even apart from the smallish minority of black marketeers, who have had the time of their lives. The independent jobbers have also done well in most cases, because of full employment. In general, the relative social and economic position of these groups has not greatly changed if anything they have done better than the average – certainly better than the salaried minor professionals or the less fortunate groups among the skilled manual workers

6 *The Higher Professions and the Managers*

This brings us to the higher professional groups, including the higher ranges of the public services and of teaching and academic research, the doctors, dentists, and other medical groups of comparable status, the practising barristers and solicitors, the middle ranges of business management, including the higher technicians, and the owners of businesses having a comparable status. The net incomes of all these groups have of course been considerably cut into by high taxation, but the gross incomes on which these taxes fall have moved very differently for different groups within this broad stratum of society – the part of the upper middle class which works for its living and gets its payment in salaries or in professional fees. Here again, the fixed salary-earners in occupations which do not result in profits have fared worst — except the medical groups, which have done remarkably well for themselves by effective and obstinate bargaining The managerial grades have, on the whole, done better than the professionals, at any rate in the more flourishing industries under private ownership elsewhere, they have not done so well, but a good deal better than most of the *salaried* professionals. Owners of smallish or middle-sized businesses have mostly flourished, because full employment and shortage of capital for investment in displacing obsolete plant have made profits easy to earn – though they are now in many trades less easy than they were a few years ago. As long as new capital goods remain scarce and demand high, profits will remain high too, and small businesses as well as large will reap the benefit of an unexpectedly long life for their plant

7. *The Top Grades*

At the highest level among earned incomes we come to those of the topmost managers and administrators, and these are not only the best placed for supplementing their incomes by means of expense allowances but also the most likely to be able to eke them out with capital gains. Only a thin line separates them from the big entrepreneurs who draw not salaries but dividends as their main source of income Whoever has suffered as a consequence of high taxation, they among the wealthier groups have suffered least, and they have been reinforced by the highly paid chief executives of nationalised industries, whose rewards help to cast a halo round theirs.

8. *The Farmers*

There remains one group that calls for separate mention, not as the highest, but as ranking undoubtedly among those which have most improved their position Farmers, large and small alike, have had a big lift as a result of the measures adopted to increase the home output of food. They are in fine feather, whether they have been 'feather-bedded' or not.

Summarising these broad generalisations, we can safely say that most 'bottom dogs', most unskilled workers, some semi-skilled workers, a minority of skilled workers, most shopkeepers and jobbing builders, most doctors and dentists, most of the higher business executives, most private employers, and nearly all farmers are both absolutely and relatively a good deal better off than they or their predecessors were before 1939; that some semi-skilled and most skilled manual workers, most blackcoats in clerical and distributive jobs and in public employments, and most professional workers in non-profit making occupations are at any rate relatively worse-off; and that it is impossible to generalise about the middle grades of managerial and technical employees This makes up a general picture of income re-distribution, as a consequence of full employment and taxation combined, embodying highly significant changes, but certainly not anything that can be regarded as carrying us far in the direction of a Socialist society. The picture needs of course to be completed by bringing in those social groups which depend on unearned incomes To these we can now turn

9 *The Small and Middle Investors*

The small investors, who hold a high proportion of fixed interest securities and preference shares, have definitely lost ground This affects particularly retired persons, including those living on pensions and insurances. It affects also the non-employed members of rich families, and also those who derive middle-class incomes partly from work and partly from property. Indeed, those in this group who depend on fixed salaries *plus* small investments have been hit in both capacities. In general, the sections of the middle classes who do not work for a living have lost a great deal of ground. Landlords of small house-property have been badly affected by rent controls, though some of them have profited by the continued occupation of dwellings that ought to have been pulled down long ago, had it been practicable to replace them.

10. *The Big Capital-owners*

The bigger investors, most of whom are in a better position to go in search of capital gains through speculation or change of investments, and who tend to hold more ordinary shares than bonds or preference shares, have fared much better, and those of them who own urban land and non-residential buildings (or premises not subject to rent control), have also done well. Agricultural landlords, where they have been in a position to revise rents, have been able to skim off a share in the farmers' gains.

These conclusions about what has been happening to unearned incomes are not very comforting from the standpoint of those who would like to believe that we have been advancing towards Socialism by easy, equitable stages. They may not be prepared to spend much sympathy on the declining sections of the *rentier* middle class, but it is hardly socialistic to weight the scales in favour of the richer capitalist as against the poorer.

Achievements of the Welfare State

The gains achieved through full employment and the Welfare State are beyond doubt considerable in terms of the reduction in the amount of sheer suffering and enfeeblement of human quality by privation. So far, they are a great good. They depend, however, at least as much on full employment as on the expansion of the social services, and are precarious to the extent to which there is a danger of severe unemployment coming back. Moreover, these gains have been secured at the expense of a narrowing of the differentials awarded for most, though not for all, kinds of superior manual skill, and *may* be reacting on the future supply of skilled workers by making it less worth while to learn a skilled trade. The supply of new recruits for the non-manual occupations which have declined in relative earning capacity is for the most part less likely to be affected because our educational system has a strong bias in favour of such occupations and because some of them are more attractive in themselves, and may still carry higher prestige, than better-paid manual jobs.

Are we Advancing towards a Classless Society?

What does all this indicate in respect of the class-structure of the society towards which we have been moving? Certainly not that we are advancing towards a 'classless society'. Except at the very bottom of the scale – the numbers in which have been reduced – there has been a diminution of economic and social inequality between skilled and less skilled manual workers, and between manual workers and 'black coats'. But there is also a tendency for a new grade, or even class, of highly paid super-skilled manual workers to develop and to increase its distance from the main body. These are not Stakhanovites; for many of them are time-workers or setters-up rather than operators of machines, and even where they are piece-workers their exploits are not announced in the newspapers or rewarded with public decorations. But they constitute a new and growing labour aristocracy, with 'money to burn' because they are only now adjusting their living standards to their increased earnings. They are still, however, in this country only a small group, not at all comparable with the much bigger labour aristocracy that has grown up in the United States. Nor is there at present any sign of a wish on their part to dissociate themselves as a group from the groups lower down in the economic hierarchy.

More widespread for the present is the economic assimilation between the large body of fairly skilled, but not super-skilled, manual workers and the main body of 'black coats': so that these too are being merged economically and to a considerable extent socially as well into a single stratum. A step above them socially, and sometimes but not always economically, the lesser professional groups and the general run of technicians constitute, together with the middling tradesmen, an intermediate stratum – a *petite bourgeoisie* which, far from dying out, is more than holding its own in relative numbers. With it go a large part of the farmers and many small employers, such as garage keepers, jobbing builders, wireless dealers, and electrical contractors so that this stratum includes groups of widely divergent fortunes and interests. It is linked on the one hand to the major professions and on the other to the group of middling profit-makers and industrial executives. A part of it has been losing, and a part gaining ground: it has no common social outlook or political allegiance, though the greater proportion tends to be politically Conservative, with some tendency to swing over when things go badly wrong.

The Rich Remain

Above all these strata the rich remain. But they have considerably changed their composition. Riches and aristocracy still go together in the case of a limited group of old families which have large holdings of urban or industrial land or have used the accumulations of the past from land to become great investors in business. To these must be added the aristocracy of banking and commerce which has bought or married its way into the 'upper classes' in the traditional sense of the term. But side by side with these, and as rich or richer, are those who have made great fortunes in business too recently to be counted among the 'idle rich', and this group of new wealth, including now many high-level business administrators who draw large salaries and have risen by personal exertions from the middle or lower grades, forms a larger proportion than ever before of those who can afford to live at a luxury level and to hob-nob, without much feeling of inferiority, with their American opposite numbers.

Is the Welfare State a Step towards Socialism?

Such a society as this is definitely not Socialist, and I cannot feel that it is even on the way to becoming Socialist. It is, of course, much less aristocratic than the society it is displacing in terms of social origins the top classes of to-day are a very mixed lot. Oxford and Cambridge are no longer gentlemen's preserves to anything like the same extent as they used to be, a much lower proportion of top Civil Servants and of the successful members of the higher professions come from a small group of gentlemen's schools, and on the boards of directors of the great business concerns there are to be found a large number of 'self-made' men who have risen, if not from the ranks, at all events from quite low beginnings. Our society has become a good deal more 'open' than it used to be, in the sense that the old distinction between 'gentlemen' and 'not-gentlemen' has largely broken down. A 'player' can not only captain England, or his county, at cricket he can also captain the Nuffield Organisation or Unilever – or, of course, the B E.A. But on the whole the new recruits to both grammar schools and universities tend to come much more from the poorer sections of the middle classes than from the families of manual workers – and to come hardly at all from the less skilled sections of the manual working class. No doubt, some children of manual workers get their higher education rather through technical schools and colleges than through grammar schools and universities, and account has to be taken of this in estimating the effects of educational development on the class structure. But in this case too the children of the unskilled workers are largely left out.

What we are getting in practice appears to be a society in which the field of recruitment for the superior positions is being considerably widened, so as to give those who can get as far as the higher ranges of grammar or technical education an improved chance of rising further even if their parents cannot afford to help them. But at the same time we are putting an increasingly difficult barrier between those who do get so far and those who do not, and this is still in the main a class barrier, though it has been moved further down the social scale. Moreover, among those who surmount this barrier only a small proportion can actually move up to positions of affluence and power, and those who do achieve this become assimilated to the new mixed upper class, take over its ways and spending habits, and with it constitute a new oligarchy of high executives which falls heir to the old gentlemanly prerogative of ordering its inferiors about.

If this is a correct picture, the question that arises is whether a society of this sort is on the road to Socialism. The question is whether it does not, as a hard matter of fact, offer the prospect of even greater resistance to Socialism than the society it has displaced. In other words, is the Welfare State, in the form in which it has been developed so far, a step on the road to Socialism, or a step in quite different direction – that is, a step, not towards a classless society, but rather towards a new stratification that is likely to persist and to become more marked?

The situation outlined in the preceding paragraph is of course only a new version of a very old dilemma. In France the peasants, when they had got the land and destroyed the old feudal privileges, turned promptly into a conservative class and became a bulwark against Socialism. They might easily have done the same in Russia had not the Bolsheviks first stamped hard on the kulaks and then collectivised the villages. In our society, the opening of higher education to wider class groups (but by no means to all, regardless of class), combined with full employment and greater social security, may well be creating barriers in the way of Socialism rather than helping its advance, especially if a child's whole chance of rising to the higher social and economic levels is to depend on the results of a single test, applied at an age when the nature of the home environment is bound to be of great influence in determining these results. This kind of test looks like leading to a new class structure which will on the one hand cut the working class into two – those with a chance of rising further and those without – and will on the other animate the upper of these two segments with a desire to protect itself against the lower, and also permeate it with a belief in the virtue of personal advancement and in the values of an acquisitive society. In short, is it towards Socialism we are tending, or towards an anglicised version of the American conception of democracy? Is our goal the classless society, or only the so-called 'open' society which is in fact still closed to a majority of the people?

The Future

What will happen to our society, will evidently depend on the conditions to which it has to adapt its ways of life and on its responses to these conditions. The days are over when Great Britain's position in the world was so commanding that other peoples had to adapt their ways to ours, and the internal trends of British development furnished, broadly speaking, a sufficient basis for predicting the future, at any rate for some distance ahead. As things now are, we cannot rely, as a nation, on getting nationally better off as we improve our productive techniques, no matter what may be the impact on us of external forces. We are caught up in a world economic process in which we are no longer the leaders, but only one people among many – and by no means the most powerful.

The Economic Outlook – First Hypothesis

Obviously one great determinant of our social future will be what happens to employment and to the national income. The real national income of Great Britain, as matters now stand, depends mainly on three factors – the productivity of British industry and agriculture, the readiness of other countries to receive British exports, and the terms of trade – that is, the rates of exchange between exported and imported goods. I do not include the level of employment as a fourth determinant, because it is mainly, though not exclusively, determined by the other three. Full employment could no doubt be undermined by ill-considered financial policies even if the other factors were all favourable, but this is rather unlikely to happen, though it could happen if the British Government were foolish enough to yield to American pressure for convertibility of sterling into dollars. Leaving that danger aside, the three factors I have mentioned are the main ones. They are, of course, to some extent interdependent. The more productive our industries are, the better will be our chances of selling our exports over whatever barriers may be set up against them and the less favourable will be the terms of trade we shall need. The fewer barriers we meet with against our exports, the more we shall be able to take advantage of the economies of large-scale production, and the better we shall be able to afford to have the terms of trade turned against us. The more favourable the terms of trade are, the less we shall be hampered by the need to restrict imports in ways that damage production and the less will be the real cost of the imported materials which constitute a substantial fraction of the value of the goods we export. On the other hand, favourable terms of trade for us mean unfavourable terms for those of our customers from whom we import, and thus reduce their purchasing power.

If all these factors act favourably, there is no reason why our real material income should not increase in future at an average rate as high as that of the post-war years, or why we should experience any difficulty in maintaining full employment. If that happens, the existing trends are likely to continue unless we deliberately take action to alter them. We shall be able to carry through fairly rapidly those further developments of the Welfare State – for example, in the field of education – to which we are already committed, and also to rectify the grievances of such groups as old age pensioners by improving social service benefits. Real wages will be able to rise, even if but slowly. Profits will remain high, and perhaps go still higher, and investment will be able to increase – including something for overseas investment, especially in Commonwealth countries. But all this, which rests on the most favourable hypothesis that can possibly be entertained, will not of itself bring us an inch nearer Socialism, and may even carry us away from it by strengthening the tendencies towards class-differentiation on the new basis and making a majority of the electorate prefer going on as they are to embarking on any risky adventures in social and economic change.

Second Hypothesis

Having taken the most favourable hypothesis, let us now take the least If productivity stagnates, if foreign markets are obstructed by fresh barriers or reduced by unwillingness or inability to buy, and if the terms of trade turn against us, it will become impossible to maintain full employment and necessary to reduce real wages and possibly social service benefits in order to cut down consumption of imported foodstuffs and materials to what we can afford to buy with our restricted exports. Such a situation, highly unfavourable though it would be to Trade Union bargaining, would almost certainly benefit Labour politically – unless the Labour Party had the misfortune to be already in office when it set in It would engender mass discontent, not only among the workers but also in the middle groups, and might clear the way for a considerable move towards Socialism if the Labour Party were minded and prepared to attempt such a move.

The economic catastrophe envisaged in the preceding paragraph is, however, unlikely to occur in any such complete form If foreign markets for our exports were seriously reduced by a world slump, the effect would almost certainly be to turn the terms of trade for what exports were left in our favour and not against us Even so, the situation would be difficult enough, and the maintenance of full employment would hardly be possible. With fewer jobs than workers looking for them, the bargaining power of the Trade Unions would be weakened, especially for the workers in the export trades and for the less skilled workers in general. Real wages would slip back the cost of the social services would rise sharply, and we should soon feel how inadequate a protection they give when the buttress of full employment is removed The effect of such a situation, though less drastically than in the more pessimistic hypothesis of the preceding paragraph, would be a growth of social discontent which would create a stronger *working-class* demand for a more socialistic programme, but might fail to swing the intermediate groups, or enough of them, over to supporting it In that event, we might easily get a Labour Government more like that of 1929 than that of 1945, impotently plastering the distress, but quite unable to make up its mind to attempt a drastic cure, or perhaps failing to carry a majority of the electors with it even if it did make the attempt.

Remedies: The Abolition of Large Inherited Fortunes

This is a depressing view, but what else can we fairly expect? Hardly anybody is at present seriously trying to make converts for Socialism, or for anything more than further advances, as occasion allows, towards the Welfare State. Indeed, no one has even attempted to think out how Socialism can be compatible with the tendencies which the Welfare State accentuates and promotes, though clearly it must be made compatible with those tendencies if we are to progress towards it *via* increasing instalments of social welfare.

The first question that arises here is that of the extent to which Socialism is to be regarded as compatible with economic inequality in its various forms I think it is clearly incompatible with any social system that allows great fortunes, or even moderate fortunes *that have been inherited once*, to be transmitted at death I see no reason why it should be regarded as inadmissible for a person to pass on to his wife or children, or perhaps to other near relatives, moderate sums which he has accumulated by saving in his own lifetime, or of course to transmit in moderation personal possessions which are not of a capital kind, and I see every reason why it should remain possible for security of tenure, subject to good use and payment of rent, to be granted to the families of farmers or householders from one generation to the next But beyond these reasonable limits I think Socialists are bound to stand for doing away with inheritance, because *they cannot recognise any able-bodied person's right to live in idleness on the labour of others or to claim on account of inherited wealth a much bigger income than he can earn by his own exertions*. Accordingly I believe that not merely higher death duties but positive abolition of the right of inheritance beyond fairly modest limits should take a high place among Labour's next steps towards its declared Socialist objective. The transition could, if it were thought fit, be eased by allowing limited additional annuities to be paid for a single further life, but beyond the permitted sums generally applicable, the capital should pass to the public, subject to such transitional charges as might be allowed.

This is, of course, a very long-standing Socialist demand. It goes back to the followers of Saint-Simon in the 1820s, if not even further, and those Socialists who have not explicitly made it have passed it over only because they have merged it in wider demands for the complete expropriation of the sources of unearned income. In a social revolution such expropriation may be possible, but for us, who are seeking a way of advance towards Socialism by constitutional methods, it is clearly out of the question. Piecemeal nationalisation involves compensation, and does not solve the problem of eliminating the claims of ownership In such a situation, these claims can be dealt with only in two ways – by levies on the capital assets of the living, or by narrowing the right to acquire wealth by inheritance. I am not ruling out the first of these methods, especially if the second proves to be too slow, but surely the second is the better, because it involves much less dislocation of established expectations and fits in best with the widespread feeling that, as far as possible, the members of each new generation should start fair, without preventible handicaps or advantages. No doubt, in the minds of many people, there is also a sentiment that a parent ought to be allowed to provide for his widow and his children, and in our class-divided, unequal society this sentiment is natural enough. Let us then concede to it, as long as serious economic inequalities remain in being, the testator's right to leave to his widow or children his house or farm, up to a maximum value, or an equivalent capital sum, but beyond that, not property, but only annuities equivalent to a proportion of what he is 'worth' at death. Under this arrangement all property above the permitted maximum would become at once public property, and the annual charge upon it would be wiped out at the close of a single further life.

A New Way of Socialisation

Such taxation of inheritance would, of course, mean that the State would have to be prepared to take over the actual property of those dying with considerable fortunes and not money payments supposed to represent their value. For it would create a situation in which there would be far too few buyers for the estates passing at death to be sold to new private owners. It would therefore mean that the Government would be continually acquiring ownership both of shares and bonds of all sorts and of other forms of property, such as houses, landed estates, and private businesses. Nationalisation, or rather Socialisation, would thus advance by a new route, even if no further industries were taken over by the methods hitherto adopted. The State would become, to an ever-increasing extent, part proprietor of a host of productive businesses, and the holder of mortgage charges on many estates and non-company businesses remaining in private hands. It could use the powers it would thus acquire to appoint its own directors to joint stock enterprises and to foreclose on concerns which failed to meet their obligations. For a time, it would find itself the partner of profit-making business men, and engaging in profit-making enterprises. But I can see no valid objection to this, if it is merely a stage in the process of acquiring total, or majority, ownership of the businesses in question, and I can see the positive advantage that it would not involve the creation of more top-heavy centralised administrations of the type of the Coal Board and the Transport Commission. Of course it would be necessary for the directors whom the Government would appoint to such businesses, not only to play an active part in their operation in the public interest, but also to work together, through some sort of collective body including all the state directors within an industry, and to follow a collective policy laid down by the Government's planning agencies. It would be necessary to train men specially for these tasks, in order to ensure well-informed intervention in the affairs of the businesses concerned, and *the long-run effect would be to establish socialised production over a wide field without setting up giant organisations in forms of enterprise better suited to relatively small-scale, and within limits competitive, operation.*

The Problem of Large Earned Incomes

The restriction of inheritance would of itself do nothing to lessen inequalities of earned income, though it would do a good deal towards levelling those who receive large incomes partly from work as managers or members of the higher professions and partly from ownership of property In the main, excessive disparities of earned incomes would have to be tackled by other methods. *As the Government now meets a large part of the cost of higher education and professional training, it is no longer reasonable for the incomes of those who have received this help to be calculated at rates meant to pay back the expenses of their professional preparation* Nor should there be any need to pay in business occupations the very large salaries which are based largely on a comparison with what is received by capitalist employers in the form of profit. It is, however, much easier to state the case for bringing down the higher earned incomes to a reasonable level than to find effective methods of setting about it. One thing that could be done would be to impose much stricter control on the granting of expense allowances, or even to abolish them altogether save in very exceptional cases. What more will be needed will depend partly on what happens to the cost of living If this continues to move gradually upward, the desired result can be secured by a simple refusal to allow the higher salaries to be increased as prices rise, and at the same time by using the influence of public directors to prevent excessive payments in directors' fees and emoluments. If, however, the cost of living falls or remains stationary, stronger measures will be called for, but these can be held over for the time being, in order to see how prices go, on condition that steps are taken to prevent further rises being given to those who are already getting too much

As for the middle incomes, no special action seems to be called for, except a steady policy of reducing trading margins so as to squeeze out the inefficient as fast as they can be replaced by more efficient producing or trading firms – which should become fully practicable if the level of new investment is made high enough to keep pace with technical progress

Wage Problems

Wage-incomes and the lower ranges of salary-incomes raise more complex problems. It is fully consistent with Socialist principles to allow whatever differentials turn out to be needed to procure adequate recruitment for the more skilled kinds of work, and also to offer whatever piecework or similar incentives turn out to be necessary in order to secure high output. Nobody, however, can believe that the existing wage-structure complies with these requirements, or is anything other than a confusion due partly to the varying fortunes of the tug-of war between employers and Trade Unions and partly to sheer accident or tradition. In a Socialist society, it will clearly not be possible to continue to allow wage-rates to be settled by a large number of unco-ordinated bargains, influenced largely by the degree of shelter or exposure of particular industries to outside competition, or to the expansion or contraction in the demand for their products. There will have to be both some general way of determining how large an aggregate of wage-payments the economy is able to afford, and, broadly, how what is deemed to be available shall be divided among the various claimants. It would be premature to-day, while non-wage incomes remain uncontrolled and while the greater part of industry is still under capitalist operation for profit, to introduce any 'national wages policy' under which a body of highly placed officials would have the right to fix wages as they might think fit. But, as we advance further towards a Socialist society, the planning of wages will become indispensable, if only because wages and prices are inevitably linked together and it will be as a rule a matter of choosing between higher wages and higher prices, with the balance of advantage shifting in favour of lower prices as the toll levied by unproductive consumers is reduced by the erosion of incomes derived from ownership.

Towards Social Equality

Class-structure is a matter, not only of incomes, but also of culture and of social prestige I regard it as a great calamity that Labour Governments have allowed themselves to fall into the evil habit of conferring titles both on persons who are barely distinguishable from those ennobled by their political opponents and – worse still – on persons who are supposed to share with them in the Socialist faith In the case of peerages, this practice is defended on the ground that, as long as the House of Lords exists as a legislative chamber, Labour has to be represented in it, but no such excuse can be put forward for the growing practice of authorising Trade Union and Co-operative leaders to stick 'Sir' in front of their names As for peerages, surely the correct course is to abolish the House of Lords at the earliest possible moment, and in the meantime, to make do with those who have been ennobled already to assist it in winding up its affairs I cannot help saying that it fills me with sheer disgust to see Labour leaders accepting titles for no conceivable purpose except that of denying their alleged faith in social equality – I mean those who become Sirs', or join the peerage without being specially needed to represent the Government in the Upper Chamber *I cannot conceive how any Socialist can defend this kind of social snobbery, which does immense harm to the Socialist cause by compromising the Labour Party with the unclean thing and spreading cynicism about the sincerity and disinterestedness of those who lead it.*

In the educational field, Labour is to be congratulated on the good fight it is putting up in many places for the Comprehensive School, for educational equality is a vital part of social equality, and as long as we allow snob schools to continue we shall have a steady stream of snobs coming out of them. Parity of esteem is impossible between schools most of whose pupils leave at fifteen and schools where most stay up to eighteen and a substantial proportion then go on to College or University. It is even impossible between the Modern School and those Grammar Schools many of whose pupils leave at sixteen or at most seventeen. There used to be an undeniable case for parents who objected to sending their children to schools where they would not only get an inferior education, but also pick up bad manners and ways of speech, and perhaps diseases too, from the children of the slums But that case has largely disappeared, thanks to the great improvement in the economic condition of the less skilled workers A residue is left, but must be dealt with by special measures and not by perpetuating the 'two nations' policy of nineteenth-century schooling Of course, in order to make the Comprehensive School workable as a general practice, we shall have to improve the quality of teaching, as well as to do a great deal of new building and equipment. These things will take time there is no danger whatsoever of our going ahead with them too fast. They must be given a high priority because, even so, they are bound to take so long in the doing.

We must, however, be careful to ensure both that our Comprehensive Schools do not keep back the quicker and cleverer children – whose brains and skill our society needs – and that we get in them a proper attention to the training of manual as well as intellectual capacities I do not mean only technical education designed to prepare pupils for particular occupations, even in a broad way. I mean also that everybody – boys and girls alike – ought to come out of school with a reasonable capability for doing ordinary manual jobs about the house and garden and with an adequate acquaintance with the household arts, and I mean too that there ought to be the fullest opportunity for each individual to follow his particular bent in the use of his hands as well as in more literary or cultural pursuits. We have suffered badly in Great Britain from an unnatural divorce between literary and technical education, not only at the higher levels but at the elementary levels as well In order to correct this, we need in every type of school teachers who know how to use both their heads and their hands and can teach their pupils to do things as well as to learn about them in the abstract. A society of social equals, as distinct from one of masters aided by servants to do the dirty work, needs an all-round training in the art of looking after itself, without calling in a professional 'workman' to do simple repairs or just letting things go to ruin for lack of aptitude for putting them right

The Supply of Ability

Some people say that a more equal society is impossible, or will lead to disaster, because there are too few able persons to run it They argue, for example, that the increased numbers in higher education have already involved a fall in average quality. I believe this to be nonsense I do not profess to know whether the supply of real first-raters can be greatly increased by improving our educational system, but I feel no doubt that the supply of good second-raters can be, and that more good second-raters are what we chiefly need to do the jobs which the advance towards a fair deal for everybody will require us to fill No doubt, it would be nice to double our supply of first-raters, but a limited number can go a long way if they have good seconds-in-command at call.

The Ageing and the Handicapped

This educational side of Socialist policy is becoming more and more important now that we are already well on the way towards solving the purely economic part of the problem of the 'bottom dogs'. Hardly less important are two other problems which we are much less near to solving – that of the residue of physically or mentally handicapped persons, and that of the increasing average age of the population Slowly, we are learning that, given the right methods, a great deal can be done to retrieve the mentally handicapped and enable them to take a useful place in society, and to help the physically handicapped to overcome their disabilities, but we have still a long way to go in these matters, which are of vital importance in the making of a society bent on diminishing social inequalities to the fullest possible extent The other matter is that of adapting our economic arrangements so as to make it easy for old people who can no longer do a full week's work at the occupations in which they have been engaged either to continue in part-time employment or to find openings for alternative work within their capacities and desires. This problem is of the same order as that of making better provision for the rehabilitation of the partially disabled and for their employment as far as possible on a self-supporting basis These matters are all important not only because an ageing society cannot afford not to make full use of every person capable of doing a useful job, but also because work, for those who are capable of it, affords much better prospects of happy living than enforced idleness and enables the aged and the handicapped to play a much more equal role in the life of the community

I should like to see the Labour Party taking up this group of problems and giving it a high place in its programme It is not a simple matter of welfare legislation it involves ensuring that industry shall be so organised as to make room for the work of the groups concerned and to devise special arrangements for them, wherever these are needed, in ways that will isolate them as little as possible from other workers, and will emphasise their capacities rather than their disabilities. What is needed is to put as many as possible of them into employment, not in segregated groups, but as the colleagues of ordinary workers, and this involves making arrangements with the Trade Unions as well as compelling employers to provide the necessary openings Above all, it involves doing all that can be done to help the partially disabled and the ageing to develop and maintain their productive capacities at the highest practicable level.

Industrial Democracy

I come now to the major problem of industrial democracy Given full employment, Trade Unions are in a powerful bargaining position, because employers cannot afford to lose the services of even moderately efficient workers *Full employment has been chiefly responsible for the great changes that have come about in factory relations and in industrial discipline as a whole.* The foreman can no longer play the tyrant as easily as he could in the past, and the higher management has to mind its P's and Q's when Trade Union susceptibilities are in question In some industries, including those which have been nationalised, there have been considerable developments of joint consultation in the workplaces as well as at higher levels, and Trade Union bargaining has spread to many trades in which it was previously almost non-existent. So far, so good, but *neither Trade Union bargaining nor joint consultation makes the worker a responsible partner in industry,* or necessarily gives the individual a sense that it is up to him to render of his best and to think of himself as a member of a team co-operating in the performance of an essentially social task. He cannot, indeed, be expected to have this sense of responsibility where businesses are still being carried on for the profit of absentee shareholders, or where the management still behaves as a caste of superiors issuing orders to inferiors to whom it recognises no democratic responsibility. Exceptionally, a few managers or employers do contrive, by virtue of sheer personality, to establish really friendly and co-operative relationships, but most managements are incapable of achieving this and will continue to be so as long as they represent a business structure in the control of which the workers have no share This applies even to the nationalised industries, in which the controlling boards are far too remote from the actual workers to give them any sense of participation – and would remain so even if the Trade Unions were allowed to appoint members to sit on them in a formally representative capacity

In the past, in a society explicitly based on inequality, it was for the workers to obey orders and for the representatives of their 'masters' to give them. Obedience was enforced partly by custom, partly by inducements such as higher earnings for greater efforts, and partly – and to no small extent – by fear of the sack or of being 'stood off' for offending the authorities, or in extreme cases of being blacklisted as well as sacked. Nowadays, these fears have become much less potent, though they still exist. Piecework incentives and other monetary inducements still retain their power, but have been to some extent weakened by the introduction of guaranteed minimum rates and by the diminished danger of getting dismissed for not producing enough. The greatest change of all, however, has been in the lessened prestige of those who give the orders and the sense of increased power to question them among those to whom they are given. The consequence is a relaxation of discipline which is bound, for the time being, to react adversely on output. This is partly to the good, where it prevents slave-driving or feverish self-driving under the influence of fear; but it is also to the bad, where it conduces to irresponsibility or to a refusal to co-operate in team work. I am not suggesting that, in most industries, average output has fallen, on the contrary, it has been going up despite a small reduction in average hours of work. But the increases have been due mainly, if not entirely, to greater mechanisation and improved working arrangements rather than to higher effort or better co-operation.

If we mean to constitute a really democratic society, permeated by the spirit of social equality, we shall have to find ways of replacing the old incentives of fear and habit with new inducements more consistent with the recognition of equal human rights. In large enterprises I do not think this can be done as long as they continue to be conducted for private profit in small ones it *sometimes* can, where the human relations are good. Social ownership will not of itself put matters right, as the experience both of the nationalised industries and of Co-operative employment abundantly shows *Social ownership is only half the battle the other half is real participation by the workers in control – not only at the top, but at every level from the work-group upwards.* By participation I do not mean merely consultation I mean *real control* This is necessary, not only for the sake of its effects in making the workers more conscious of their responsibility for high productivity, on which the standard of living must depend, but also because it is impossible to have a really democratic society if most of the members have to spend most of their lives at work under essentially undemocratic conditions. What a man is at his work he will tend to be also in his pleasure and in his activities as a citizen. Industrial democracy is therefore an indispensable part of social democracy – that is, of Socialism

Productivity and the Standard of Living

That the possibility of maintaining a satisfactory standard of living and adequate social services to protect the individual against the contingencies of life depends on high output should be self-evident, for even an absolutely equal distribution of incomes, after making due allowance for the portion of the current product that must be set aside for replacing worn-out capital goods and for new investment, would have only a small effect on the standard of living of the majority of households.* In the past, it was possible for social reformers to advocate that social services should be financed by taxes on the wealthy and higher wages paid, at least in part, at the expense of profits To-day, in view of what has been already accomplished, what can still be done in these ways is narrowly limited, for though profits are high a large part of them is not available for consumption but is needed for investment in capital goods in order to keep our industries efficient and responsive to changing demands It does not of course follow that the sums needed for this purpose should be allowed to be appropriated by private persons merely

---

*By equal distribution I here mean of course equal as between adults with smaller allocations for juvenile earners and with proper dependents' allowances for children and young persons not at work

because they own the assets of the businesses by which these profits are made. Indeed, as socialisation of business assets proceeds this form of appropriation will progressively disappear But public ownership of such profits will not render them available for consumption when they are needed for investment, and for as far ahead as we can see the need for investment is likely to remain high, both because we have big arrears to overtake and because the pace of technical change is likely to continue to be rapid.

Improved standards of living must therefore come mainly out of higher production. Indeed, unless we keep up a high rate of investment we shall not be able to maintain even the standards of living we possess now; for in face of intensified competition in the international market in which we have to sell our exports and buy our imports we shall need at the least to keep pace with the rise of productivity in the countries which are our chief competitors – notably Germany, Japan, and the United States. Great Britain has lost the favoured position in the world market that it used to enjoy when, aided by cheap and abundant supplies of coal – which was then the key material – it profited by being first in the field in the Industrial Revolution and was able to stimulate demand for its export both by its imperial position and by having a large surplus of capital for investment overseas Nowadays, competition in efficiency takes place on more equal terms between the leading countries, and the ability to supply capital for overseas has passed mainly to the United States – for a country can in effect export capital only if there remains a surplus on its balance of payments after paying for imports and such other current charges as it has to meet

Great Britain, therefore, has to depend on increasing productivity for improving, and even for maintaining, present standards of living This means that the working classes can no longer afford to regard high productivity and low costs of production as exclusively the employers' business, and their own role as simply that of extracting as high wages and as good conditions as they can from their employers, and of demanding, by political action, improved social services to be financed mainly by taxing the rich. It is to their own interest – indeed, it is of vital importance to them as a class – that the national product shall be as large as possible. This means both that they need to use their political power to insist on proper organisation and planning of industry, and also that they need to use their industrial power to bring about better organisation of productive processes and factory relations, so as to eliminate the inefficiencies that necessarily arise when managements and workers are pulling in opposite directions.

Responsibility and the Worker

This brings us back to the question how far it is psychologically possible or socially desirable for the workers and their organisations to accept any sort of responsibility for the efficiency of profit-making industry.

Psychologically, any such notion encounters very strong resistance, both rational and irrational 'Why should I work harder, or produce more,' says the Socialist workman, 'in order to swell my capitalist employers' profits?' That is the rational objection, and with it, over a much wider field, goes the non-rational resistance to a change of traditional attitudes which rest on the long experience of exploitation to which the workers as a class have been subjected Socially, too, there are powerful arguments against collaboration, because it is liable not only to destroy the fighting spirit of the Trade Unions but also to break up class-solidarity and put in its place a loyalty to the particular firm which unscrupulous employers can use as a means of undermining Trade Union influence.

The Conditions of Responsibility

These arguments are so strong as to be conclusive against collaboration, save under certain indispensable conditions The workers as a class cannot properly be invited to collaborate on any terms which envisage an indefinite continuance of the toll levied on their labour by profit-making employers or shareholders, or the continued private appropriation of that part of their product which is needed to finance new investment. They need to be assured that the toll levied on labour by the claims of ownership will be brought to an end as speedily as possible and that immediately a beginning will be made with the transfer of profits needed for investment to public ownership.

We have seen already how, by means of the abolition of large inheritances, the ownership of existing capital assets could be transferred to the public by stages not too prolonged. Side by side with this gradual transfer, the State could begin at once to assume public ownership of that part of profits – or of a part of the part – that is needed for new investment. This could be done by (*a*) *statutory limitation of dividends* – that is, of the part of profits that can be paid out to shareholders as incomes, (*b*) *statutory allocation of a share in profits to a capital fund which would become at once public property* and, if invested in the business, would carry shareholding rights to be exercised by public nominees. The public would thus acquire holdings of capital in what are now private enterprises by a double process – through the lapsing of shares to it at the owners' deaths and through the new shares to be created out of profits placed to reserve By rapid stages private ownership of joint stock enterprises would be extinguished they would become public property, and the State would be free to make what arrangements it might think best for their future conduct It could, for example, sell or lease some of them to the Consumers' Co-operative Movement, convert others into Producers' Co-operative Societies, and arrange for others to continue as publicly owned joint-stock companies It could amalgamate businesses into larger concerns where this seemed likely to increase efficiency, but it would be under no necessity to set up huge organisations except where the technical conditions required them *The outcome would be a highly varied and flexible system of socialised ownership and control, which would not preclude leaving as many small enterprises as might be considered desirable to continue under private ownership and control, subject to due provisions to ensure good working conditions and compliance with planning requirements.*

Given a clearly defined Socialist programme of this sort, I do not see why the workers should not be prepared to collaborate with the dying capitalist under the control of a Socialist Government pledged to carry it through to the end. There remains, however, the obvious difficulty that under our political system no Government can be sure of remaining in office for more than five years, and that accordingly the carrying out of the programme might be broken off short by the return of the Conservatives to power after an election victory. To be sure, this difficulty applies to every attempt to advance towards Socialism by non-revolutionary means *it is part of the price we pay for preferring parliamentary government to dictatorship under a one-party system*. There is no doubt that most people in Great Britain do prefer parliamentary government, and the Socialist who wishes to see his ideas carried out has to proceed on that assumption. This, I agree, makes it much more difficult than it would be if continued office could be assured to persuade the workers to modify their traditional attitudes indeed, they cannot fairly be asked to modify them in any way that would reduce their ability to resume their fighting posture in face of any attempt by a Conservative Government to undo the achievements of its predecessor. This means that any collaboration that can be advocated under present conditions must be carefully safeguarded so as to preserve, and where possible to increase, Trade Union power.

Towards Real Workers' Control

This I believe to be entirely practicable, provided that the policy receives the full backing of a sympathetic Labour Government – but not otherwise. What it involves is, first, that the Trade Unions shall set out deliberately to *extend the area of collective bargaining* to include much that employers still regard as belonging to the sphere of 'managerial functions' and therefore outside Trade Union competence, and secondly that they shall use this extension to *transfer to the workers, under Trade Union supervision, certain of the functions of workshop discipline and organisation* that are at present in the hands of foremen and supervisors appointed by the employers to order the workers about. Under this second head I have in mind the replacement of foremen by elected supervisors chosen by the workers themselves from among properly qualified candidates and the substitution, in suitable cases, of collective contracts under which groups of workers will undertake to carry through a particular job, or series of jobs, at a collective price, making their own arrangements for the organisation of the work and sharing the proceeds in accordance with rules drawn up by the Trade Unions to which they belong.

The effect of these changes would be to throw upon the workers responsibilities which they would exercise, not jointly with nominees of their employers, but by themselves, under arrangements negotiated by their Trade Unions with the employers and their associations The transfer of functions to the workers, far from undermining their collective power, would add to it, and would provide the foundation for extending their authority into further fields. Such arrangements could, and should, operate both in nationalised industries and in those remaining in private ownership or in transition from private to public ownership. *They would constitute the reality of 'workers' control' where the putting of a few Trade Union nominees on National Boards would give only the appearance of it.* Indeed, I feel sure that Trade Union representation on National Boards can be desirable only after a measure of real 'workers' control' has been established in this more real form – if even then.*

The Danger of Stabilising Inequality

I have written this pamphlet in the belief that since 1950 Labour's official leadership has shown clear signs of not knowing how to make a further advance towards Socialism and perhaps even of not much wanting to Certainly some Labour Party leaders, notably Herbert Morrison, have made no bones about saying that what is needed now is a pause for consolidating what has been set on foot rather than a venture into new projects. I do not agree with this view, partly because I do not believe there is any satisfactory halting place between a mainly capitalist and a mainly Socialist economy, but also because I am afraid that *the effect of what has been done, if we halt at the point we have reached, will be to establish a new class-system rather than to clear the road for a further advance towards a classless society.* We are in danger of coming to regard large salaries, titles for Trade Union and Co-operative leaders, and the control of industry and the workers by highly paid administrators imposed from above, not as necessary evils of transition, but as right and proper elements in the new society we are attempting to create. We are in danger of accepting 'reasonable' profits and the maintenance of capitalist operation as legitimate for the major part of industry, provided only that the Government holds certain very broad powers of planning and control – powers which, under such a system, it is very difficult to use effectively in any matter upon which the capitalists are not prepared to 'play ball'. We are in danger of failing to carry through the major reorganisation and large investment programme which many of our industries need because capitalist insistence on profit-taking, which provokes workers' insistence on higher wages, does not leave enough resources for capital development or make it possible to guide investment into the right channels.

Our Socialism badly needs, I think, a 'new look', based on a fresh

*For a fuller discussion of this issue see my recent book, *An Introduction to Trade Unionism* (Allen and Unwin, 1953)

angle of vision. I can sum up what I have been trying to say very briefly in the following propositions

A Summing Up
We need
1. *a forthright attack on economic inequality based on the ownership of capital.* The best approach to this is by the abolition of inheritance beyond certain fixed limits, subject to such transitional alleviations as may seem to be desirable.
2. *a no less forthright attack on social inequality* This involves abandoning the practice of handing out titles on any account, abolishing the House of Lords, and ceasing to create a new class of very highly paid administrators in the nationalised services.
3. *a real attempt to diffuse economic responsibility*, especially by extending the range of collective bargaining and by transferring managerial functions at the workplace level to groups of workers acting under rules established by Trade Union bargaining.
4. *a rapid advance towards greater educational equality*, especially through Comprehensive Schools and greater attention to technical and manual education for those whose bents lie that way.
5. *greater attention to means of enabling elderly people to remain at work, and disabled or handicapped people to receive better rehabilitation, education and training*, both in order to increase production and thus raise living standards, and because such measures will increase happiness.
6. *limitation of dividends and compulsory allocation of part of profits to new capital which will become the property of the public, and not of the shareholders.*
7. *extension of public ownership and control of industry not only by further measures nationalising entire industries or concerns but by the progressive taking over of shares and direction through inheritance taxation and the creation of public shareholdings out of profits.*

Socialism – or what else?
There will, I am sure, be many objectors to the new programme outlined in this pamphlet. Some who regard themselves as Socialists will object to it on the ground that it is bad electioneering. To them I answer that I do not care if it is – for the time being. I am a Socialist and a believer that Socialism means, above all else, a classless society. I am not in the least interested in helping the Labour Party to win a majority in Parliament unless it means to use its majority for advancing as fast as is practicable towards such a society. I do not expect a majority of the electorate to agree at present with what I have said, for the simple reason that it differs from what they have been used to hearing. For the same reason I do not expect a majority even of the active leaders of the Labour Party to agree, for it is not what they have become used to saying. For a long time now, many of them have given up talking Socialism and have been talking instead about nationalisation and the Welfare

State. They have now, thanks to the enterprise of the Labour Government between 1945 and 1950, got nearly as far as they can go along these lines, until they set about doing two other things as well – smashing the class-system by a direct attack on property rights, and putting real responsibility into the hands of ordinary people.

It took a considerable time and a great deal of apparently fruitless effort to get the working-class movement solidly behind the programme which the Labour Government carried through between 1945 and 1950. It will take a great deal of effort to get similar support for a new programme that will carry us on towards Socialism. Therefore, the sooner we begin on this essential task of education and propaganda, the less long shall we have to wait for its results.

The alternative is to rest content with what has been achieved, and to give up trying to establish a Socialist society. That, I fear, is what many who continue to call themselves Socialists are really minded to do, sheltering their apostasy behind the assertion that the majority of the electors could not be induced to vote for it. But what is the use of winning an election, except as a means to an end? To win an election without a policy is the surest way of losing the next, and of spreading dismay and disillusionment among one's supporters. If the end is no longer Socialism, but something else – what else? If it is still Socialism, let us tell the electors frankly how we propose to advance towards it.

NOTE. I have not discussed Labour's international policy. If I did, I should need to say far more about it than I could compress within the limits of a single pamphlet covering home policy as well. I propose to deal with the all-important international aspects of Socialism in a second pamphlet.

WHAT IS WRONG
WITH THE
TRADE UNIONS?

G. D. H. COLE

FABIAN TRACT 301

ONE SHILLING AND SIXPENCE

G D H COLE is Chichele Professor of Social and Political Theory at Oxford and President of the Fabian Society

FABIAN TRACT 301

This pamphlet is based in part on a series of articles which appeared in *Tribune* early in 1956

THE FABIAN SOCIETY,
11, Dartmouth Street, S W 1

Note—*This pamphlet, like all publications of the FABIAN SOCIETY, represents not the collective view of the Society but only the view of the individual who prepared it. The responsibility of the Society is limited to approving the publications which it issues as worthy of consideration within the Labour Movement*

September, 1956

WHAT IS WRONG WITH THE TRADE UNIONS?

G. D. H. COLE

1. THE WAGES QUESTION

TO begin with, is anything wrong? If the only purpose of a Trade Union is to strike the best possible bargain on its members' behalf in the matters of wages, working hours, and physical conditions of employment, I do not think there is much amiss The present leaders of the Trade Unions, by and large, are competent negotiators and honest men who have found themselves during the past sixteen years—that is, since 1940,— in a position of unprecedented bargaining strength, but also in one of very considerable difficulty It has been within their power at any time, thanks to full employment, to exact higher wages and a shorter working week than they have actually attempted to secure, but in practice what they have secured has amounted to a quite considerable improvement in real as well as in money wages, a moderate reduction in the length of the **standard** working week, and therewith an improvement in overtime earnings

Earnings Rise

As compared with October 1938, the last pre-war year, average weekly earnings in the industries covered by the Ministry of Labour returns had risen by 242 per cent in April 1955, and wage-rates exclusive of overtime and piecework payments by about 145 per cent Actual hours worked had increased over the same period by rather under half-an-hour a week, but average hourly earnings had increased by 240 per cent—almost as much as weekly earnings—mainly because men, who are more highly paid, work more overtime than women or juveniles

Of course, these increases in money wages have been largely cancelled by higher costs of living According to the official indices, the cost of living rose by about 30 per cent between 1938 and 1947 and, on a new basis of calculation, by about 50 per cent between 1947 and 1955—that is to say by about 95 percent in all These figures, I know, are seriously misleading, especially for the period 1938—1947 But even if the actual rise from 1938 to 1955 is put at well over 150 per cent, which I hold to be a fairer estimate, the increase in money earnings is still a long way ahead, and that in wage-**rates** only a little way behind.

Another way of looking at the situation is in terms of the share of wages in the national product and in the total of personal incomes, excluding such elements as reserved profits The share of wages in the total national product of all kinds was roughly 37 per cent in 1938 and 39.2 per cent in 1954 It was highest in 1948, when it reached 40 per cent, and has since fluctuated between 38 7 per cent and 39 7 per cent, without any steady tendency either way In terms of their share in the total of personal incomes the wage-workers have done rather better Their share was 37 9 per cent in 1938 and 42 4 per cent in 1954—the highest point yet reached, though only a small improvement on the 41 6 per cent of 1948 **What these figures show is that by both tests the main shift to the workers' advantage occurred between 1938 and 1948, and that since 1948 there has been no further advance in the workers' share.**

Inflation Produces Restraint

In face of this, is it possible to say that the Trade Unions have done a good job in recent years? Why have they not used their power to continue the advance in the proportion of total wealth-creation paid to the wage-workers? The main reason has been that the Trade Union leaders have been afraid that to press for higher and higher wages would involve an inflationary rise in prices and a crisis in the balance of payments that would make it impossible to pay for the foodstuffs and materials from abroad that are needed to maintain full employment In this I feel sure they have been correct, on the assumption that the economic system as a whole would continue to operate much as it actually does now For, as things are, higher wages and higher profits go together, and higher wages cannot be got at the expense of profits, but only on terms which lead to inflation and thus both increase living costs and decrease exports and the power to pay for imports There is a vicious circle, which can be broken only by a fundamental change in the economic system as a whole

In fact, up to the present, the major part of increased productivity has been going, not into the spendable incomes of the dividend receivers, but into investment either out of the reserved profits of business or out of taxation used to finance public capital expenditure—for example, on houses, schools, roads, and other public services This expenditure is necessary—indeed, it ought to be much higher than it is if industrial equipment is to be kept properly up to date and social services are to advance at a satisfactory pace The Trade Union leaders are well aware that Great Britain cannot afford to fall behind in either of these respects, and that until we have put a great effort into mechanising industrial equipment and developing the capital equipment of the social services there cannot be *much* room for improving real wages, at any rate unless means can be found of preventing every wage-increase from being passed on to the consumer in higher prices

But how, as matters stand to-day, can this be prevented? Not by Trade Union action, for the Unions have no control over prices Only by strict price-controls and prevention of monopoly practices, designed specifically to squeeze the profit-makers and explicitly limit dividends and keep down interest rates It cannot be done at all under the so-called 'free economy' which the Tories have been trying to bring back since their return to office in 1951 Moreover, even if prices and monopolies were brought under effective control, the need would remain to invest, instead of spending on consumption, a very large part of the total product so that working-class, as well as other, spending would have to be held down in order to enable the British economy to bring its methods thoroughly up to date The great difference would be, not that the wage-earners could have much more to spend in the immediate future, but that the benefits of higher productivity, as they are achieved, could be passed on to the workers instead of being appropriated by capitalist investors through reserved profits, as they are at present

Keeping Up the Pressure

Trade Union leaders, whose business it is to have such facts as these in mind, cannot properly be blamed for not having pressed hard for the highest wages they could exact at the cost of letting inflation rip, for serious inflation would hit the workers a disastrous blow The leaders, however, cannot afford on this ground to refrain from wage-pressure that will at any rate prevent the workers' share in the total of personal incomes from actually falling off They have at least to meet any measures which threaten this—e g the Tories recent financial manoeuvres with equivalent wage-demands, and any failure to do this would soon lose them their members' confidence and lead to a rank-and-file revolt I do not, however, feel that they can be charged, so far, with any grave failure on this account

That is not to say that I believe the leadership of the Trade Unions to have been equally wise in other respects Subsequent sections of this pamphlet will show where I think it has gone wrong **What I am saying in this opening section is that in respect of wages the Trade Unions have managed to hold up to now the substantial advantages gained during the war years, and could not have done much better than this unless there had been a frontal attack on capitalism as a system— an attack requiring political action of a drastic Socialist kind.**

2. WHAT IS RIGHT WITH THE TRADE UNIONS

BEFORE I begin discussing what I believe to be the shortcomings of the Trade Union movement I want to make clear that I have a deep admiration for its achievements No movement in the country elicits from its members anything approaching the same amount of devoted voluntary service or gets so high a proportion of its essential work done by volunteers who labour for it because they believe in it and without any prospect of personal advantage over their fellow-members Nothing that I shall have to say about the widespread apathy among Trade Unionists is inconsistent with this notable fact, on which the strength and vitality of the entire movement depend However well the paid officials serve their Unions—and the great majority of them are competent, hardworking and faithful servants of their members—the basis of Trade Union power is in the unpaid day-to-day service of the local activists who attend branch meetings, serve as shop stewards or committee members, and take the trouble to understand how their Unions work and to master the problems with which they are required to deal

Most of these activists, I rejoice to say, are animated by loyalty, not only to their own Unions, but to the wider working-class movement as well They are Socialists as well as Trade Unionists, and play their part politically as well as on the workshop floor They have every reason to be proud of what they have achieved, and the shortcomings of which I shall have to speak are not at all their fault It is largely owing to them that the Trade Unions have been able so greatly to add to their power and prestige during the years since 1939, and I have nothing but praise for them

Outstanding Achievements

Trade Union officials too deserve on the whole to be congratulated on their successful efforts to improve the status and conditions of the organised working class My personal memory goes back not only to the bad times of the depression in the 1930s, but further to the years of ' Labour unrest ' before the world war of 1914 Nowadays I occasionally hear young Trade Unionists, who have no clear memory of either of these periods, denying that there has been any real improvemnt in the condition of the workers, or even suggesting that it has got worse because of the increasing ' contradictions ' of capitalism What nonsense!

Since 1914, and indeed since 1939, there has been an enormous improvement in the position of the workers, not only in respect of standards of living, but even more in social and economic status, and with this has gone an immense advance in Trade Union power and prestige What above all else has made these advances possible has been full employment, which has forced the employing class to treat the worker with much greater consideration for fear of losing his services and not being able to replace him, and has thus radically changed the character of workshop relations and the behaviour of managers and supervisors in their handling of human problems With this has gone a far-reaching change in the workers' own attitudes, for they are no longer haunted, as so many of them used to be, by the fear of unemployment and by the continual insecurity of their conditions of life They can now stand up for their rights with far less risk than used to be involved, and most of them are well aware of the change and know how much they owe to Trade Unionism for helping to bring it about

Defending Full Employment

It is precisely for this reason that there is so much talk nowadays, in reactionary circles, about ' overfull employment ', and so much desire to bring back a situation in which workers will once more be hunting for scarce jobs instead of employers hunting for workers, so that the old ' discipline ' can be restored and the concessions that have had to be made can be cancelled in the interests of the exploiting classes But despite these desires, both employers and Government have so far hesitated, in face of the strength of Trade Unionism, to challenge it to direct combat, and have limited themselves to attempts to whittle away the workers' gains by such indirect means as the removal of food subsidies, the raising of rents, and the 'credit squeeze' designed to restrict the demand for labour

If the Trade Unions were to accept these indirect attacks without offering the most lively resistance, the champions of capitalism would soon seek to press them further and to shove the working class back to the inferior status and conditions from which it has begun to emerge The gains that have been made are still insecure their preservation depends on the maintenance of a fighting spirit in the Trade Unions—on the absolute refusal to give up what they have won and dogged determination to use every chance of advancing to further victories

This, however, cannot be achieved merely by pressing for wage-advances, for, as we saw, such claims, pressed too far, may help to destroy the very 'full employment' on which the Trade Unions' power so largely depends The Government's attempts to bring about a re-distribution of real incomes to the detriment of the workers need to be met by political as well as by industrial action—by carrying the Labour Party back to political power with a programme for maintaining full employment, reducing rates of interest, and curing the disequalibrium in the balance of payments by controlling imports and ensuring priority for those forms of expenditure, on both capital goods and consumers' goods, that are most useful socially and for the improvement of economic efficiency, whether or not they are also most profitable to the capitalist class.

Industrial Responsibilities

At the same time it is necessary to recognise that the standard of life in Great Britain depends absolutely on British industry keeping pace with the growth of technical efficiency in other parts of the world, and that the workers however hostile they may be to capitalism, cannot afford to allow British industry to fall behind The Trade Union leaders, in stressing the need for the highest possible productivity, are not being false to their members' interests on the contrary, they are doing only what is indispensable to safeguard these interests, and they have a right to look for the fullest support in the campaign for higher output at the lowest cost compatible with good wages and conditions of work

The workers cannot afford to ignore the fact that the crisis through which the British economy is passing is a real crisis that can be cured only by putting British industry in a position to sell the exports that are needed to pay for the imports without which full employment cannot be maintained or the standard of living be prevented from falling In such a situation there is no room for forms of militancy which, in making trouble for the employers, at the same time damage production and worsen Great Britain's position in the world market The Trade Unions have to look for ways and means of defending their members' interests that will not have this effect If the employers and the Government attack them, they have to fight back, but they must be at the same time ready to co-operate in measures designed to improve productivity and must avoid all forms of 'trouble-making' calculated to hamper British industry in its competitive effort

This means that, in the present situation, it is necessary to attack capitalism politically, rather than industrially, in order to get a Government that will put the working-class claims first, will break down the capitalist monopolies that hamper production, and will prevent scarce capital from being frittered away on luxury output while urgent claims are left unsatisfied, Trade Unionism alone cannot accomplish such tasks, but it can, if it will, powerfully reinforce the Labour Party as an instrument for their achievement, both by a much more intensive effort at the political and economic education of its members and by insisting that the Labour Party's programme shall be stiffened up for a much more determined advance towards Socialism and planned control of the economy as a whole

Tory-voting Trade Unionists

The need for such a campaign is evident in view of the fact that in recent General Elections **well over one-third** of the manual workers who have cast their votes have voted for Conservative candidates No one knows how many of these Conservative working men and women are Trade Unionists, but clearly a great many of them must be, and it is no credit to the Trade Unions that such a situation should exist and so little attempt be made by the Unions to correct it Of course, many more Trade Unionists vote Labour than vote Conservative, and the Trade Unions do, at election time, make some attempt to throw their organised weight on the Socialist side But between elections they do far too little to educate their members politically, and even at election time they fall a long way short of mobilising their full resources for the political struggle

This is folly, from their own point of view, for the maintenance of the great advances they have helped to bring about depends fully as much on how the country is governed as on anything they can achieve by industrial bargaining or strike action In a later section of this pamphlet I shall show how tenuous the existing links between the Trade Union rank and file and the Labour Party are and shall suggest ways of strengthening them The main answer, however, must be in terms of a great Trade Union campaign of economic and political education, and in failing to launch such a campaign the Trade Unions, despite the immense services they have rendered to the workers, are showing a disastrous lack of foresight Only an educated democracy can effectively exercise power, but it is no less true that an educated democracy is needed for winning power and for preventing the great gains of the past two decades from being frittered away.

3. APATHY AND CENTRALISATION

THERE are at present about 9½ million Trade Unionists, of whom more than 8 million are affiliated to the Trades Union Congress, as compared with 6 million and 4¾ million in 1938 The number of Trade Unionists has thus increased by more than one half, whereas the number of Trade Unions has been falling sharply—in the TUC from 216 in 1938 to 183 in 1955 Individual Unions have been getting bigger, as a consequence both of amalgamations and of successful recruiting of new members Over the same period, Trade Union bargaining has been getting more centralised, as well as spreading over a wider field

Branch Interest Lost

In most industries to-day, wage-rates and general conditions are settled by nation-wide bargaining or arbitration, which applies to large masses of workers This type of bargaining is necessarily done by quite small groups of full-time national officials and executive members, so that the local branches and shop organisations of the workers have only a remote part in it, though the members may be called upon to vote for or against a particular agreement, either directly by referendum or through some sort of delegate conference The result is that the average Trade Union branch or district has much less say than it used to have in bargaining about such matters and has come to deal much less with the fixing of wage-rates and general working conditions than with applying national agreements to local circumstances and traditions Such application, moreover, has to be done largely in each separate establishment, through shop stewards and shop committees, rather than in a whole town or district so that the branch or the district committee has lost power both to the centre and to the workplace organisation—above all, in engineering and in coal-mining These changes tend to make branch meetings both less important and less interesting than they used to be when bargaining was largely local and a go-ahead branch or district committee could affect local wages and conditions much more directly than it can to-day

The rise in membership has had another important effect Trade Unions, when they had fewer members, consisted mainly of those workers who were keener and more active than the rest But nowadays a great many workers belong to a Trade Union not because they are keen on it but because they have to in order to get or hold their jobs It is a natural consequence that the proportion of apathetic members has increased

Devolution the Answer

Thirdly, it must not be forgotten that Trade Unions, like many other bodies, have to face the competition of many more rival attractions than were open to their members in past years A Trade Union branch meeting needs to be more interesting and important than formerly in order to induce more than a small number of members to attend it, but it is not at all easy to make such meetings interesting when they are dealing only with routine questions and there is nothing special afoot. It is so easy to argue that it will make no difference whether one attends a particular meeting or not, and the habit of not attending, once formed, is not easily broken. Moreover, the very acceptance of Trade Union membership by most employers as normal and natural makes it seem to many Trade Unionists less necessary to put in an attendance in order to manifest their solidarity with their fellow-workers.

This makes it vitally important to do all that can be done to make branch meetings attractive, by cutting down sheer routine to a minimum and making them as far as possible social occasions for good fellowship as well as opportunities for free discussion and debate. This, however, cannot easily be done unless there is really important work for the branches to do, and it therefore comes back to the need for more devolution of power and responsibility from central offices and officials to the rank-and-file members, and to the necessity of basing branches as far as possible on actual working units that have common problems to discuss and to resolve.

The General Unions

Thus three factors have been operating together to increase apathy. There are more members who are apathetic by nature, there are more counter-attractions, and there is also less to attract even the less apathetic to attend branch meetings or to play an active part in Trade Union affairs which seem to be largely beyond their influence. In addition, the rise in membership has been greatest among the less skilled workers, who tend to take a smaller part in Union affairs than the skilled craftsmen. There has been a prodigious rise in the membership of the two huge general Unions, which consist largely, though not exclusively, of the less skilled, and these Unions have exceedingly high rates of membership turnover—which means that members are continually passing in and out of them and that a considerable proportion of the members have no continuous interest in their affairs. Moreover, in the General and Municipal Workers' Union especially and also in the general sections of the Transport and General Workers, branches often consist of highly miscellaneous groups which have little to discuss in common as compared with more homogeneous branches. This also makes for apathy, and for leaving it to the full-time officials to do the job without active participation by more than a tiny fraction of the rank and file.

Remedies for Apathy

How far, we need to ask ourselves, are these tendencies unavoidable, and how much can be done to counteract them? It would be quite impracticable to propose that nation-wide bargaining should be given up and that there should be a return to purely local bargaining about wage-rates and general conditions, for national bargaining has undoubtedly done much to level up wages and conditions in the worse-paid areas, and employers are now nationally organised on a scale that makes purely local bargaining impossible. What is needed is not to undo national bargains, but to give clearer recognition to the importance of *workshop* bargaining over the implementation of national agreements and the development of collective negotiation in each particular establishment, within the general terms of such agreements—in other words, fuller recognition of the powers and functions of shop stewards and Trade Union workshop and works committees, and also much greater representation and influence to such bodies in the control of Trade Union policy. Shop stewards, especially in engineering, have a good deal more recognition in the Trade Unions than they used to have, but still not nearly enough—and there are still not a few industries in which they hardly exist.

As for the second cause of apathy—the enrolment of those who would not have joined a Trade Union at all unless they had been virtually compelled to—the remedy must clearly be sought in much greater efforts at elementary Trade Union education and training in Trade Union work, especially of new recruits. Many Unions are doing a good deal more than they used to in this respect, but most still lag a long way behind. Every Trade Union member ought to be strongly encouraged, even if he or she cannot be compelled, to go through at least a short course of learning both about his Union and its problems and about the wider movement of which it is a part. There is no other way either of ensuring that enough competent persons will come forward to do the work the Union needs or of making the Union work democratically. Nor is there any other way of preventing a sectional minority from getting control if it sets out to do so. Much more Trade Union education is a vital need—more vital than ever now that the Unions include a higher proportion of the entire working class.

Encouraging Participation

The third cause of apathy—the rise of the huge general Unions—presents a special problem which can be met only by much more encouragement for members of these Unions to play an active part in their work. This requires big changes in internal Union organisation—the breaking up of oversized branches into smaller, more homogeneous units, more self-government for the main sections of the membership through trade or industrial groups, and less power in the hands of full-time officials in relation to local and workshop affairs. Broadly speaking, however, the Trade Union leadership, instead of encouraging such changes, opposes them for fear of losing its centralised control over the rank and file. Trade Union democracy is opposed on the ground that it might add to Communist and left-wing influence.

I do not, of course, mean that Trade Union leaders wish their members to be apathetic. I am sure they deplore the apathy as much as I do. Nevertheless, they are not prepared to attempt to cure the evil by giving greater power to shop stewards or works committees, because they are afraid that this might open the road to control by irresponsible minorities that are out to make trouble rather than to improve the efficiency of the Unions as instruments of collective bargaining The leaders would be only too pleased to see the members more alert and active if they could be relied on to be sensible as well, but, as matters stand, they are too fearful of the consequences of diffusing power more widely to be prepared to take the risk Yet, unless it is taken, I do not believe there is any way by which the apathy can be overcome

This is so important an issue that I propose to devote most of my next section to discussing it in greater detail

4. THE FEAR OF COMMUNISM

FEAR and hatred of Communism and of anything that can be, plausibly associated with it are an occupational disease of modern Trade Union and Socialist leadership. I say this, not as a Communist or a 'fellow-traveller'—for emphatically I am neither—but because I am sure this attitude is the most disastrous obstacle to necessary and practicable reforms in the structure and working of Trade Unionism under the conditions of to-day

One great effect both of the centralisation of collective bargaining and of the increase in the proportion of apathetic members has been a growth of power in the hands of full-time officials and of national executive members who spend a large part of their time on Trade Union work It is in man's nature—in that of Trade Union leaders as well as of other men—to love power and to be reluctant to share it with others more than they must Trade Union leaders who enter into great nationwide bargains on behalf of their members accept therewith a responsibility to employers that these bargains will be kept, and therefore become responsible for disciplining their members in order to enforce obedience Thus, national Trade Unions become, as their power grows, more and more agencies for imposing discipline on their members rather than for responding to such of their members' demands as come from activist groups and minorities and not from the membership as a whole As most forward movements begin as minority movements, or at least as movements of particular sections, this means that rank and file initiative is sevsrly discouraged, and that disciplinary action is readily taken against discontented branches or groups Branches are dissolved and are re-formed under 'safe' leadership, and the apathetic majority is brought in to reduce the active minority to order

The use of these disciplinary powers cannot be altogether avoided, for some discipline there must be if the Union is to do its job But their use tends to be pushed much too far when the leaders come to be dominated by the notion of a Communist conspiracy to overthrow them, and to see every revolt against their policy as an expression of this conspiracy It is of course true that Communists, constituting a small but very active minority in the Unions, do their best to take advantage of the widespread apathy to get themselves elected to key positions and to get their resolutions passed at meetings which only small minorities attend. But it is none the less disastrous to meet such attempts by excluding Communists from office or by shutting down branches in which they get the upper hand—and much more disastrous to smear as a Communist or fellow-traveller everybody who ventures to criticise the attitude and policy of the official leadership For this results either in killing every sort of progressive initiative in the Union or in perpetual troubles and a most dangerous lack of communication between the leaders and the active members on whom the real strength of the Union is bound to depend **The remedy for Communist infiltration is not to repress all rank-and-file initiative in order to defeat it, but to encourage other forms of initiative and to increase the proportion of active members by better training and by giving them more responsible Trade Union tasks.**

Neglected Functions

No organisation, whether it be a Trade Union or of any other type, can be properly called democratic unless a considerable proportion of its members plays an active part in its affairs, or unless it accepts a reasonable amount of responsibility for equipping them to do so Similarly, no organisation is truly democratic unless it does its utmost to encourage active participation by offering opportunities for responsible tasks to a sufficient part of its membership to ensure that, if the national leadership were put out of action, its groups would continue to operate effectively and a new leadership could be speedily recruited from its ranks I very much doubt whether the Trade Unions of to-day are meeting these tests as adequately as were the Trade Unions of a generation or of two generations ago, despite the improvements that have taken place both in standards of living and in general education

This is partly because there is now more opportunity for clever young people to rise out of the working class, and also because there are more rival interests and activities competing with the Trade Unions But it is, I feel sure, also largely because Trade Union leaders have paid much too little attention either to Trade Union education and training or to the need to diffuse power and responsibility instead of allowing them to become concentrated in fewer and fewer hands This neglect, in turn, has been partly an outcome of the leaders' desire for power, but also partly of their exaggerated fears of Communism and of 'leftism' in general

It is a most dangerous situation when a Trade Union becomes more concerned with disciplining its members than with encouraging them to think and act for themselves. Such discipline is, in some degree, inseparable from power, for clearly agreements, once made, ought to be honoured unless new circumstances arise to render them invalid. Discipline, however, is properly acceptable only where those who are subjected to it are allowed a fair chance to push their views and projects without being held up at the very outset by charges of 'disloyalty': it becomes intolerable as soon as the leaders come to regard the members as their property, whose only duty is to obey.

Why Unofficial Strikes?

I feel sure that the prevalence of unofficial strikes in recent years is due largely to over-centralisation, which has brought with it long, roundabout processes of negotiation that are often intensely exasperating to the workers directly affected by them. These processes can be used deliberately to delay consideration of real grievances, and are largely so used by bad employers when they dare: so that, all too often, the men on the spot have to choose between striking without official support and allowing an employer to introduce some new practice to which they strongly object, or to dismiss a worker who has stood up strongly for Trade Union rights. Employers attempt, more and more, to enforce their claim to refuse negotiations as long as a strike continues, and to tie the Trade Unions down to accepting this limitation on their members' rights, and Trade Union leaders are apt to be so fearful of left-wing influences in their Unions as to acquiesce in this employers' claim. The answer must be sought in more decentralisation of Trade Union power, and not in making the Unions into bodies, one of whose main function is to keep their members in order for capitalists to exploit.

5. TRADE UNION STRUCTURE

ON what basis ought the workers to organise themselves in Trade Unions? There are a number of alternative ways open to them and, in Great Britain, no one way has prevailed over the others. There are *craft* Unions, such as the United Patternmakers or the London Typographical Society, there are what may be called *departmental* or *sectional* Unions, such as the Associated Society of Locomotive Engineers and Firemen, which organises not only engine drivers but also firemen and cleaners—that is to say, all grades, less skilled as well as skilled, attached to the locomotive department, there are *industrial* Unions, which set out to organise together all the workers belonging to a particular industry, whatever their grade or degree of skill—for example, the National Union of Railwaymen, or the Shop, Distributive and Allied Workers, there are *general* Unions, such as the National Union of General and Municipal Workers, and the Transport and General Workers' Union, which are open to workers from any industry or trade, though in practice they do not enrol those for whom well-established Unions of other types effectively cater, and finally there can be Unions which actually attempt to unite the entire working class in a single Union—the One Big Union of which the American Industrial Workers of the World was once the outstanding example

These are the main types, but not all Trade Unions can be clearly assigned to one or another of them. For example, is the powerful Amalgamated Engineering Union to be regarded as an industrial Union because it is open to many kinds of workers, unskilled, semi-skilled and skilled, who work in the engineering industry? On the whole, yes but it must not be forgotten that the A E U also includes large numbers of engineers of various sorts who work in other industries and are attached to it because of the crafts they practice rather than because of the industry in which they work. The A E U or rather the A S E out of which it arose, when I first knew it was mainly a craft Union enrolling workers from a number of *kindred crafts*. It has developed gradually into something more like an industrial Union through opening its ranks more effectively to the less skilled machine-minders, but it still falls a long way short of including all engineering workers. Many such workers belong to separate Unions, such as the Electrical Trades Union, the Amalgamated Union of Foundry Workers, or the United Patternmakers' Association. And a high proportion of the less skilled, though eligible for the A E U, are actually members of either the T and G W U or the N U G M W, and in the railway workshops the A E U competes for members with the N U R.

Principles of Organisation

It is tempting to suggest that, in order to avoid Unions competing for members, one principle or another ought to be adopted as a common basis of organisation. This is the case in some countries, where there exists a central Trade Union Commission with power to decide to what Union each kind of worker shall be assigned. Thus, in the Soviet Union, the *industrial* principle is adopted so completely that every sort of person employed in an industry is assigned to the Union catering for that industry, from the top technicians and managers down to the least skilled workers. But in most countries, even where the central body has much more power than in Great Britain, uniformity of structure is carried much less far, even if the industrial form of organisation is quite widely used. For example, non-manual workers are quite often organised separately from manual workers, as here the Transport Salaried Staffs Association (formerly the Railway Clerks') is separate from the N U R, and it is common to find that, whereas in some industries the workers are organised on industrial lines, in others *craft* Unions confined to special types of skilled workers exist side by side with these more inclusive Unions. In the United States for example, where the two rival central Trade Union bodies—the American Federation of Labor and the Congress of Industrial Organisations—have recently joined forces, the combined body includes both craft and industrial Unions— the latter drawn mainly, but not exclusively, from the C I O and the former from the A F. of L.

Why do these differences of structure exist, and what is there to be said in favour of one or another basis of organisation? Historically, in most countries, craft Unions have been among the first to establish themselves—with the compositors very often taking the lead. For highly skilled workers following a common craft or a closely related group of crafts can organise more easily than less skilled workers, and have a closer common interest to bind them together. Employers find it harder to victimise bodies of highly skilled craftsmen, who cannot be easily replaced, than workers who have no such monopoly of skill. Accordingly, as a rule, organisation begins among the skilled workers and spreads only later to the less skilled, and there have been in the past cases in which particular groups of skilled workers have done nothing to help the less skilled to organise, or have even opposed their efforts, in the hope of improving their own position by building up an effective monopoly of their particular kind of labour. More and more, however, with the development of mass-production, there have come into existence large bodies of semi-skilled workers intermediate between craftsmen and labourers, and it has become indispensable for the craftsmen to make common cause with the semi-skilled in dealing with their employers—so that one craft Union after another has opened its ranks to less skilled workers and turned into something more like an industrial Union.

Sometimes, however, the craft Unions have put up a long fight before joining hands with the less skilled, and there remain to-day whole industries—notably building—in which the main basis of Trade Union organisation is still that of craft, with separate Trade Unions of carpenters, painters, plasterers, plumbers, and so on, loosely federated in a National Federation of Building Trades Operatives which negotiates for them all in some matters, but not in others.

Craft Versus Industrial Unionism

Wherever *craft* Unionism exists, it means that each employer and each employers' association is confronted not by one Union but by a number, which either negotiate apart or work more or less completely through a federation to which they delegate some of their powers. As against this, the aim of *industrial* Unionism is to confront each employer and each employers' association or federation with a single body competent to bargain on behalf of all the workers employed. This aspiration is seldom realised in full, for as we saw blackcoated workers and officials usually insist on maintaining separate organisations of their own. Even in the coal mines there exists, side by side with the powerful National Union of Mineworkers, a separate body representing Colliery Officials, though the N U M comes a good deal nearer than most to being an effective industrial Union for all the manual workers concerned.

Why do skilled craftsmen, in so many cases, prefer to maintain separate Unions of their own? Largely because they are afraid that the less skilled, who are usually more numerous, will not understand their special claims or back them up when they demand the wage-differentials and the special working conditions which they regard as reasonable in view of their particular skills. In recent years wage-differentials have in many instances been considerably reduced, especially during the war, and the skilled workers are apt to feel that, with the less skilled pressing for higher basic wages, their claims may be set aside nor can it be said that they are entirely mistaken in this view It is a real moot point in many disputes whether the claims of the worst-paid workers should be given priority over those of the better-paid, especially in times of rising prices and above all under conditions of wartime scarcity It is not surprising that skilled workers who are still in a position to maintain their monopoly of a particular type of necesary skill tend to cling to their craft Unions—as, for example, the London Typograptical Society does, with its long tradition of closely knit organisation open only to skilled workers

Effects of Mechanisation

The case for industrial Unionism is strongest in the industries that have been most invaded by mass-production, which tends to break down the barriers between the main bodies of skilled and semi-skilled workers and to confront the entire body of employees with huge employing concerns they can cope with only by uniting all their forces under a common control In America the workers in most of these industries never became effectively organised till the C I O, thrusting the older A F of L aside, adopted the method of industrial Unionism and compelled the great capitalist businesses to accept collective bargaining, against which they had previously stood out As more industries resort to highly mechanised methods, industrial Unionism is likely, here too, to gain further ground But it is unlikely, from this cause alone, to oust the other kinds of Unionism altogether

There is another factor to be taken into account In as far as Trade Unions are simply agencies for collective bargaining about wages and conditions of employment, the only relevant consideration in deciding what basis of organisation is to be preferred is what will most strengthen the workers' bargaining position, and there may well be cases in which, though industrial Unions could serve the majority of the workers best, craft Unions will be to the bargaining advantage of particular skilled groups If, however, the workers are aiming at getting any sort of 'workers' control' or share in the management of industry, they evidently need a common organisation covering all those employed in the same establishment and in the industry to which the establishment belongs so that industrial Unionism, or the nearest practicable approach to it, is clearly to be preferred. **I propose to discuss this question of workers' control in a subsequent section of this pamphlet; and I shall accordingly say no more about it here than that I regard it as an indispensable ingredient in the making of a democratic Socialist society, and therefore wish to see the Trade Union movement develop, as** far as possible, a structure through which an advance towards workers' control can be effectively made.

As for the *general* Unions, of the type represented by the T and G W and the N U G M W, the reason why they have developed on so vast a scale is plain They are largely a by-product of craft exclusiveness, for where the skilled workers were not prepared to admit the less skilled workers to their own Unions, the less skilled, if they were to organise at all, could do so only in separate Unions, and there was a strong case for making these open to a wide range of occupations in preference to setting up separate 'labourers' Unions in each industry or occupation Such separate Unions, as the chequered history of Unions of Builders' Labourers shows, cannot easily maintain themselves alone They need large numbers and variety, in order that each group may be able to rely on the help of others when trouble comes As industrial Unions develop, the scope for general Unions becomes less, but as against this the growth of mechanisation brings into existence large bodies of machine-workers who can shift fairly easily from one industry to another—and the general Unions can cater most easily for workers of this type, as well as for the large mass of workers in scattered industries not clearly enough defined to maintain Unions of their own The general Unions are accordingly likely to remain very important

A Single General Union

What is absurd is that there should be two of them, competing over practically the whole range of industries and getting continually in each other's way What I should like to see is the splitting off by agreement of the Transport Workers' section of the T and G W. from the rest, and the amalgamation of the remainder with the N U G M W to form a single Union open to all workers for whom no distinct effective craft or industrial Union exists The transport workers do not appear to be too happy inside the huge amorphous Union of which they form the central group, and there seems to be a good case for an industrial Union including all branches of transport except the railwaymen and perhaps the seamen I shall no doubt be strongly criticised for daring to suggest so drastic a change in the established Trade Union structure, but my task in this pamphlet is to write what I believe without taking too much care not to tread on important persons' toes

6. TRADE UNIONISTS IN POLITICS

OUT of the 9½ million Trade Unionists, roughly 5½ million belong to the Labour Party as political contributors through their Unions' political funds, but only a tiny fraction of these contributing members plays even the smallest further part in the Labour Party's affairs or receives any account through his Union of what the Labour Party is doing, either nationally or locally. Of course, a substantial number of Trade Unionists join the

Labour Party as individual members, in addition to paying their Union levy, and these members can play as active a part as anyone else in the Labour Party's affairs, if they wish to do so But it remains true that the Labour Party membership of the great majority of affiliated members is purely nominal, and that most Trade Unions make no attempt to interest the contributing members in Party affairs or to give them any control over Party doings.

Voting at Conference

Trade Union branches seldom discuss political questions or, even if they are affiliated to Divisional Labour Parties, receive any regular reports from their delegates to such bodies, and, at the centre, the Labour Party's relations with the Trade Unions are almost wholly a matter of dealings with Union head offices and national executives, with practically no contacts with the Trade Union rank and file It is not uncommon for the voting of big Trade Unions at Labour Party Conferences to be settled by Union executives without any attempt at consulting their members so that a huge block vote may depend entirely on the opinions of a few men chosen as leaders on mainly unpolitical grounds

In other cases, Trade Union delegates to the Labour Party Conference are specially elected and hold a preliminary meeting as a delegation, before the Conference assembles, in order to decide how to cast the Union's vote, which they may either cast as a block vote, ignoring any minority within the delegation, or divide so as to reflect the actual division of opinion among the delegates. But even, this, though more democratic than leaving the whole matter to be settled by the Executive, does not achieve any real consultation of the main body of contributors to the Union's Political Fund

Some people argue that this does not matter, or even that it is a good thing because it allows the weight of a Trade Union to be thrown solidly into the scale on controversial issues instead of being scattered so as to express differences of opinion Trade Unions, it is said, owe their power to their ability to act as solid bodies—monolithically, to borrow a favourite Communist term In industrial matters this is no doubt often necessary one cannot wish to have half a group of workers striking, and the other half staying at work In political matters, however, there is usually no good reason why a Trade Union should wish to act monolithically, so as to suppress differences of attitude among its members, or why control of its political activities should be concentrated at the centre, so as to allow the ordinary member practically no voice in what is done in his name

More Political Discussion

Is there a remedy for this unsatisfactory state of affairs? The situation could be made much better if most Trade Unionists who pay their Union political levy would also become individual members of their local and divisional Labour Parties and attend their meetings. **A bigger Trade**

Unionist membership in the local Labour Parties would add greatly to the influence of these bodies and would much strengthen their claim to an effective voice in controlling the Party and to a larger representation on the Party Executive. This, however, is not to be hoped for save as the outcome of a successful attempt to reduce the apathy of Trade Unionists in relation to their own Union affairs, for the apathetic Trade Unionist, even if he is a political contributor, is not very likely to become a Labour Party activist.

Short of that, it would be possible for Trade Unions to arrange for special branch meetings for the discussion of political questions At such meetings, the branch delegates to the local Labour Party would report on its work, and matters of Party policy, national as well as local, could be freely discussed It would not be easy, at any rate at first, to secure a large attendance at such meetings but even smallish attendances would serve to bring the local Trade Unionists into much closer relations with the Labour Party than exist at present, and they could be used as opportunities for elementary education in political problems of special concern to the Trade Unions, as well as over a wider field There could also be inter-union local meetings for political discussion and small branches could join forces for political meetings.

Channels of Communication

If this were done on any scale, it would become necessary for the Trade Unions to establish machinery for political discussion and decision at higher levels Resolutions from political branch meetings could be sent up for consideration at regional and national levels, and Trade Unions could begin democratically to work out political policies and programmes of their own to be put before the Labour Party, not as the fiat of a few top leaders, but as the considered opinion of the active members Trade Unions would be induced to take politics more seriously and to take greater account of the members' views Indeed, without something of this sort, tension is bound to arise between the Trade Union leadership and the local Labour Parties, which, as their members do most of the work for the Party, do not like being overridden at the Party Conference by the block votes of a few big Unions whose members have never been consulted about how their votes are to be cast It would become impossible for Trade Union leaders to look down with contempt on the Local Parties as expressing the whims of irresponsible intellectuals and trouble-makers, and the entire Labour Party would benefit by getting the Trade Unionists to participate on the ground floor, instead of coming in for the most part only at the top level, and even there only in the most indirect and unrepresentative way.

The difficulty, of course is not only that many Trade Union leaders prefer the political influence of the Unions to be concentrated in their own hands, but also that many of the leaders of the Labour Party suffer from the same disease of oligarchy, which, as we saw, besets all large organisations. The local Labour Parties themselves are not so popular at Transport House (South Block) that it wishes to see them reinforced by much more local Trade Unionist participation and support. From the standpoint of oligarchs democracy is always a nuisance, unless it is reduced to the most formal terms of majority control, so as to allow minorities, the bearers of new ideas, to be nipped in the bud.

Therefore, only Trade Unionists who want to increase active rank-and-file Trade Union participation in political affairs can be looked to as possible makers of the change, by insisting on their right to discuss political issues in their branches and to receive regular reports on the Labour Party's doings, national as well as local. Until they do this, the Labour Party's association with the Trade Unions will continue to rest on undemocratic foundations and the main body of Trade Unionists will remain politically uneducated, to the grave damage of the Labour Party as a political force and of the Trade Unions themselves as bodies whose functions, in the world of today, necessarily extend a long way beyond purely industrial affairs.

7. THE QUESTION OF WORKERS' CONTROL

TO-DAY, most Trade Union leaders neither believe, nor even profess to believe, in 'workers' control'. Most workers, they say, show no sign of wanting it, and, if they did, they would not know how to set about it. Both these contentions are, of course, largely true. The demand for workers' control comes only from a small minority, and even this minority is often not at all clear what it wants. It is also true that, with the advance in the scale of production and the rapidly growing application of science to industry—up to the extreme point of automation—management becomes more and more a highly specialised and exacting profession, far beyond the capacity of the average operative at the bench or machine. That is why societies are heading towards a 'managerial revolution,' which is transferring power from mere owners of capital to scientifically trained wizards and higher technicians, as the far-sighted Saint Simon prophesied would happen a good century and a half ago. At present, these wizards are in the service of the propertied classes, into whose higher ranks they rise by virtue of their skill. Under modern conditions of production society cannot do without them, but it can by socialisation compel them to change their allegiance and to become the servants of the people instead of its masters.

Restraining the Technocrats

Socialisation is needed, not only to put an end to the private appropriation of surplus value, but also to compel the technocrats to take proper account of the rights and interests of those who work under their orders.

The ordinary workman cannot control industry in the sense of planning either what is to be produced or how production is to be organised He does not know enough, and cannot, for this to be possible in a society in which new methods of production are continually being discovered, and any country that allows its technical efficiency to lag behind will be unable to hold its position in the world market, or to sustain a satisfactory standard of living for its people But, although the ordinary worker cannot know enough to be in a position to say what should be produced or what new techniques are called for, he does know a great deal about where the shoe pinches when methods and processes are changed without his consent

Workers' control can mean nothing unless it begins on the workshop floor, in relation to matters which the ordinary worker can understand and which affect his working life Joint consultation at the workshop and factory levels is a step towards it, wherever it includes real prior consultation about proposed changes in workshop practice But consultation is not control, because it still leaves the final decision in the hands of a management responsible to the owners of the business, and not to the workers—or to a state-appointed Board or Commission where the industry is publicly owned The workers must still either obey or strike they have still under joint consultation no positive right to participate in *deciding* what is to be done

Extending Joint-Consultation

I want them to gain such a right, by building on joint consultation an extended kind of collective bargaining, under which, in each establishment, the rules and regulations governing workshop practice will be embodied in negotiated agreements, accepted as binding upon both parties and backed by the Trade Unions as an integral part of the structure of collective bargaining Such factory or workplace agreements would, of course, need to be sanctioned by the Trade Unions at the regional and national levels, in order to prevent them from being misused to break down Trade Union standards I can see no good reason why this cannot be done It would, of course, involve the Trade Unions in building up improved machinery for workshop negotiation and in giving greater powers and fuller recognition to shop stewards and factory committees But this would be a great gain because it would diffuse responsibility more widely and would counteract the tendency towards increasing centralisation of Trade Union affairs.

With the kind of so-called 'workers' control' that begins and ends at the top, with putting a few Trade Union leaders on the Boards of nationalised industries, I have very little sympathy Trade Union leaders have not been trained to manage or administer large industrial concerns, and only a very few of them are likely to do so even tolerably well Nor will their presence on such boards give the workers any real control unless control has also been built up from the bottom, on the workshop floor. Without this, the Trade Union directors will only become isolated from the workers and will cease to represent them in any sense As for allowing the workers to nominate some of the directors to private businesses, I am again not much interested unless the businesses have begun by building up a workshop structure of joint control, and even then I am suspicious of anything that would convert the workers into co-partners of profit-seeking capitalist employers.

'Democratic Partners'

I remain, however, convinced that there can be no way of making industry work well under socialisation without enlisting the workers as democratic partners in control, above all at the workshop and factory level. If only a minority wants this, it is nevertheless well worth while, for a minority can leaven the majority with its spirit It is vain to suppose that in a Socialist society it will be possible to compel men to work harder or better than most of them feel like working, or that they will mostly feel like working well unless they can be given a sense that it is up to them to do their best—and this they will be likely to feel only if the responsibility and the power are placed squarely upon them, by leaving them, in their working groups, as much freedom as possible to settle their own working conditions. Only in such a set up will it be possible to train those who are suitable for managerial and technical posts without alienating them from their fellow-workers, or to advance towards a truly classless society in which there will be differences of function and authority without division into contending social or economic classes

I am convinced that the Trade Unions, in order to square up to their growing responsibilities, need to make a growing measure of workers' control, beginning at the bottom levels, an integral part of their policy and that the best way of setting about this is to give much fuller recognition and negotiating rights, within the framework of wider agreemens, to shop stewards and works and workshop committees directly chosen by the workers concerned To do this would make the Trade Unions, as well as industry, much more democratic, and would be a real contribution towards the creation of the democratic Socialist society most active Trade Unionists profess to want.

8. A SUMMING UP

WITHOUT doubt, the primary function of Trade Unions is to look after their members' industrial interests, and any Union that neglects this is being false to its task. But such a statement requires qualification. Hardly anyone outside its own ranks would praise a Trade Union which, however successfully, pushed its sectional interests in entire disregard of everybody's else's claims. If a particular Trade Union, holding a monopoly of some kind of skill that was in high demand, used its power to improve its members' conditions without paying any attention to the effect of its action either on other industries or on the less skilled workers in its own industry, it would be rightly accused of holding the people to ransom in a thoroughly illegitimate way.

There have, indeed, been instances of this sort, where a group of craftsmen has not merely done nothing to help the less skilled in the same establishment, but has actually opposed their organisation and joined with the employers in resisting their claims. One historic case—now half a century old—is that of the highly skilled steel workers, whose selfish policy was defeated only by the rise of a new Union—the Steel Smelters—which espoused the cause of the less as well as of the more skilled workers, and gradually drove out the abominable practice of sub-contracting, under which the skilled pieceworkers employed the less skilled at grossly inadequate time-wages. There were similar experiences in coal-mining, under the 'butty' system, till the Miners' Federation drove it out.

No Single Responsibility

We cannot, therefore, say that the function of a Trade Union is simply to get as much as it can for its own members it has also to pay some regard to the claims of other workers, and to act, up to a point, in a spirit of working-class solidarity. Nor can we say that the Trade Unions as a whole should set out simply to raise wages to the highest possible fraction of the total product, for they have also to consider the claims of the children and of the aged or disabled, and to recognise the need to provide, in one way or another, for enough capital accumulation to keep the economic structure up to date and to meet the capital claims of the social services. It is doubtless true that, as long as Trade Unions are relatively weak, there is little or no danger of their claims on their members' behalf conflicting with the general interest, but, the stronger they grow, the more account they need to take of the effects of their claims on other poor people and on the economy as a whole.

This, however, is a reason, not why Trade Unions should press less hard, but why they should to some extent alter the nature and direction of their pressure For they may reach a point at which merely to press their sectional claims to the full will so dislocate the whole economy as to do them serious harm—e g , by causing unemployment or a balance of payments crisis—unless the basis of the economy is radically changed

This sort of issue forces the Trade Unions into politics, both in order to press for changes that can be made only by legislation and in order to square their particular demands with those of other under-privileged groups. In general it has forced them to ally themselves with the Socialists, as the only substantial political body that stands for an alternative economic and social system This, however, has never meant that the Trade Unions have gone over solidly to Socialism or have pressed the Labour Party in the direction of a more socialistic policy. On the whole, ever since they broke away from their old allegiance to Liberalism, they have been mostly on the Party's right wing, though never ranged solidly in one camp Only when a quite clear class-issue has made its appearance, as it did in 1931, have they been even momentarily on the left, and such deviations have not lasted long.

The New Dilemma

The Unions' present dilemma is essentially new. They have to admit the need of and even to press for, a high level of capital accumulation out of current production, in the long-run interest of their own members as well as of the whole economy But hitherto the principal source of capital accumulation has always been private profit. Nor is there any alternative source, except taxation, which has increased in importance in this respect with the growth of public capital expenditure As long as the funds for business expansion continue to come mainly from reserved profits, these profits must be high, and must be allowed to increase as the need for new capital gets bigger This, as we saw, limits the possibility of raising wages without either raising profits also or bringing investment to a standstill **The only way out of this impasse is for the State to take over the responsibility for new investment, either through higher taxation or by appropriating the surplus profits which are at present re-invested as the property of the shareholders**—which would be much the easier method. It would, of course, be denounced as sheer confiscation, but to talk of Socialism without confiscation has always been nonsense All Socialists wish to expropriate the capitalists somehow even those who wish to pay compensation have every intention of cancelling it in the long run by taxes on capital or by the limitation of inheritance, or by some other method that will not discriminate unfairly between one capitalist and another Most Trade Union leaders, however, have not yet fully appreciated the logic of the situation they see only that they cannot go all out for higher wages under capitalism, and have not seen that the remedy is to do away with capitalism now instead of allowing their aspirations to be stultified by its continuance.

Nor have most of their members seen this, for many of them still believe that wages and consumption could be increased at the expense of profits, whereas in practice high money wages and high profits go together, as the Labour Government discovered while it was in office after 1945 This delusion is possible because few workers are investors in industry or realise the indispensability of high investment to the future prosperity and level of employment in this country Here again, the only remedy is more and better Trade Union education to bring home the hard economic facts and prevent Trade Unionists from being deluded by over-optimistic false prophets This education is needed, not in order to persuade Trade Unionists to acquiesce in 'wage-restraint' in the interest of profit-making, but to bring home to them how indispensable it is to transfer these profits from their present owners to the public, and to get and sustain in power Governments that will ensure that the benefit of rising productivity accrues to the workers as fast as more can be spared from the requirements of *public* investment.

Education a Priority

A Trade Union movement of the kind that is needed for escape from the present dilemma will have to be much better educated, and much less beset by apathy and centralisation, than the Trade Unions are today It will have to be a movement whose leaders can afford to trust their members to think and act for themselves, and will do their best to spread power and responsibility over the widest possible area, instead of concentrating it in their own hands Maybe to hope for such a movement is wishful thinking but to give up hope of it is in effect to give up hoping at all A working class that lacks both knowledge and self-reliance neither deserves power nor is likely to win power to re-organise society on a really democrtic basis Without *enough* active democrats, democracy in any real sense cannot exist, either in the Trade Unions or in society as a whole

* * *

I MUST now briefly summarise the principal practical suggestions that I have made in this pamphlet

1 It is neither possible nor desirable to go back on the system of national as against local collective bargaining that has led to an increasing centralisation of Trade Union power and has reduced the scope for local and district action, but it is both possible and desirable to develop workplace bargaining by shop stewards and works committees within the framework of national agreements, and by so doing to re-vivify local Trade Union action and to diffuse power and responsibility over a wider field

2 It is wrong to be deterred from doing this by fear that workplace bargaining machinery may be captured by Communists or 'fellow-

travellers', for, though this danger is real, the rank-and-file apathy that results from over-centralisation is a much greater danger.

3   Even if industrial Unionism is generally to be preferred to craft Unionism, it is not practicable at present to re-organise the Trade Union movement on a comprehensive industrial basis It is, however, practicable to speed up the process of amalagamation, and it would be particularly advantageous if the two big 'general workers' Unions were amalgamated, and if the transport workers' sections of the T and G W U were re-organised as a separate industrial Union

4   Trade Union 'apathy' is largely a consequence of three things—the extension of Trade Union membership to a higher proportion of the workers, over-centralisation, and the increase in alternative attractions for the use of leisure time But this apathy is made much worse than it need be by the failure of most Trade Unions to take any effective steps to educate their members to a knowledge of the working and problems of their Trade Unions and of the working-class movement as a whole A great campaign of Trade Union education and training is therefore needed

5   Trade Unions have now won so much power and recognition that they are forced to act with a high sense of responsibility not only for the direct interests of their members, but also for the efficient working of the whole economy, even under capitalism This means that they have to co-operate in raising productivity and that it is imperative for their leaders to make clear to the members why this is necessary in their own interests This, too, calls for a great educational campaign for better understanding of economic realities

6   Trade Unions have made great conquests in recent years, but the maintenance and extension of these conquests depends on political as well as industrial factors and requires a Government pledged to give priority to working-class interests It is therefore imperative for Trade Union education to include political as well as economic education, in order both to reduce the number of workers who fail to vote Labour and to impel the Labour Party towards a more forthright Socialist policy

7   The links that bind together the rank-and-file Trade Union contributor to his Union's Political Fund and the Labour Party are far too tenuous and far too much concentrated at the top level of Trade Union officials and Executives Trade Union branches should hold special meetings for political discussions and many more Trade Unionists should take an active part in the work of the constituency Labour Parties

8   The development of workers' participation in the control of industry should be made a definite and important part of Trade Union policy, and should be pursued first and foremost at the level of the individual workplace The winning of Trade Union representation on national Boards or Commissions is of little value unless it rests on a foundation of real participation in control at the workplace level.

9. Accordingly, a determined effort should be made to advance from mere 'joint consultation' to actual participation in control of policy at the workplace level, by extending the range of collective bargaining to include bargaining at that level about the arrangement of work, engagements, promotions and dismissals, and other matters now usually regarded as falling within the definition of 'managerial functions'

10. Finally, and above all, Trade Unionism can be healthy and militant only if it enlists the active and responsible participation of a substantial proportion of its members, and it should be a foremost task of Trade Union leadership to promote, for this purpose, a greater diffusion of power and responsibility among the members, as well as to do all that is possible to ensure that every Trade Unionist understands the democratic working of his own Trade Union and is equipped also to play his part in the wider activities of the working-class movement

APPENDIX: A FEW STATISTICS

AT the end of 1954—the latest date for which full figures are available—there were 674 Trade Unions known to the Ministry of Labour, with a total membership of 9,495,000 Of these, 217 Unions, with 8,107,000 members, were represented at the Trades Union Congress of 1955, leaving 1,388,000 Trade Unionists not represented The largest Unions outside the T U C were the National and Local Government Officers' Association (NALGO) and the National Union of Teachers The apparently small proportion of Trade Unions included in the T U C is misleading, as some federal bodies which count as single Unions in the T U C are counted as a number in the Ministry of Labour figures

In 1938 there were in all 1,024 Trade Unions, with 6,053,000 members The number of Unions had thus fallen by 350, whereas the number of members had risen by 3,442,000 The fall is due mainly to amalgamations the number of Unions in the T U C had fallen by 34, from 217 to 183, whereas T U C membersip had risen by 3,438,000, or nearly 74 per cent

* * *

Trade Union membership is highly concentrated in a few big Unions The biggest is the Transport and General Workers' Union, with 1,240 000 members represented at the T U C of 1955 The Amalgamated Engineering Union comes second, with 823,000, followed by the National Union of General Workers with 787,000, and the National Union of Mineworkers with 675,000 These four Unions have together more than 3½ million members, or 43 5 per cent of the total T U C membership The three next largest—the National Union of Railwaymen, the Union of Shop, Distributive and Allied Workers, and the Electrical Trades Union—add another 942,000, bringing the total for these 7 Unions to nearly 4½ millions, or about 55 per cent of the T.U C There are 8 other Unions with from 100,000 to 200,000 members, making a further total of 1,179,000, and bringing the combined total for the 15 biggest Unions to 5,646,000, or nearly 70 per cent of the T U C total Seventeen further Unions, each with more than 50,000, raise the number in the 32 biggest to 6,873,000, or over 84 per cent

* * *

The size of a Trade Union, of course, depends both on that of the groups for which it caters and on its success in enrolling members A relatively small Union, such as the Cotton Spinners, may represent a highly organised group, whereas a very big one, with a wide coverage, may be weak in relation to the numbers eligible for membership It is not possible to say what proportion of workers in the various industries and occupations belong to Trade Unions, because the occupational and Trade Union classifications do not coincide The two big 'general' Unions cut right across industrial divisions and include members drawn from almost every industry and service It can, however, be said that the most strongly organised groups include miners, printers, cotton operatives, and civil servants, and that the major sections of steel, engineering and shipbuilding, electrical, and railway workers are also highly organised So are dockers, some, but not all, sections of the building industry, boot and shoe operatives, and a number of less numerous but highly specialised groups, such as dyers and musicians Generally speaking, organisation is weaker among less skilled than among skilled workers and among clerical than among manual workers Railway clerks, however, are highly organised and to a lesser extent so are bank clerks and insurance workers So, outside the T U C , are teachers and local government officers

* * *

Women Trade Unionists numbered in 1954 about 1,789,000, or nearly 19 per cent of the total Women in the T U C numbered 1,332,000, or 16¾ per cent The T and G W had 152,000 women members, the N U G M W 158,000, and the Distributive Workers 152,000 The A E U had 56,000, the Printing and Paper Workers 63,000, the Weavers 71,000, the Cardroom Operatives 41,000, the Tailors and Garment Workers 99,000, the Boot and Shoe Operatives 33,000, the Civil Service Clerical Association 72,000, and the Union of Post Office Workers 40,000 The rest were widely scattered In general, Trade Unionism is less strong among women than among male workers, but since 1938 female membership has risen by 93 per cent , as against only 50 per cent for males

* * *

The total Trade Union membership of nearly 9½ millions at the end 1954 compares with a total working population of 23,667,000, of whom 839,000 were in the armed forces, leaving 22,828,000 But this total includes employers, managers and self-employed persons as well as employed workers It is not possible to say at all accurately what proportion of those who could be members of a Trade Union are actually enrolled, but there is clearly still a wide field for expansion, especially among non-manual workers, but also among the less skilled manual workers Growth has been slow in recent years Total membership reached 9 millions in 1947 and was nearly as high in 1951 as in 1954 The big increase over 1938 took place during and immediately after the war